MASON'S WAY

The 20 Universal Ways of Oneness

Taught by the Spirit of an Enlightened Dog

RACHEL FIORI

MASON'S WAY

The 20 Universal Ways of Oneness Taught by the Spirit of an Enlightened Dog

Copyright © 2022 by Rachel Fiori.

All Rights Reserved. Printed in the U.S.A.

ISBN: 978-1-94-7276-04-8

All rights reserved. No part of this book may be reproduced or transmitted in any form or by any means, electronic or mechanical, including photocopying, recording, or by an information storage and retrieval system - except by a reviewer who may quote brief passages in a review to be printed in a magazine or newspaper - without permission in writing from the author.

Publishing and Design:

EPIC AUTHOR
PUBLISHING

Ordering Information: Quantity sales. Special discounts are available on quantity purchases by corporations, associations, and others. For details, contact the publisher at the address above. Orders by U.S. trade bookstores and wholesalers.

Please contact: 561-601-9871 | info@epicauthor.com | EpicAuthor.com
First Edition

For my Mason.

*You are the most precious gift that life has given to me.
Thank you for choosing me to be your mommy,
for the 14 priceless years that you were by my side.
I love you always & forever.*

TABLE OF CONTENTS

CH 1: The Universal Ways Of Oneness — 1

CH 2: Mason — 17

CH 3: The Way of Responsibility — 23

CH 4: The Way of Patience — 35

CH 5: The Way of Surrender — 49

CH 6: The Way of Truth — 59

CH 7: The Way of Presence — 75

CH 8: The Way of Connection — 85

CH 9: The Way of Compassion — 111

CH 10: The Way of Harmlessness & Gentleness — 121

CH 11: The Way of Equality — 149

CH 12: The Way of Trust — 161

CH 13: The Way of Honoring — 171

CH 14: The Way of Selfless Service — 183

CH 15: The Way of Loyalty — 207

CH 16: The Way of Unconditional Love — 221

CH 17: The Way of Humility — 235

CH 18: The Way of Integrity — 245

CH 19: The Way of Forgiveness — 257

CH 20: The Way of Purity — 267

CH 21: The Way of Wisdom — 279

CH 22: The Way of Harmony — 299

CH 23: Mason's Final Days — 315

CH 24: Grief — 335

CH 25: Living In Oneness — 355

CHAPTER 1

The Universal Ways of Oneness

THE UNIVERSAL WAYS OF ONENESS

Our planet and everything on it is going through a global transformation, a global dark night of the soul that is needed to launch humanity into a global awakening. This is necessary in order to bring to the surface every aspect of shadow living so it can be seen and transformed, so human evolution can elevate to a higher level of consciousness. The time has come in human history to command Oneness with all. Old belief programs of separation must be dismantled. A new understanding of how to relate to one another through ways that are absent from violence, hate, separation, and forceful control need to be birthed. A truly free society is one where everyone shows love and support for one another and for all things. Humanity has historically created their experiences on Earth from such limited perceptions, using only their five senses to perceive what's tangibly in front of them. If they can't see it, touch it, taste it, smell it, or hear it, it isn't real or doesn't exist. Extrasensory perceptions, intuitive gifts, or energetic healing were reserved for the few such as saints, masters, or priestesses. And everyone else either thought it was nonsense, or they believed that they themselves could never possess such special gifts. Humanity is now going through a tremendous evolutionary shift. People are being challenged more than ever before to raise their level of consciousness and open to the divine gifts that they are capable of experiencing and using. Opening to the nonphysical world that can't be "proven" and is real means opening the door to freedom from suffering. When people limit their perceptions to what they can touch or see in front of them, they close themselves off from their nonphysical support team. Every person has formless teachers, spirit guides, and even guardian angels that are there to assist them and support them throughout their lives. But most deny their existence, claiming these things are the stories of fantasy and fairy tales. Or that the people who believe in these things are "woo woo" and "out there." The truth is that these things aren't fantasy at all. They are the ways of being that enlightened people and enlightened societies are divinely led by. Your higher soul is one of these beings, and your divine soul is not tangible. It's a formless aspect of divine consciousness that is moving through a human experience. This aspect of divinity, this aspect of you, is what is meant to be the director of your human life. How can one listen to their divine natures if they fail to realize that it even exists at all? How can one step onto a path leading them to enlightenment when they close themselves off from the Light that they are? If you resist the Light, the Light that you are, how can you ever embrace the ways that will lead humanity into a new enlightened state of civilization?

Enlightened societies are created by and structured from the Universal Ways of Oneness. These are the enlightened characteristics of the highest level of divinity itself. To be guided, led and even healed by these Ways of Oneness means to individually, internally transform oneself so that you become the Ways. These Ways represent universal truths of the nature of all things. It's how enlightened societies function. Using your free-will choice to awaken to the Ways *is* the way to create peace on Earth. Peace on Earth starts with creating peace and harmony within yourself. We as humans have spent centuries robbing our souls of the nourishment of love while incarnated in human form. That era must end. And that can only happen through the willingness to see that you are running programs of separation and to put forth the effort to dismantle them within yourself. To awaken to the Ways doesn't just mean to read about them or speak of them. It means to embody them. It means doing the real work on yourself to rid yourself of every other way of being that you offer to yourself and to others that are out of alignment with these Ways of Universal Oneness. It means to wake up. To grow up. To die the ego death several times over and move through the rebirth process as many times as necessary until all aspects of your former self no longer exist. This is the way to heal the lineage of suffering and separation that were passed down to you from previous generations. It means thousands of years of unconscious ways of thinking, believing, and behaving must be disassembled, and a new understanding of relating must be birthed, embraced, and nurtured. It means systems, governments, corporations, and patriarchy must all be knocked down and restructured from the ground up. A new framework must be built that secures a foundation of Oneness with all things. This is the only way to prepare for and to co-create the age that is coming upon us and that functions in Oneness: The New Golden Age of Harmony.

THE UNIVERSAL WAYS OF ONENESS

Humans have a long history of creating and acting out violence, conquering, pillaging, raping, controlling, hating, lying, hiding, dominating, oppressing, and teaching and encouraging sexism, racism, and inequality in almost every way conceivable. Humans continue to pollute and destroy Mother Earth without a second thought. Humans torture and murder animals and justify it in the name of science. So many people fighting for their freedoms are the same people paying for and supporting the enslavement of animals and the massacre of Earth's precious forests. Our arrogance and sense of entitlement has reigned long enough. Living in contrast to peace and unity for thousands of years has fueled us to make the necessary changes that are required for a global level of transformation. Spiritual unconsciousness is rooted in selfishness and separation and has spread like a plague on this planet for far too long. It destroys everything in its path and it replenishes itself on denial, greed, and domination. There are many people alive today that are truly beginning to "wake up." These people are trying hard to ignite transformation within themselves while spreading that awakening to others. Many are doing what they can to heal the planet and to educate others on the harmful effects of consumerism, as well as trying to end the maltreatment and abuse of animals and nature. But there hasn't exactly been a "rulebook" to follow on how to actually achieve all of this. Many spiritual teachers have stepped up and used their wisdom to teach individuals how to heal themselves and even on how to become self-actualized. Some focus on teaching what it means to be Present. Others focus on parapsychology and our intuitive abilities. Still others try to teach and focus on emotional health and mental wellbeing. All of them are wonderful way-showers of healing and human potential. On the downside, they're all piecemeal and basically separated from one another. You need to learn from countless teachers and do your best to put it all together on your own.

The truth is there is a code of Universal Ways of Oneness that can be used to create and "govern" enlightened societies. Govern doesn't mean to control or to dictate. Enlightened governing is a structured roadmap of freedom that has cosmic love as its central theme. These divine laws are ways of living that create peace, empowerment, and enlightenment within oneself and within communities and societies. As it spreads, it will take on a global effect. The shadow side of elevated consciousness, human unconsciousness, has been moving through a process to bring everything ugly and unloving to the surface for transmutation. All the lies, disharmony, greed, and control is being exposed so people can become aware of them. Nothing heals or transforms without acute awareness. That's true for healing at the macro level (the collective or global level) and at the micro level (the level of your own individual healing and transformation). The first step is becoming radically self-aware of all of the things that are hidden in your blind spot. Once seen and taken responsibility for, anything can be healed. This is happening all over the world on large scales. It sometimes takes what looks like travesty—say, a pandemic, for example—to help to expose all of the inequality, hate, judgment, oppression, and separation that exist among individuals while simultaneously exposing the inequality, injustices, and corruption that exist at the level of those in power and in systems that exercise authority over societies. Because of the upheavals taking place all over the world, it's time to introduce a structure to replace how we operate and relate to each other. We need a guidance system that teaches us how to relate to all things from a place of loving congruence. The Ways of Oneness make up the divine goldprint on how to create peace on earth. These are the Universal Laws that create and govern enlightened societies because they are rooted in unity. It creates freedom from an elevated state of consciousness. Divinely free societies live from a place of honesty and full transparency. In order for that to be achieved, you must achieve it as an individual. You see, the Ways are aspects of Cosmic Love that guide the individual to becoming self-actualized while forming the foundation for societal and even global enlightenment.

This book is going to introduce and teach what each Way of Oneness is. Every chapter will focus on one of the Ways as well as teach you how you can integrate and become that Way of being. Once you are well on your way to integrating or becoming that Way, you will organically open up to learning and adding a new Way. It's almost like moving up grades in elementary school. You first learn what letters are, then words, until you can eventually read full books. You learn. You practice. You integrate. You become. You move to a higher level and repeat. All the while your new skills are dependent on the mastery of your previous skills. This is why many can't understand why it's so hard to change toxic systems that are plagued with sexism and racism. The people running these systems haven't learned the basics of Oneness, let alone mastered the more advanced stages of divine Oneness. They fight to keep the old systems in place. Meanwhile, those that demand and fight for change haven't mastered the internal transformation necessary to create a more conscious and loving society. Many people protesting and fighting for big changes have yet to make those big changes within themselves. You will never create peace on Earth if you yourself are not the beingness of peace. You will never see equality in society or culture while you still practice exclusion and separation in any form. Learning and living in the Ways of Oneness is a way to heal yourself, to heal generations of ignorance and suffering, and to heal society as a whole. These Ways shine the Light on our own blind spots, all of which need to be healed from within before we see entire countries heal. Every Way described flows with sacred nectar. Each Way that you focus on and begin to integrate within yourself is the act of drinking that sacred nectar and experiencing the transformative power of becoming more sacred yourself. Each one of the Ways is a divinely powerful gift of transformation waiting for you to choose to drink its sweet Light.

THE UNIVERSAL WAYS OF ONENESS

The Light from the Ways of Oneness is what will transform our current world into an enlightened one so we may enjoy living in the New Golden Age of Harmony.

It's also important to understand that you have a choice. You always have. Many people get stuck on making choices, worrying over whether they are making the right or wrong ones. You may have wondered if you're choosing the "right path" at various times in your life. It's really important to understand that you can't ever actually pick the "wrong path." But you can pick the more treacherous one. Since our minds are conditioned to run duality programs, your mind may jump immediately to, "I want the easy road. Not the treacherous one. How do I do that?" This would be a mistake in understanding the journey that you are to experience while living in the Earth School. Picking the treacherous path of learning means that you are not yet aligned with your soul. It means that you unconsciously choose all that you experience with no idea that you have the power of choice. You only believe what you can physically see with your own eyes. You have little to no faith in the divine, or you have blind faith, which allows you to take no responsibility for your own life. Blind faith and no faith are two sides of the same coin of the duality of spiritual unconsciousness. Both keep the doors closed and locked to allow your higher soul to enter into your humanness and to become your main guiding light throughout your lifetime. When aligned with your soul, your life is going to be filled with beauty, joy, and delightful experiences. It's also going to be filled with challenges, some really extreme ones, and pain. You need these for your soul's evolution. All of it is beautiful and perfect. This includes the most painful times because those changes are filled with lessons to be learned and gifts to be gained.

When you're not yet aligned with your soul, you're choosing the path of treachery. This path is filled with repetitive lessons that go unlearned, mistakes that you make over and over again, and unloving, selfish choices that cause you and others harm. You often become bitter, depressed, angry, and resentful. You blame others, life, the universe, or God for your pain and problems. And you refuse to take responsibility for your life while you continue to drown in victim consciousness, spewing to anyone who will listen how unfair life is. You are living in suffering, and you see life as cruel and unfair.

People who choose the treacherous path because they're not yet aligned with their souls continue to reenact the programs of suffering that have plagued humanity for centuries. They contribute to ignorance, righteousness, destruction, inequality, oppression, racism, misogyny, and sexism, all while being in denial that they contribute to any of it. People not aligned with their souls will drown in victim consciousness while claiming to be fighting for real change, but also while hating who they view as their enemies. This is ignorance. You cannot hate, be rageful and resentful, and ever evoke positive change. You are just like your enemy, but you can't see that because you're blinded by your program of ignorance.

The willingness to align your human self to your soul self means making the conscious decision to evolve. When a person begins to spiritually awaken, they have a moment when their personality realizes there is more to its identity than just its human self. This begins the birthing process of a divine level of awareness. The awareness is the realization that there is a higher consciousness, a soul, that is having a human experience and that this soul is the *real* You. This is where the awareness of the real you, the divine you, becomes the observer of your human self you. This is the Human-Spirit Integration Point™. This is an energetic point where the consciousness that is you begins to energetically detach from its human identity. This is the byproduct of consciousness "awakening" to itself in human form. The higher Self can now begin to observe its human experiences from a place of neutrality. Your consciousness becoming a neutral observer opens one up to allowing this divine aspect of you, your higher soul, to begin to guide you in all aspects of your life. This is the true path to authentic awakening and to moving towards the enlightened characteristics of the Universal Ways of Oneness.

Aligning with one's soul means activating the process of the integration of divinity within oneself. Once your soul has the freedom to flow through you . . . to guide your life on Earth, the veils of ego illusion begin to dissolve away. The ignorance that once ruled your beliefs and actions fades, and you awaken to encompassing the gift of divine sight. Gaining divine sight is one step to the alignment of one's soul. Divine sight allows you to see the truth in how you are *actually* showing up in the world, in your relationships, or at your place of work, instead of how your ego likes you to think you're showing up. Divine sight opens you to become more self aware. Self-awareness is what illuminates the path to healing and to the Ways of Oneness. And you can choose to walk on this path at any point in time. You reading this right now is a sign that you are ready to walk the path, to learn about the Ways of Oneness, and to put forth the necessary effort needed to integrate them until you become the Ways. This requires that you learn how to heal the aspects of your personality that reflect your shadow self.

Such a giant leap in evolution requires a new, upgraded foundational model for healing, wellness, and wholeness. That model is based on spiritual psychology, energetics, and mysticism. It acknowledges the fact that you are made of four bodies: a spiritual body, mental body, emotional body, and a physical body. The principles of Oneness embrace the fact that you are a divine soul having a human experience, and therefore, no aspect of you (your four-body system) goes unrecognized when moving through a healing, transformation, illness, or life challenge. Denying your soul self prevents you from fully healing and becoming whole. Denying your human self and only focusing on the spiritual aspects of you has the same negative effect. This is what births the programs of separation that you then manifest and carry out throughout your life on Planet Earth. While you carry out programs of separation within yourself, you'll never achieve wholeness. And you'll never experience wholeness in your life or relationships. For humans to grow out of the experiences of suffering, caused by the deeply rooted beliefs in separation, soul healing needs to occur, while healing at the level of the personality must also simultaneously occur. And as both aspects of you are moving through the transformational-healing process, the integration process gets activated so that the healed aspects of your divine soul can integrate with the healed aspects of your human personality. Once this is achieved, you will move through life being completely guided by your own intuition. . . your higher soul. You'll gain understanding of universal laws and divine wisdom. You'll see the Truth in situations like you never have before. You'll elevate to levels of consciousness not yet experienced by you. Psychic, intuitive, and healing gifts will open, blossom, and expand within you. Self-actualization will no longer be a thing that only an elite few get to experience. It's what you will move through simply by learning about the Ways of Oneness and integrating them within yourself. You will not only heal your human self, your soul self, and every aspect of your life while living on Earth, but your Light will become so powerful that you'll be healing the planet and all beings that reside on Planet Earth as well. This is the next phase of human evolution and of elevating the collective level of consciousness in all of humanity. Understanding and implementing the Universal Ways of Oneness is the illuminated path to take humanity into the New Golden Age of Harmony. There are twenty Ways of Oneness to master. It used to take souls thousands and even millions of incarnations to achieve enlightenment in human form. You now have access to the secrets of how this is achievable. And you can achieve this for yourself in just this lifetime. And all it takes from you is willingness and devotion. You must have the willingness to learn each and every Way at its depths and the devotion to fully healing every aspect of you that prevents each Way from integrating into who you are. This is how to create mental, emotional, and spiritual freedom. And it's also how to create harmony on Earth.

You may now be wondering how *I* am the one who knows of the Universal Ways of Oneness. Well, I learned them from my dog, of course.

CHAPTER 2

Mason

MASON

Mason was a gift to myself for my thirtieth birthday. My first rescue, Madison, was getting up there in age. She was a Black Lab and German Shepherd mix. I knew when the day came that she crossed over to the rainbow bridge would be incredibly difficult for me. Madison was my first baby and my first soul companion dog. I wanted to bring another puppy into the family before Madison was too old. I didn't want it to be stressful on her and decrease her quality of life by waiting until she was too elderly. And I wanted another dog that could be by my side when Madison's day to say goodbye to me inevitably came. On March 9th, Mason was born. I was able to take him home with me two months later in May. The day that Mason came home with me was a day that set me on a deeper spiritual trajectory of spiritual awakening.

Mason was an English Yellow Lab filled with pure handsomeness, goodness, and vitality. I knew the first minute I met him that he was something really special. He had the spunk and wildness of a Lab puppy, but he also somehow had a profound gentleness to him. He'd ignite into running zoomies and then charge at you, running full speed. But then he'd stop just short of you, careful to never actually jump on you. . .well, mostly, anyway. He'd pounce in front of you, posing in the play stance with his butt high in the air, his thick, powerful tail wagging so hard it would almost create a wind tunnel in the room. Boy, did he play like crazy with Madison. He absolutely adored her and fell madly in love with her. She tolerated him. She was more interested in playing with her ball than playing with Mason. But when I took them to the park and threw Madison's ball, Mason would chase after her with no chance in hell of outrunning her or getting to that ball first. But he chased her down every time like he had a chance to beat her to that tennis ball. He never did. But it didn't matter. He still played the game with full gusto and had the time of his life. I of course held Madison's collar at times to prevent her from getting the ball, allowing Mason enough time to get there first before letting her go so Mason could feel like he beat her. When he succeeded, the joy that radiated from that dog was palpable! He was so incredibly happy! And then he was only slightly less happy the next twenty times that Madison beat him to the ball. But his joy was in the act of playing, of just being together and having fun all together. He really didn't care what we were actually doing. He just loved that we were all doing something together.

As Madison aged, she began to develop spinal arthritis. She couldn't run as fast or wrestle with Mason anymore. I noticed the way that he played with her evolved. Even though she couldn't wrestle anymore, she still loved to play. So when they started to play, Mason would lunge into the play stance at her, but instead of jumping onto her to wrestle her, he started nudging his nose on her. She'd jump around and playfully bite at him. And his face would light up in the biggest smile. He started running circles around her at full speed. He'd run by her and bite her side or butt on his way by. She'd jump at him and try to catch him on his way by. It was his turn to be the fast one that *she* couldn't catch. The roles reversed. And an amazing thing occurred to me one day. Never once did Mason jump on her or get too rough with her. He would've seriously hurt her if he had. She was at least eight years older than him after all. But once she reached a point where she could no longer wrestle, and she was slower, he adapted to her level of play, still having fun with her, but being very careful never to harm or hurt her. He also waited for her. He'd let her go first out of the door or up or down the stairs. He waited for her to get to the bottom before he came barreling down. Or he'd wait for her to reach the top before charging up after her. But he never competed to be first. It was like he was so cautiously aware of her physical state. He was selflessly aware enough of her to be sure to never harm her or put her in danger. He was consciously careful of her and on behalf of her. It was a remarkable thing to witness.

Over time, I noticed many things about Mason that were extraordinary. As my level of awareness increased, so did my observations and realizations about what Mason was actually doing, offering, and showing. I realized he was *teaching*. He was demonstrating ways of living and being in the world that were authentically divine. He was role modeling how to show up in the world, how to interact with others, and how to selflessly consider others in a deeper, more loving way. He was like a spiritual teacher that taught, not with words, but by modeling divine ways of being. He was a spiritual teacher of the

Ways of Oneness. I was his pupil here to learn the Ways from him. I didn't know it at the time, but once his mission of being my guru was complete, he would leave this physical world and pass the torch to me. I would be left with the teachings and inherit the responsibility to pass those teachings on to others. Mason was by my side for fourteen precious years. Well, fourteen years, one month, three weeks, and two days to be exact. He taught me the Ways of Oneness in a sacred way that only a soul as powerfully divine as his could teach. He has been the biggest blessing of my life to date. These teachings have touched my soul so deeply, and elevated my consciousness so extraordinarily. And now I feel the weight of divine responsibility to pass these teachings on to as much of humanity as possible. I was taught all twenty Ways of Oneness. They are outlined in this text, one by one. To gain the most out of this book would be to read through the entire manuscript to get an overview of all twenty Ways. Then go back to the first Way and spend a considerable amount of time mastering that one Way. I have found that practicing and integrating one Way for an entire month is a good way to ignite that Way into your beingness. If you feel like that would take way too long—after all, that would mean nearly two years of focusing on becoming the Ways—simply remember that you're here to participate in this Earth School for an entire lifetime. Twenty months is merely a blink of an eye in the grand scheme of things. And you really feel called to learn what these Ways are so you can enhance yourself, your relationships, your life in some way, then you're ready to dive into the first Way. The Way of Responsibility.

CHAPTER 3

UNIVERSAL WAY
OF ONENESS № 1:

The Way of Responsibility

THE WAY OF RESPONSIBILITY

Mason taught the Way of Responsibility by his soul choosing to manifest into a physical form that another being would always have to be responsible for. His soul chose to incarnate as a dog, and he chose me to be his caretaker. As puppies, dogs require a tremendous amount of care, training, and attention. They require your nurturing and your love. They must learn what they can chew on and what they cannot chew on. Of course, they don't know the difference without you teaching it to them. Everything is a chew toy because they go through the teething process. All of their baby teeth need to fall out while their adult teeth come in. This is uncomfortable for them, and it causes them to chew, chew, chew, and chew some more. Constant chomping on your shoes, the bedsheets, or even your arm will do if it's close enough to their mouths! As a dog owner, you are the one who is responsible for teaching them. You are responsible for learning how to properly and effectively train a dog and then to consistently carry these teachings out for as long as your dog needs until he learns what he needs to learn. And you don't do this for a day or two. Or for a month. You do it until. You do it for as long as you need to until your doggy moves out of that phase and masters the skills that you've been responsibly teaching to him. This is what Responsibility looks like.

Humans often fail to learn what true Responsibility is until they are in the position to care for another being. Once in that position, you get to see pretty quickly how responsible you are or how irresponsible you are. Irresponsibility is seen every single day when puppies and dogs at one or two years old or in their elderly years are dumped on the side of the road to fend for themselves or dropped off at kill shelters. Life is showing you that you're not a responsible person when you fail to do what it takes to care for, teach, and nurture another. So many also do this with their children. Once they have a child and realize how much work it is, many regret it on some levels. This is when parents resort to being a disengaged parent, or permissive, rigid, or even enmeshed. These are the four most common dysfunctional ways to parent, and they are also the methods that cause the most long-term damage in the children that were raised by them. The difference between children and pets is that it's harder to abandon your child at a kill shelter because you've realized you weren't mature or responsible enough yet to raise them in ways that will set them up to realize their full potential and internal power. So they're stuck with you. As awful as it is that so many give their pets away, at least they have the chance to be adopted by a loving owner who is responsible. Most children don't have the luxury of this option. And more often than not, parents rob their children of their power, and they do this to their pets as well. They do this because they haven't yet learned what true responsibility is.

When we're not responsible enough yet, it means we're stuck in programs of selfishness. We still think that living on this planet and one's life experience is all about "me." Not learning the real meaning of divine Responsibility keeps people trapped in perpetual spiritual and emotional immaturity. This allows us to be filled with greed, materialism, and objectification. Because of this, many get pets or have babies because they think these things will fulfill them. The perfect pet or the perfect baby will make them happy. This is extraordinarily selfish. It's selfish because it means you're using that little being to fill you up. You're a user. A divine being knows the tremendous amount of responsibility that it takes to raise a baby, a puppy, a child, a dog. You never get a dog or have a baby for *you*. You bring a being into your life *for them*. To be this Responsible means that you would begin by educating yourself in every way possible to better prepare yourself for that role. You would gain the knowledge and the skills in order to provide that helpless being with everything she needs to thrive. This takes work. This takes devotion. This takes consistency. It takes energy. It takes the willingness to learn. All of these are characteristics of the Way of Responsibility.

The Way of Responsibility teaches you that it's not up to others to fulfill you or to make you happy. No one else on this entire planet is responsible for your quality of life. That Responsibility belongs to you and to you alone. When you can finally understand that you and only you are responsible for your life, you are ready to evolve. You are ready to heal. You are ready to gain the gift of divine sight. You are ready to release your shadow self, the parts of yourself that are inadequate, unhealthy, selfish, dysfunctional, and unloving. The parts of you that create separation, suffering, and harm to yourself and to others.

If you continue to blame other people for your struggles, your conflicts, your pain, then this is living as an irresponsible, disempowered person who is making the choice to do anything but heal himself. Only once someone chooses to finally take full responsibility of his life can someone walk the path of spiritual awakening and authentic, transformational healing.

The Way of Responsibility requires you to change the relationship that you have with power. Blaming other people or circumstances for your emotional and mental state of being is an example of having a very unhealthy relationship with power. It means you are coming from a place of no power. You are disempowered. Your wellness, or lack thereof, is not another person's fault. It's your Responsibility to be well. To make yourself well and to keep yourself well. It's your Responsibility to awaken to conscious choice versus unconscious choice and then to be Responsible enough with every choice you have, to choose consciously instead of allowing your unconscious programs to run by default. Being Responsible means to become aware of every aspect of yourself that is inadequate. That is harmful to others. That is spiritually blind. That is selfish. That functions as an immature child. And that refuses to offer love in certain situations. The Way of Responsibility means choosing the path of healing. It means growing up and releasing all excuses and justifications for your anger and your judgment of others. It means to no longer live in shame and to shift to the powerful perspective of, "I now take full Responsibility of my actions, my choices, my emotions, my life." Being Responsible means being accountable for everything that you create. The good karma as well as the bad karma. And to see that you have indeed created both for yourself and for others.

Responsible accountability means no longer using the excuse that you didn't know any better at the time. And instead to shift your focus on how your choices at the time harmed others and how you're going to heal that or make amends with that and with those that you have harmed. It's never about blaming yourself or others. It's about taking Responsibility for your ignorance and no longer justifying what you've done because of your ignorance. Imagine the generations of trauma that could be healed if parents were willing to live at this level of divine Responsibility. If they were to embrace their internal power by acknowledging to their children how unprepared, unskilled, and uneducated they were when they had children. That they are willing to dive deeply into understanding how aspects of their parenting contributed to harmful mental, emotional and behavioral programs in their children. That, instead of expecting your children to just get over the fact that you made mistakes and didn't know any better at the time, that you are willing to go to counseling and coaching and do the work together as a family to heal. This is what the Way of Responsibility looks like. It's not just reading the words or even saying you're sorry. It's taking action to right your wrongs. A deeper way to see this is that you are taking action to create positive karma instead of allowing the old, negative karma to continue to run on autopilot and play out in your lives. When you made a harmful choice in the past that affected another person, the question to ask yourself is what have you done since then to heal that aspect of you that was capable of harming another? Let's say that you cheated on a partner, for example. What have you done to heal the infidelity program that you carry inside of you? If you blame the relationship or your ex-partner for your cheating, you've failed to take Responsibility for your lies and lack of trustworthiness. You deny taking Responsibility because you blame your ex or make excuses for yourself so that you can feel better about yourself. No matter the partner or what was happening in the relationship, you still make the choice to cheat. That means you also lied. You snuck around. You plotted. You planned. You acted in unloving, harmful ways. You used and objectified another person. And if your partner became suspicious, you most likely also gaslighted, lied some more, became defensive, or called them crazy. Or you took the narcissistic stance that they dared to question where you were or what you were doing. Wow. And you think your ability to do all of those terrible things simply escapes you just because you change partners? Or that a long time has passed? Now who's the crazy one?

The Way of Responsibility means you're finally willing to grow up. You're making a conscious choice to look at all the unloving aspects of your personality that cause negativity, hurtfulness, and harm to yourself and to others and take full ownership of them. No more justifications as to why they're there. No more excuses. No more pretending that they're not a part of who you are. No more looking the other way. Divine Responsibility means gaining the willingness to see all of the ugly aspects of yourself, shine the Light onto them, and to do whatever work necessary to heal every last one of them. Many people claim to want to heal. They want to stop suffering. They claim to want to stop hurting their partners or loved ones. But then when it comes time to take a hard, deep look at the parts of them that are "evil," they run in the other direction. They'll choose spiritual bypassing instead. They'll participate in ceremonies, become a yoga teacher, a meditation master, a coach. They'll lie to themselves and to others by claiming that because they became spiritual, that means they're an awakened being and healed now. That they're "woke as fuck" because they wear crystals and channel the Pleiadeans. The fact that you teach yoga now or post your cacao ceremonies on social media doesn't mean that you've shifted into a good relationship with power. If you're bypassing the whole 'taking Responsibility thing,' then you're still living as a very disempowered, unawakened person.

It's also important to understand that taking Responsibility isn't simply stating that you did something wrong. "Yep, I admit it. I cheated. Can we get past this now?" That's the attitude of a cheater who is always going to be a cheater. The attitude of someone who consciously chooses that it's time to grow up is, "I'm ready to heal the wounds that I hold inside that causes me to lie, sneak around, cheat, and harm the person I claim to love the most. I'm ready to heal my relationship and the harm I've caused by healing myself." This is someone who just shifted his relationship with power from dysfunctional to healthy. This is someone who is ready to learn about becoming powerful. Living in the Way of Responsibility is consciously choosing to step into your divine power. It's taking ownership of every choice you make and learning to choose conscientiously. It's accepting the consequences, AKA karma, of every choice that you make. And it's realizing that the karmic consequences that you are indeed experiencing are because you and you alone created them. There is no more blaming others. There is no more being a victim of your gender, sexuality, or race. For using these as excuses for your suffering are examples of powerlessness. Divinely powerful people living in the Way of Responsibility use adversity and challenges to rise above, to expand themselves to a level of enlightenment that allows them to transform systematic oppression from the inside out. Powerful people never use these things as excuses as to why they can't get ahead. For this would be relying on other people, on external factors, to get you ahead. This means that you have no power, no ability to rise above and move yourself ahead. If you're a woman or a person of color, for example, to "get ahead" and rise to the top means that you have a million things in your way, actively blocking you and trying to stop you from reaching the top. So many fight to keep systems and laws in place that keep you oppressed. This is glorious. It's glorious because when you step onto the path of divine Responsibility, it means that you will gain a power so sacred, so awe-inspiring, that you will transform into a true force of change. You will have the ability to clear the way for countless others that come after you. You become a way-shower. And when you tap into this power, you realize that the very people that try to keep you oppressed only ever held the illusion of power. They are completely disconnected from divine power. Divine power is free from inequality and oppression. True power functions in the Way of Oneness. When you take Responsibility for your life in this way, you gain true power. The more holy power you gain, the more you not only transform yourself, your life circumstances, and your relationships, but the more you also help to transform the world. Once you've made the choice to live in the Way of Responsibility, you're ready to do the work that it takes to gain all of the characteristics of an enlightened being who functions in the Ways of Oneness. Being radically Responsible allows you to gain the characteristic of the next Way. A Way that is foundational to all levels of healing and transforming: The Way of Patience.

CHAPTER 4

UNIVERSAL WAY OF ONENESS № 2:

The Way of Patience

THE WAY OF PATIENCE

Mason had the patience of a saint. He modeled the Way of Patience every day of his life. He would watch me as I prepared his meals for him. Although extremely food-driven, he didn't beg or become restless while he waited. When I placed the bowl down, he would look at it and then look at me patiently, waiting for me to tell him "Okay!" so he had the green light to eat. One early evening, I arrived home at the time I typically fed Mason dinner. After letting Mason out to go to the potty, I started to prepare his dinner for him. I saw that my sister was calling me, so I grabbed the phone and started to chat. At the beginning of our conversation, I took Mason's filled dog dish into the laundry room where I always fed him and placed his dish in the food stand. I left the room and went to sit on the couch in the Florida room off of my kitchen. Melissa and I chatted for about ten minutes or so when, all of a sudden, Mason came barreling in the room, running right towards me. When he reached the couch, he pounced at the ground right in front of me, then turned around and ran back to the laundry room. I burst out laughing. "What the hell was that crazy move?!" I belted out to my sister. Then I told her what Mason had just done.

She laughed too and said, "What the heck?"

I responded, "I have no idea what that was." I waited for a minute and saw no sign of Mason. So my sister and I went on chatting. Approximately ten more minutes went by, and suddenly, Mason came running into the room, the same as before. He charged at me full speed. Right before he got to me, he pounced on the floor while grunting, then turned back around and ran like a bat out of hell through the kitchen and back to the laundry room. "What the hell is this dog doing?!" And as I started to tell my sister that he just "did it again," it dawned on me. "Oh my God! I know what he's doing!" I yelled. I jumped up and ran into the laundry room while my sister was trying to figure out what was going on. When I got to the laundry room, I couldn't believe my eyes. There was Mason, standing over his food dish with his nose just centimeters away from his kibble, with a downpour of drool saturating his food. I realized when I had put the dish down for him twenty minutes before, I never said, "Okay." I never gave him the command to eat his food. It slipped my mind because I was talking to my sister. I just walked away from him and went into the other room after setting his dish down in front of him. And Mason never touched that food. He patiently waited for the command that never came. As I realized all of this in an instant, I yelled, "Okay, Mason! OKAY!" And Mason dove into that food and gobbled it up like he hadn't been fed for three days.

What's so remarkable about this is that Mason waited so patiently for a good ten minutes before running into the other room to find me, to let me know he wanted permission to eat his food. And when I didn't initially understand what he was communicating to me, he waited *another* ten minutes before he came back out to tell me once more. A two-year-old, food-driven Lab exhibiting that level of patience is nothing short of a miracle. But then again, Mason himself was a miracle, so it really shouldn't have surprised me at all. Now, before some of you dismiss this as a behavior that reflects obedience versus patience, understand that being obedient requires patience. If you have no patience, you can't be obedient. So what I'm focusing on here and singling out is the level of patience Mason demonstrated that allowed him to "be obedient" and not eat his food until he had the command to go ahead and eat it.

Mason's energy and personality was so magnetic that people and other animals would flock to him when they were around him. Our three cats, Lilly, Sonia, and Sage, were no exception. They often would lie next to him, rub all over his face, rub their bodies under his chin, and, quite frankly, make it impossible to just relax. They always bothered Mason with their love. As soon as they were near him, they'd turn their love motors on, and the purring would get louder and louder while they rubbed all over him and then typically lay on top of his legs or some part of him that completely invaded his personal space. And although you could tell Mason would get annoyed at times, with a cat tail wrapped around his snout, and the cat butt right in his face, preventing him from laying his head down, Mason would just sigh, moan, and be patient. He never growled. He never "warned" them that they were too much and that he'd had enough.

He just demonstrated loving patience and took the first opportunity he could at laying his head down, right when the cat would make the turn around his head and circle back to repeat the rubbing, tail-wrapping, and headbutting. Once he got to lay his head down, they usually resorted to licking his head and ears for ten minutes or so before they walked away. Mason would let out a long moan at this and patiently allow the cats to get their fill of him before they moved on to something else.

Patience requires stillness. To be impatient means you are in the energy frequency of "wanting." If you're in "wanting," that means you're not accepting of something that is. You want something to be different than what you're experiencing. It means you're in the energy of lack or scarcity because you don't yet have something that you want. Being impatient shows a lack of appreciation for this very moment. Whatever that moment is. It shows a lack of gratitude for what you already have. Impatience reflects a denial of Presence. Patience requires a healthy relationship with yourself to just be. It requires emotional and spiritual maturity. It requires you to master your mental programs that are running that tell you that this moment should somehow be different than it is. The emotional maturity it requires is for you to master being provoked, restless, irritated, or annoyed with whatever you are experiencing or witnessing in this moment.

THE WAY OF PATIENCE

* * *

Back when I was still working as a pediatric occupational therapist, I required all of my patients, from toddlerhood on, to use "the waiting chair." This typically looked like a brightly colored cube chair that was the perfect size for their little child bodies. From their very first therapy session with me, I introduced the waiting chair. No matter what play therapy modality or piece of equipment we were going to use that day, they first had to sit in the waiting chair quietly before getting to play. I was teaching them patience. Many pediatric patients' favorite thing to do was to utilize the different swings that we could hook up for them. For them it was awesome fun to swing, and for me it was a magnificent way to rehabilitate them and work towards achieving our therapy goals. A bolster swing can increase core strength, balance, endurance by holding on, help to regulate their vestibular system, and it's just plain fun to swing! It was a great motivator to get them to work hard without them realizing how hard they were working. It takes a couple of minutes to hook up a huge swing like that. So the child had to learn to sit in the waiting chair while I hooked up the big swing. Some would resist sitting at all. Some would only last a few seconds at first before jumping up and fleeing from the chair. The child was redirected back, sometimes a dozen times or more, and he was reminded to, "First sit. Wait. *Then* swing. Waiting chair *first*. *Then* you get to swing." Over time, when a child would pick a game or their favorite swing, I would ask them, "Okay, what do you have to do first before we can swing?" And they would shout, "Waiting chair!" and run right to it and sit patiently until I told them it was okay to leave the chair.

This exercise was teaching kiddos as young as two years old how to master patience. They were learning how to control their bodies and increase their level of impulse control. They were learning how to energetically ground themselves by sitting with their feet planted on the floor. They were learning safety. I had to take my eyes off of them to hook up the swing. But they were safe while I turned my back for a few moments because I knew exactly where they were. And of course I never turned my back until they gained enough self-control to sit without being redirected for at least a minute at a time. They were learning self-control. They were combating the nasty characteristic that plagues so much of humanity: instant gratification. They were learning how to be calm instead of irritated, and they were emotionally maturing. All of these things together make up the Way of Patience. Over time, most kiddos would come to their therapy session and immediately head to the waiting chair and sit down. After a while, I never even had to ask them to use it. They just sat in it automatically every time they transitioned between activities. They felt calmer and safer in that waiting chair. It represented stillness, and they learned quite quickly how incredible the body feels when it has periods of calm stillness. When I coached parents, I would teach them to use this technique at home. This one simple strategy works miracles for children's behavior and emotional development at home, when used properly. It's never, ever to be used as a punishment. It's only to be used in a proactive, positive way to teach a child self-control, impulse control, stillness, safety, emotional maturity, and how to energetically ground themselves. For this is how to internally develop the Way of Patience.

Patience is a foundational characteristic required for every aspect of life. And yet many people have poorly honed or developed this rudimentary skill. You need patience to wait in the grocery store line. When raising children. With your spouse. When dealing with traffic. With your elderly parent who has dementia. With deadlines at work. While waiting to find out if you got the job or not. While renewing your driver's license at the Department of Motor Vehicles. With your puppy you are training or with your elderly dog who won't walk through any part of the house without you right by his side. Patience is an elementary but vital skill to master in order to gain higher-level skills that allow us to move through life with divinity, maturity, and flow.

Being patient is such a gift. It's one of the most selfless gifts you can offer to another. When you're impatient, you show a complete disregard for anyone else involved while making the entire situation about you and only you. Your impatience makes this scenario about how *you* feel with no consideration of how this is impacting the other person involved. You're thinking only of yourself because you've been taken over by impatience. This is a form of selfishness. On the flipside, patience creates a selfless spaciousness for all involved. In this way, it's a gift to yourself as well as to others. The energetic flow of patience is calming and relaxing to your physical body, your mental body, and your emotional body. Being impatient often means we are trying to force something to happen. Trying to force a higher level of success in your career for example. You may not have the necessary skills, training, or experience yet to be where you wish you were. If you attained that level of "success" while not adequate enough to sustain it, it would crumble before your very eyes. The Way of Patience, when embodied, means that you may have a big dream, but you employ the maturity needed to patiently acquire the knowledge and skills needed to be gained for you to not only reach your goals but to have the capacity to deal with all that comes with that level of success. So if you're impatient and trying to force something to happen before its divine time, you're creating a lot of unnecessary stress for yourself. A lack of patience means there are stressful mental programs running. For example, your mind might be telling you, "This is taking forever. Why hasn't this happened yet? Is this ever going to go my way? I'm a failure. This isn't fair." Your mental programs will then trigger negative emotional programs. You may feel frustrated, overwhelmed, angry, or even hopeless. This of course causes your physical body to run in overdrive, which is exhausting and may overtax your adrenal system. You may experience weight gain or weight loss. Your sleep may be disrupted. What you eat and how much you eat may be impacted. Not to mention you're likely to also demonstrate unhealthy behavioral programs. You might be quick-tempered. You may snap at your spouse or children. Harshly punish your dog. Unfairly treat colleagues or employees at work. Get triggered into road rage. Project your frustration about your life as blame onto another. And all of these things are a domino effect of the deficit of Patience that you carry within yourself. Any Universal Law of Oneness that you have yet to develop within yourself will have a ripple effect in every aspect of your life. Developing Patience challenges you to emotionally mature, for Patience is one aspect of emotional intelligence. It's commonplace for so-called adults who don't get their way to throw a tantrum like a toddler. To smear a product, service, or defame someone's character all over social media simply because they were made to wait, because someone made a mistake, or because you didn't like the answer or response they gave to you. To err is human. To lack Patience when someone inevitably makes a mistake is to deprive yourself of your own divinity, for Patience is a divine trait. Furthermore, when you fail to offer another Patience when they err, you are inevitably shaming them, making them wrong, and hence placing them as inferior to your superiority. That says so much more about you than it does about them.

Patience helps to eliminate the activation of shame in another. You can course-correct with loving Patience and still set healthy boundaries and appropriate consequences. Offering Patience to your child, your pet, a friend, spouse, or colleague when they make a mistake means that you are refusing to shame them for their error. Shaming someone doesn't teach them to be better. It teaches them to be bitter. It plants the seed of resentment, and no one drowning in resentment chooses to heal or to grow. Instead, their growth is stunted because resentment that one holds inside of himself is a direct block to self-growth and expansion. This may sound profound to some of you. To hear how the times that you don't offer Patience can have such a negative effect on others. But those who are unable to currently connect those dots are the ones who don't understand what Oneness is or how they themselves create, perpetuate, and live in separateness.

The reason why impatience permeates in people is because they don't trust, and they lack faith. First and foremost, when impatience gets triggered, it's a reflection of the absence of trust that you hold regarding yourself, your inability to emotionally handle what you are currently experiencing. "You can't handle this" because you have low emotional resilience. You have low emotional resilience because you don't trust yourself to move through challenges or negative situations with power and grace or without "falling apart." Not having trust within yourself is a reflection of the lack of faith that you carry within at a deeper level. Having no faith means you are missing the wisdom and understanding that comes purposefully and that's hidden within every single life experience. Every challenge that you face is an opportunity to learn a particular lesson so that you may receive the gift that blooms once that lesson is integrated into the beingness of who you are. Faith is knowing and accepting this universal truth and therefore is reflected in your showing up as the Way of Patience as you move through life.

If this seems to be a little bit over your head, don't worry. There's no need for you to bite off more than you can chew. Just focus on increasing your own level of Patience for now.

For, if you never master Patience, you'll never be able to achieve Surrender. If you don't have the ability to Surrender, you don't have the ability to eliminate your suffering. If you truly want to no longer suffer in life, then you'll need to dive deeply into the next Way of Oneness. The Way of Surrender.

CHAPTER 5

UNIVERSAL WAY
OF ONENESS № 3:

The Way of Surrender

Mason would often get some cooked food mixed in with his kibble or other healthy treats added at mealtime. The aroma of some of those feedings was very enticing to the cats. I'll never forget one of those times when I fed him and walked across the kitchen, turning my back to him as I continued to cook dinner. When I turned around, there were all three cats, Lilly, Sonia, and Sage, standing on their hind legs with their heads in Mason's bowl, eating his food. Mason was standing over them and over his bowl looking at me with this smile on his face as if to say, "Well, look at these sillies eating up all of my food! Yep, this is really happening." He was in full Surrender to what was happening. He never growled. He never snapped. He didn't get anxious. He just stood there in Surrender, aware of what was happening and patiently waiting for whatever was going to happen next. I of course ran over, shooed the cats away, and Mason just happily wagged his tail and continued eating like nothing had ever been wrong. And nothing had been "wrong." He accepted things as they came to him. Every experience to him was just what it was. He lived his entire life in Surrender in the deepest way.

As Mason got older, he developed arthritis. He could no longer run, jump, or swim like he used to, but he handled his aging with grace. He surrendered to the fact that his body moved and worked differently than it had before. His excitement and happiness never diminished no matter how limited his physical body became. He didn't suffer. He would occasionally wobble and miss a step with his back leg during a walk, but he behaved as if it made absolutely no difference. Because it didn't make a difference. Not to his happiness. He *loved* his walks. And walking more slowly and stumbling sometimes never, ever impacted his ability to be happy. This is the Way of Surrender. Surrender frees us from suffering. It does not free us from pain. They are not the same thing. Pain is a part of life. You cannot escape pain. But suffering is a choice. Mason would struggle to stand up, and it was clear that he was in physical pain doing so. But once he was standing, he would wag his tail and put those happy ears on and smile at you as if to say, "It took me a while, but I'm up! So let's go!" Utilizing holistic treatments of arthritis including CBD and feverfew made a world of difference for him. But prior to figuring that out and waiting for those treatments to combat the inflammation and pain, Mason had moments of significant physical pain. But he was fully accepting that this was a part of his experience, and he never once showed any signs of suffering. He simply never allowed it to get him down. He chose to continue to enjoy life as it came.

People can learn a lot from Mason's ability to be fully surrendered to the experience that he was having at any given moment. There is no such thing as moving through life and never experiencing pain. You will have life experiences of physical pain as well as emotional pain. This is inevitable and unavoidable. But suffering from our painful experiences stems from our inability to surrender to what is. This means to be in full acceptance of what is happening or what has happened. Patriarchal conditioning teaches us to avoid pain at all costs. This leads us to suffer when we do experience pain. We're so busy resisting "what is," often shown as anger, fighting, or denial, that we never develop the emotional muscle required to process our pain. Weak, disempowered people employ strategies to cope with, avoid, ignore, deny, or suppress pain. Powerful people are aware of the fact that this situation is causing emotional pain and choose to drop into the heart space to process, unconditionally love, and nurture the pain while it's there. This is the powerful essence of sacred feminine energy. Surrendering to the reality that you are in fact in pain opens you to the possibility of experiencing that pain with divine grace. This is what processes the pain and prevents it from turning into an unhealed wound or emotional block that you will inescapably project onto your partner later or onto other people that trigger you. This is the transformational power and wisdom of the feminine at work. You are only triggered because you have unhealed wounds and emotions that you carry within. Nothing can trigger a clear, open, healed soul. To become fully healed and clear begins with the ability to fully surrender with no resistance to the reality that you are experiencing. Resistance to reality activates suffering. Suffering is a chronic inability to process pain. Resistance, or energetically fighting against the reality that is, comes from a childish spiritual and emotional immaturity that is expressed when "I just don't like what I see happening here." This has been taught to us from the reign of patriarchy that breeds domination, selfishness, entitlement, and competition, which are also characteristics of emotional and spiritual immaturity or functioning in life from a very low level of consciousness.

The Way of Surrender is the ability to see 'what is' and accept what is because 'what is' *is*. To deny 'what is' is mental insanity. And this is how most people's minds function. The mind automatically resists what it doesn't like and therefore slips into delusion while simultaneously claiming that what they are experiencing is what's delusional. To resist and fight against 'what is' is not only delusional, but it's a form of entitlement. Only when you enter into the surrendered state of divine spaciousness can you access the Wisdom and power of the universe. For that's where it resides. In the surrendered state of nothingness, one can find the realm of divine reality. Here is where guidance patiently awaits your arrival. Being in resistance to 'what is' blocks your ability to enter into the realm of divine reality where Wisdom can be accessed. This is offered to you by your Higher Self in the form of intuition. Intuition can only be received by you when in the state of Surrender. For the state of Surrender is an aspect of Oneness with divinity itself. To be in Oneness with the very Source of Sacred Wisdom is to be led and guided by Her. To be in resistance to what you don't want to be experiencing is to be in resistance to Her. To be in Resistance to Her Wisdom means to be in resistance to divinity itself and to the only reality that is actually free from egoic delusions.

THE WAY OF SURRENDER

The act of surrendering instead of fighting against the reality you are experiencing takes impenetrable courage. To willingly and wholeheartedly dive all the way into the depths of pain, such as grief, for example, requires the wisdom and power of Sophia. . .the Sacred Feminine energy that can be found in all things created because she created all things. Being in the place of true surrender connects you to power. The power to rise. The power to be at peace. The power to heal and transform. The power to take inspired, divine action. The power to use your voice against injustice. The power to be patient. The power to forgive. The power to be whatever this situation needs you to be in order to receive the divine gifts that are offered to you in every life experience that you move through. Surrender is the releasing of all resistance and taking action towards stillness. It opens doors of awareness, of the opportunity for healing, and for change. Surrender places us on the path of our divine journey to expanding and maturing. It allows us to deal with a person or situation free from resisting, fighting, opposing, or controlling. It requires you to release all rigidity and flow with what life is offering to you in this current experience. It allows us to break free from the mental commentary of our minds as it guides us to find our way within to be in the body. In this way, being in Surrender is grounding. And when you're grounded, you have the ability to see the truth in all situations.

Surrender never means giving up. It's quite the opposite. It means to choose quietness while you gain clarity on a situation. True clarity can only happen when our mental programs and the stories that our mind wants to tell or project onto the situation cease. When in Surrender, you are taking steps towards quieting the egoic mind and opening the heart. Being in the state of Surrender leads us to respond versus react. To mature out of patterns of forcing life to happen. It's also the place that leads to success. Cultural conditioning teaches us to force life. You may attain status, fortune, fame, and materialism by working eighty hours per week, but at what cost? If you neglect family and loved ones in order to make more money for your fourth luxury car, if you're stressed, mentally exhausted, emotionally drained, and have no time for physical exercise, if you have children but rarely spend any quality time with them, if you expect to continue to rob your spouse of emotional intimacy and quality time, but are then puzzled why your sex life is deteriorating, then you are not successful no matter how much money you have in the bank or how big your mansion is. These are the byproducts of forcing life and not learning how to live in the Way of Surrender. True success stems from the ability to let go of the grips on life. No longer forcing life is the opposite of what we've all been taught. When surrendered, you have the faith that the Universe will bring to you the people, conversations, solutions, insights, and opportunities in the perfect divine timing. There's no more stressing out or pushing to make things happen. Surrender allows things to come to you with ease, for it puts you in a position of receptivity and removes all resistance to what's coming your way. Surrender is a step towards emotional freedom. No more stressing to make things happen. No more immature resistance or tantrum-throwing to things you don't prefer regarding your life circumstances or experiences.

Being in the energy of resistance causes you to contract to a smaller, powerless version of yourself. This non-surrender to "what is" creates the energy of rigidity to penetrate your experience and the people you associate with. What you resist persists because it blocks your ability to flow out of the current scenario. Being in the energy of resistance chokes off your connection to your Higher Self and to Divinity. Resistance comes from the ignorant belief that life happens *to* you instead of *for* you.

The most efficient way to change circumstances that you don't want to be experiencing is to completely let go of all of your resistance and control programs and learn to surrender to what the current experience is. Every life experience holds valuable lessons within it, no matter how uncomfortable that situation is. When you stop resisting, and surrender, you'll gain the lesson that is meant for you and flow out of these particular circumstances. Currents, like life challenges, can either pull you under and drown you, or they can propel you forward and move you swiftly to where you are meant to go.

It's time to gain the aspect of Oneness through becoming the Way of Surrender. Choosing to surrender opens the door to the power to change your circumstances because you're no longer offering the resistance that makes unwanted things persist. You're becoming One with the flow of the Universe. To master the Way of Surrender means having the ability to eliminate any and all suffering from your life experience. It opens the door for grace to flow into and through you. With the flow of grace moving through you, and the removal of resistance, the Way of Surrender therefore evokes the onset of what stillness is within oneself. A person is then better able to see the truth in situations and interactions with others. Most people perceive conflicts, for example, through the eyes of their mental programs, emotional woundedness, or unhealed inner child. Surrendering to "what is" allows you to see the actual truth in any situation versus your misperceived interpretation of what's happening. Living in the Way of Truth allows you to live with honesty, transparency, and trust with yourself and with others. So the more you learn to release your resistance to life and life challenges, the more you are learning to master the Way of Surrender. This opens you more and more over time to receive all the gifts that the universe has in store for you. And it strengthens your mental and emotional bodies, evolving them to be capable of living in the next Way of Oneness. The Way of Truth.

CHAPTER 6

UNIVERSAL WAY
OF ONENESS № 4:

The Way of Truth

THE WAY OF TRUTH

You might be wondering how in God's name can a dog be truthful. A part of truthfulness is honesty. And Mason was very honest. Sasha, our little dog, would of course be fed at the same time as Mason. Their dog dishes were right next to each other. Sasha would often try to sneak over into Mason's dish and eat his food in addition to hers. But Mason would absolutely never do that. He knew the Truth. That Sasha's dog dish was hers, not his. So he never touched it. There were times when Sasha would snub her nose to her meal and walk out of the room leaving a full bowl of food there. Mason would certainly notice it. He'd inch his way close to it, using that powerful sniffer of his to confirm what it looked like: an entire meal sitting right there in front of him, free for the taking. And Mason was an eater. He was *very* food-driven. If you'd give him ten bowls of food, he'd eat himself to death. But not if the bowls didn't belong to him. He'd see Sasha's food and sometimes go right up to the dish and put his nose in it. But he never dared to eat what wasn't his. He was too honest for that. He knew that food didn't belong to him. He was tempted for sure. But he'd always walk away from what wasn't his. So he demonstrated a level of integrity that only living in the Way of Truth can offer. He didn't take what didn't belong to him. He honored that fact. He walked away from her dish every time. Now, if you told him "Okay!" and let him know that he could eat it, he'd devour it right away. But on his own, he remained in this honest level of integrity. . . in the Way of Truth: that that small dog dish didn't belong to him. He surrendered to the fact that her food wasn't for him, so he never touched what wasn't his. He knew the Truth, and this truth wasn't distorted by his hunger or his interest in Sasha's food. Mason never lost sight of the Truth, and he role-modeled what it was to surrender to what is and live from a place of honesty and integrity.

It's important to understand that the more you successfully surrender, the more you'll organically transform to become a person that is peaceful. So, instead of misperceiving or projecting your mental or unhealed-wounded programs onto the situation or person involved, when you remember to surrender and walk onto the stage of stillness, it activates the process of dissolving the veils of falsity that distort your sight to the Truth. There is only ever one universal truth in any situation. This isn't "your truth" or "my truth" nonsense. "Speaking your truth" comes from ego, woundedness, and the perceived need to be right, seen and heard. All of those are aspects of your shadow self. Being in surrender means you've let go of all resistance to what's before you. When there is zero resistance, the ability to see the truth in the situation exists.

My biological father died exactly one week after my fifth birthday. From around 5 ½ until I went off to college, I was raised by a man who became my stepfather. He was a medical doctor. A radiologist. He was bipolar and extremely abusive. Mental, verbal, emotional and sometimes physical abuse were a part of every day throughout my childhood. Living in survival mode of flight, fight, or freeze impacted my emotional body and my nervous system sometimes hourly. Until about the age of 13, I was constantly striving to prove that I was worthy to him. I reacted to the constant belittling and criticism with programs of, "If I just run faster, play my sports better, get better grades, take first place, etc., he'll give me the validation I deserve." But when I got straight A's and top awards in my sports, he would react sometimes with hours of screaming at me, telling me that I was so pathetic I didn't deserve to play that sport or that I was still stupid because I didn't have a 4.0 grade point average. And he'd even threaten to pull me out of the sport altogether, telling me that I didn't deserve to be on the team. Or if I earned MVP, he'd snicker and tell me it didn't mean anything unless I got MVP every single time, every single year, until I graduated. Only then would he be impressed. In a thousand different ways, he constantly told me that no matter what I did, no matter what I achieved, it was never good enough. I was never good enough. Then the day came when I had my first shift into awakening that showed me that all of that was bullshit.

I was mortified after earning a B-plus in one of my classes. At 13 years old, I understood that only stupid failures got B's. The fact that I didn't have straight A's meant I was going to get one hell of a dose of verbal abuse and most likely be grounded as a punishment. My stepdad loved to give extreme consequences for...well...pretty much anything. So I put my head down, focused on bringing that grade up, and worked my ass off so I could earn the A. The problem was I wasn't earning the A for me. I was earning an A for the validation and approval of someone outside of myself. I was trying to earn the approval of a mentally ill, emotionally broken, abusive dictator of a man who oozed toxic masculinity from every pore of his being. So fast-forward a grading period, and I got the A. Well, it was an A-minus. When my stepdad came home from work, I rushed over to hand him my report card. I stared up at his face with anticipation. I was eagerly waiting for his expression to change into a smile filled with pride and maybe even receive a "Good job, Rachel" for all of my hard work to bring up my grade. But instead, his face changed to disappointment and even disgust. He immediately began ranting about my A. "This is barely even an A!" he scolded. "This doesn't even count as an A!" And then he went on to tell me how stupid and worthless I was for not being capable of getting higher grades and how I was a loser that would never get into college and blah, blah, blah. But here's the magic in this. When he first changed his facial expression to a negative one, and I knew what was coming, I felt the fear and numbness sweep throughout my body. That extremely familiar fight, flight, or freeze response that got activated on a daily basis. But, this time, as he opened his mouth to spew out the diarrhea of abusive nonsense, I had a sudden revelation. Well, more accurately, I had an out-of-body experience. My soul left my body. It was slightly behind and above us watching the scene. And my soul consciousness suddenly had the epiphany that, "Oh my God, this has nothing to do with me." I instantly received the divine truth that he was running abusive programs that he received from childhood, and all he was doing was projecting those programs onto me. It wasn't personal. His abuse had *nothing* to do with my grades, or how well I did in sports, or was personal to me at all. It had everything to do with how he perceived and felt about himself. I was just the scapegoat for his own self-loathing and hatred. The feeling of a smile crept onto my face while he was rattling off how incapable I was, and I felt an energetic weight of hundreds of pounds lift off of my shoulders. This was my first authentic shift into awakening. From that moment on, although the abuse of course continued and it was awful, I never took it personally. Never. Studying and learning, getting better at the sports I played, were all for me. I did those things to improve who I was as a person and to show up in this world better today than I was yesterday. And not because I wasn't good enough yesterday, but because as a divine, infinite being, I'm capable of being even better today. You see, in that moment at 13, I let go of trying to change my stepdad's perception of me. I never again offered resistance to who he was choosing to be towards me. I surrendered. Because I surrendered, I suddenly was able to see from the realm of Truth. That although my stepdad's behavioral programs were abusive and filled with maltreatment of me, they were absolutely not personal or had anything to do with me at all. I also saw that my soul chose to have this childhood experience so I could learn something valuable from it. In one mystical split second, I shifted out of victim consciousness into a more empowered state. That was the first step into emotional freedom, a higher level of consciousness, and it set me up to walk the path of becoming a spiritual teacher of Truth and Oneness. It allowed me to receive the gifts that were hidden in the abuse and in the mentally ill man who was raising me. It allowed me to move through painful and challenging experiences in order to integrate the "fierce spiritual warrior" that I was meant to become. I cannot offer this world what I am here to teach without the integration of the fierce warrior. No teacher of Truth is a teacher of Truth without the embodiment of the fierce warrior. I came into this world with the divine characteristics of a sacred mother already fully anchored into my beingness. Nurturing and loving was as easy for me as breathing. But to live my life's purpose, it required me to fully integrate the fierce spiritual warrior with the sacred mother. That required challenging-enough experiences to give me the opportunity to bring forth the fierce warrior spirit that was ready to teach and express itself through me during this human lifetime. All of that discovery and understanding started first with my ability to Surrender. If you are offering even a tiny crumb of resistance, you are not surrendered. And if you don't have the ability to fully Surrender, then you won't have the ability to see the Universal Truth in the situation.

The ability to see the full Truth, to function from Truth, to Live in Truth allows you to live your life with integrity. It takes a very powerful person to live their life with integrity. This is because integrity is the practice of being honest and showing a *consistent and uncompromising* adherence to strong moral and ethical principles and values. In ethics, integrity is regarded as the honesty and truthfulness of one's actions. The opposite of this, telling half-truths and lying by omission, is not only manipulative, but they are cowardly. Cowards lie because they are too weak to handle the Truth of the situation and face the fact that they were the ones who created it to begin with. Which leads us to another aspect of dishonesty: going into denial or running from the Truth. The Truth truly does set us free. Free from the bondage of darkness that is created from lies and evil secrets. Denial is just another form of lying and dishonesty. It's just a form of lying to yourself. Aspects of your life or your relationship cannot be healed if you refuse to see what's really there. Truth, however, shines the Light on everything so every single thing can be seen, considered, and dealt with. Truth is fundamentally required in order for healing to take place.

Are you refusing to see that you are being lied to or that you are being treated poorly? Are you being dishonest with yourself about how you really feel? Are you too scared to admit your relationship needs to end or that you've grown out of your friendships and it's time to move on and connect with others who are of a higher vibrational frequency?

It's time to see how you are actually showing up in your life and relationships versus how you'd like to think you are showing up. It's time to become honest with yourself and face the music of how things need to change, of how *you* need to change.

Many people will run programs of defensiveness when they feel attacked. And yet most of the time, the Truth is the person isn't even being attacked. It's only *perceived* that way because an unhealed inner child wound got triggered within them. So they'll project their feelings of inferiority onto another, claiming that the other person is being judgmental, critical, or superior. When, if they take the time to self-assess, the Truth is an inner child wound got triggered. And the feelings from being judged, criticized and feeling inferior or not good enough that was created from childhood flooded the body through the activation of an energetic memory. This is what it means to have mental, emotional, and inner child programs activated. Then the behavioral programs of defensiveness, attack, and deflection, for example, are played out, and then you have your fight with the other person. You project onto them what you perceive they were doing. They defend themselves, get triggered into their old patterning or woundedness, and no one wins. Everyone's miserable. Both people claim to be right, making the other wrong. And when we make another wrong, we automatically create opposition instead of unity. Both parties are in the hamster wheel of egoic delusion. Neither being capable of seeing the Truth in the situation.

When living from Truth, one can say, "Oh wow, I just got triggered by what you said to me right now. I'm very aware of the programs that are running because of it. My mental programs say that you are a jerk; you think you're better than me; that I'm never good enough. My emotional programs are expressing anger and sadness. My inner child feels like she's about 12 years old. My behavioral programs that want to show themselves are to yell at you and tell you what an arrogant jerk you are. But I won't allow myself to do that. Instead I'm going to go take 10 minutes to sit inside of my heart center with all of these activated programs and love them. I'll come back after I'm done nurturing and loving my wounded inner child that just perceived you as being such a jerk for attacking me."

Seeing the actual Truth in this situation completely derails any fighting or being at odds with another. It allows you to take radical Responsibility for your own triggered states and woundedness that still need to be healed. When you live at such a level of Truth, you can heal anything. The Way of Truth would deter most divorces, rectify all misunderstandings, and even prevent wars. It would allow for mistakes and poor choices to be seen for what they are, rectified and healed. It would ratify claims of racism and sexism that simply weren't true and were instead misperceived projections coming from woundedness and victim consciousness. Then, and only then, can the actual and *true* acts of racism and sexism be seen for what they are and dealt with appropriately. Until then, people's misinterpretations as well as their projections of previous experiences will always muddy the water and make it incredibly difficult to see and respond to what the actual truth in the situation is. Your own individual lack of living from Truth, speaking Truth, seeing Truth, and responding to Truth and only Truth, is what prevents all of humanity from waking up to the Way of Truth. It has to happen within each individual so it can spread like a glorious plague. And a Truth-plague is exactly what every government, every financial institution, every CEO, every world leader, and every partner in a relationship needs to be infected with. "The Truth shall set you free." And it does. It frees you from the hold that your ego has on you. It frees you from seeing things through the murky vision of your old, unhealed wounds and negative experiences. It frees you from contaminating interactions and relationships with others based on your biases, ignorance, prejudices, or lack of experience. Truth expands you. It educates you. It opens your eyes to seeing with divine sight instead of being limited to your physical vision and egoic sight. The Way of Truth allows you to respond fairly versus unjustly. It empowers you to walk your life's path as a divine being instead of someone who lies by omission, refuses to grow up, or keeps himself blind by not being able to see through the veils of illusion. Truth pierces through the veils of illusion that our egos love for us to be diminished by. Truth nudges us to be understanding and forgiving towards others. It guides us to become more conscious as we are no longer seeing through the eyes of unconsciousness. Truth is the bridge to a higher level of consciousness. For those who continue to lie, or hide, or cover things up, or only offer partial truths aren't living in Truth at all. You lack integrity when you offer behaviors like those. And what's worse, most who choose to do that also defend their dishonorable positions like a mother bear would defend her cubs if under attack. It takes humility and vulnerability to live in Truth, to be honest at all times even when no one is looking. *Especially* when no one is looking. What do you try to get away with when no one is looking? When your spouse or partner isn't there to witness? The Way of Truth teaches you to be honest, transparent, and Truthful always, no matter what. Because when it's not *always*, you're not truly truthful. Whether anyone bears witness or not. And in fact, when no one is watching is actually more important. This tends to show your true colors. If you think someone is watching you, that's when most put on their masks. The masks that hide certain aspects of yourself so you can portray yourself to be what you want others to see and believe about you. Your unwillingness to see the Truth about yourself is what prevents the Way of Truth from becoming an attainable goal.

To live as the enlightened definition of Truth may not always be easy, and in fact can sometimes be scary, but it is absolutely essential if you are to be aligned with the divine aspect of you. To be true to yourself means to always be truthful with others. If the temptation to be dishonest has presented itself to you, this is your reminder to keep walking on the path of your Light. Free yourself from manifesting karma created from dishonesty and allow the Light to continue to guide your choices and actions. Remain truthful to the divine aspect of you and you'll live a life that creates peace and harmony for yourself and for others around you.

Maybe you've learned to hide your sensitivities because your culture shames men who show what's misperceived as weakness. Women may hide their sensitivities because the sexist label of overemotional or "out of control" might be thrown at them, so they show up with too many masculine characteristics. Neither one of these examples are examples of people living in the Way of Truth. They are wearing masks out of fear of judgment and criticism. Some will portray themselves with a mask of the positive, loving persona on social media. But as soon as someone is a little unkind, they'll judge, criticize, and complain about them. What happened to being loving and positive? Part of being loving is to offer Patience to someone when they're having a bad day and maybe didn't show up as their best self.

They're human. It happens. How *you* respond to that is what's important. Drop the masks and live in Truth. Living in Truth... seeing what is *actually* True in any given situation allows us to experience what it means to be Present. Truthfulness leads us to the baseline of our divinity, which is Presence. When we are incapable of seeing the actual Truth over our misperceptions, masks, old wounds, or current fears, we are unable to be in Presence. Being in Presence opens the channels for divine wisdom to flow in and guide us. So, mastering and elevating into the beingness of the Way of Truth leads us to the next Way of Oneness, which is the Way of Presence.

CHAPTER 7

UNIVERSAL WAY OF ONENESS № 5:

The Way of Presence

THE WAY OF PRESENCE

Almost every person who ever met Mason commented that he was a healer. And he was. He was a healer because he lived in the Ways of Oneness. And one of those ways was that he was capable of being in total Presence all the time.

One year Mason and I lived with two roommates. One of them had her friends come over for the afternoon. This couple brought their six-month-old baby girl with them so we could meet her. She was absolutely adorable. They were a little nervous about Mason at first because he was so big, and he looked extra enormous next to this tiny little baby. But there was nothing to worry about because Mason read the room and was fully Present with everyone. So he gently and slowly approached the baby on her mother's lap. I of course verbally made sure they felt comfortable with Mason coming over and saying hello to their little one. They gave me the green light, so I told Mason "Okay, go ahead." Because this infant was so delicate, so fragile, being in Presence allowed Mason to read her energy. When he read her energy as such, he changed his energy to match hers. Being in Presence allowed him to be divinely guided to adapt based on what this infant needed from him. She needed him to be extra gentle, slow in his movements towards her, and delicate. He was all of these things during the time spent with her.

When I would take Mason to the dog park, he was so fully Present that he read the energies of the other dogs and would raise or lower his energy to match theirs. If a younger, strong, and rambunctious dog wrestled with him, Mason would turn into a bull and wrestle back with the same amount of force. If a puppy played with him, he would match the puppy's energy and play happily but gently so as to not hurt the puppy. Elderly dogs were the same way. He'd run around them playfully but never jump on them, and when they "wrestled," he did so with carefulness and caution. The times that I took Mason to work with me at a skilled nursing facility in La Jolla, CA, Mason would exhibit the perfect dose of calmness, tenderness, obedience, or silliness that each elderly resident seemed to need from him in order for them to receive a healing effect from his Presence. Mason's ability to be fully Present with each and every being he encountered allowed him to adapt his energy in such a way that the being felt seen. . .understood. . . selflessly accommodated for. What a precious gift to offer to another.

When you can be fully divinely present, you are offering the feminine aspect of openness. To be open is to be in the energy of receiving. To be open is to be free from running programs like judgment, resistance, or separation. To be open is to be divine. It's divine feminine energy that is open, receiving, and freely flowing. This is the energy of divine Presence. To be Present is to be nothing and everything all at once. When you offer the Way of Presence to another, there is no expectation of them being anything different than they are. It's the ability to actively listen with an open expansiveness that speaks the unspoken message of, "I'm fully with you right now. I see you with divine eyes. I hear you with divine ears. My divine heart is open to you now." Presence requires the ability to release the mind's constant verbiage and storytelling of every little thing that's happening, while anchoring into the heart center. No one can be fully Present when they're trapped in the mind. Presence only arises with the ability to drop into the heart space and live from there. When you understand that, it's easier to grasp the gift that dogs, in particular, role-model for us. They live and move through life from their heart centers. Which means they automatically offer Presence to us. This is why they make such great therapy animals and why dogs are masters of teaching people things like empathy. Prison inmates experience a deeper level of transformation after working with dogs as a rehabilitative method. Children open up more and gain the courage to read out loud when they get to read to a dog. A dog doesn't judge you or shame you because of your past. A dog thinks nothing of your skin color, race, sexual orientation, or stutter. Dogs freely offer their Presence to you. And they focus on the deeper aspects of you that matter much more than the superficial aspects of you like gender, ethnicity, or society's definition of attractiveness. They see through the surface layers and penetrate straight to the heart... to *your* heart. When you are able to be Present, unconditional love has the ability to flow. The Presence of love is blocked when we're trapped in our mental programs of judgment, resentment, blame, viewing another as inferior, etc. Offering the Presence of heart-energy comes naturally to dogs, and it's part of how healing can be ignited in people who rehabilitate with or are around dogs.

The moments when we can be fully Present are the moments that open us up to the ability to form healthy, loving connections with others, instead of forming egoic attachments. This discernment is critical to create and nurture thriving relationships. To function in a thriving relationship requires Presence. When we are not Present, we are running programs. Programs of unhealed inner child wounds. Fear of abandonment programs. Programs of codependency, enabling, neediness, blame, and shame. Programs of expectation, entitlement, and self-absorption. When we don't have the ability to be Present during challenging times, we react instead of respond. We make things worse and add fuel to the fire instead of being the water that can put the fire out. For this is the power of Presence. The Way of Presence allows us to master the art of energetic detachment. It shifts a person into the divine quality of being the observer. The ability to observe another person and not become energetically, egoically attached to their story, their pain, their behaviors or choices in life. Presence guides us to master energetic detachment of our own pain, emotions, and programs, to realize that our unhealed traumas or the programs that we run are not actually who we are. Energetically detaching from our programs requires the divine level of awareness that only Presence can bring. That detachment is what separates us from the unconscious belief that we are our programs, our behaviors, our pain. It further enhances the Truth that those are just energies flowing through us and that we can choose at any given moment to detach from those energies (AKA behaviors, emotions, pain) and bring the Presence of our heart energy to them. When we consciously choose this, instead of unconsciously choosing to allow those programs to run through us, we are energetically detaching from them. And when we choose that, we are truly igniting the process of alchemizing those very programs into a permanent form of healing.

Presence opens us to higher conscious qualities that allow us to have harmonious relationships. Active listening is one such quality, and yet it is missing in so many relationships. Active listening is the ability to listen with 100 percent focus for the sake of understanding the other person. If you're trying to fix them, you're not actively listening. If you're waiting to respond, you're not actively listening. If you're eager for the person to stop talking so you can share about you, you're not actively listening. If you're interrupting, yep, you guessed it. No active listening is being offered. Active listening is a higher quality because it requires Presence. To be Present for someone while they're sharing, or while they're in emotional pain, is to actively listen to them and to show up for them in a way that offers emotional safety. Feeling safe to express, to share, or to be vulnerable requires an emotionally safe space, AKA Presence, to be there. So creating a safe emotional space for someone is another highly conscious quality that is an aspect of Presence. And yet another aspect of Presence is understanding. When you're Present, you're a safe person to share with. You're actively listening, and because you're listening and engaging with stillness, the absence of mental chatter, and with divine focus, you gain understanding. To be understood is a gift. To be understanding is a gift you get to give to others that is birthed from your ability to offer Presence.

The beautiful thing about the ability to be in Presence is that the higher qualities such as active listening, creating an emotionally safe space, and truly understanding another, organically arise out of this divinely still place. You don't have to try to learn those characteristics. They simply arise out of you by being Present. So if you are the Way of Presence, you are also these other characteristics. Presence is the fertile soil that sprouts these flowers of consciousness that offer your vibrant colors and fragrances to the world. Everyone and everything gains benefit from you living in this particular Way of Oneness. And you begin to open to the mysticism and magic that life is always offering to us. For example, have you ever experienced a hummingbird fly right up to you and just hover like a helicopter about a foot in front of your face for a few moments? If you're not in Presence when this happens, you'll completely miss the absolute bliss in this. If you're stuck in your thinking mind, you'll only be able to engage with this tiny bird and with the energy of this moment in a superficial way, from the level of thinking. You won't experience the sheer magic of it that comes from being fully Present with this moment. The physiological and emotional delightfulness that derives from experiencing this hummingbird in front of you is a reflection of the marvelous wonder that is floating around us all of the time. But you'll miss the mysticism of it 100 percent of the time that you remain trapped in the mind. Presence requires you to get out of your head and drop into your heart. To open your heart to every single thing that comes your way. The more you open your heart to everything, including what we like to label as bad or negative, the more you'll anchor into your heart center. Heart-centered living requires this. It requires you to fire your mind as the CEO of your life and to demote your mind to being a dedicated employee of the new CEO: your heart. Heart-centered living allows joy, magic, and wonder to flood into your emotional experiences and your body's physiological experiences. It's incredibly healing to allow these energies to enter within you and to become a part of who you are. It's also only with an open heart that you can heal emotional pain. And an open heart center is a powerful contributor to healing physical diseases and illnesses. For it's the closed heart center and compilation of unhealed emotional pain that creates most illnesses in the first place. Opening our heart centers allows us to be in Presence. Being Present opens our heart centers. This is the avenue for experiencing the beauty, wonder, and magic of life as well as opening the door to allowing miracles in.

Finally, being in Presence is a prerequisite for healthy, loving connections to form between and among other beings. If we're not the beingness of the Way of Presence, then superficial, codependent, or dysfunctional connections form. But Presence allows us to form pure, non-egoic connections. So being in Presence leads us to true and healthy Connection. Which is the next Way of Oneness. . . The Way of Connection.

CHAPTER 8

UNIVERSAL WAY
OF ONENESS № 6:

The Way of Connection

Great spiritual teachers say that you're never truly alone. We humans sometimes drown in our loneliness. We feel so desolate at times. We feel lonely when we're not understood, or supported, or when single and not sharing our life with someone else. Some understand on an intellectual level that we each have formless beings supporting us and looking out for us at all times. Every person has a guardian angel that loves and supports them throughout their incarnated life on Earth. But when we feel disconnected from others, we tend to feel isolated. And then loneliness can creep in. Loneliness can run so deep that people take their lives because of the unbearable internal feeling of it. It's during these times that seems to block the comfort of an intellectual knowing that your guardian angel is with you. After all, you can't really see her. You can't feel her embrace to comfort you or listen to her words of encouragement. And even for those of us who can psychically feel their divine presence of support and love, and yes, even communicate with them, it's not the same as someone being there in person to give you that tangible hug or put their hand on your shoulder while you cry.

Typically, humans live their lives in such disconnection from Oneness that if they don't have a tangible connection with another, especially during times of sadness or grief, they feel isolated, maybe even deserted, and lonesomeness begins to creep in. The reason this occurs is because we live in separateness, the opposite of Oneness.

Much of our emotional suffering stems from the programs of separation that we create, live in, and continue to perpetuate as our reality. The Way of Connection means living in Oneness and awareness of your Higher Self. It's that powerfully connected sensation and knowingness that you are in Connection to life itself, which means you are connected to all things divine, at all times. If you learn to live in the connectedness of all things divine, you can never feel lonely. Because the truth is you're never truly alone.

Mason was a master connector. He was always connected to everything and everyone. When he went outside to potty, he would just stand there: eyes partially closed, head raised, nose twitching, paws embedded into Mother Earth. He was in full Presence, which allowed him to be connected to the ground, to the smells, to the wind that was caressing his handsome face. He smelled the grass and the flowers very purposefully. He took everything in. He connected to everything he smelled, everything he saw. On our walks a bunny would run across our path, and Mason's ears would perk up, and he would slightly quicken his pace in the direction that the bunny was running. He connected to it in a way that said, "Hello, little bunny! It's so nice that you crossed our paths. Love to you! Enjoy your day, little one! Thanks for saying hello!" He did this with every other animal, whether they were lizards, birds, cats, or other dogs. He demonstrated the Divine Knowing that we are all connected to everything all at once. That we are One. He connected to every person he met, whether they were open to connecting to him or not. He just energetically lived with an open heart and the loving gift of Connection.

* * *

Sage came into our family very unexpectedly. I headed off one morning for work and stopped at a stop sign just a few miles from my house. At this intersection there was a semi truck that was crossing through. I glanced down at the ground in the middle of the intersection and saw a tiny gray kitten almost get smashed by the massive front tire of this truck. I threw my car door open and ran into the middle of the intersection and stopped traffic. I scooped the terrified kitten up and placed him on my lap as I got back in my car. He was so tiny I couldn't imagine him being weaned off of his mother's milk yet. I for the life of me couldn't fathom how the heck he ended up in the middle of a busy intersection without getting killed yet. And there were no other kittens or a mommy cat nearby. As I started to drive him to the nearest animal shelter, I looked down at him. He stopped trembling, pressed himself against me, and looked up at me. He dead-locked into my eyes and didn't look away. He connected to me at that moment. As I drove I kept glancing down at him staring at me. I heard his name during this; it was given to me. "Sage," I heard. "His name is Sage."

I responded, "Well, Sage it is then." Then I looked down at him and said, "Okay, stop staring at me like that, Sage. I don't keep the animals I save. I'm taking you to the shelter, and you'll get all fixed up, and someone will adopt you. I'm doing my part. I already have two cats and a big Mason dog at home. There's no way in hell I'm taking another animal in right now."

One week later, I brought the newly adopted Sage home to meet his animal siblings. Lilly and Sonia are sister cats from the same litter. They did really well when they met Sage. I had this teeny-tiny blue-tabby mix in a carrier in the living room. The cats walked around the carrier, checking him out. He looked back at them with curiosity and nervousness. That first introduction went really well. But then Mason walked over to look inside. And that tiny little peanut of a kitten fluffed up, curled his back, hissed ferociously, growled, and then started spitting at Mason. I couldn't even believe it. Sage was so scared of this big yellow giant, he was completely freaking out. He attacked the door of the crate to get at Mason. I never knew cats could spit until I saw him spitting at this yellow boy. Mason just watched all of this with his golden-brown, gentle eyes and then did something only Mason would do. He energetically connected to Sage. He sat down right next to the carrier, lowered his body to the ground, and rested his head right next to the cage door. And he closed his eyes and fell asleep. All the while Sage was acting like a devil-monster that wanted to kill Mason. I felt Mason's energy just *connect* to Sage's. He didn't take Sage's rejection of him and attack on him personally. He understood his fear and simply connected his heart energy to Sage's and slept by him. He energetically showed Sage that he wasn't a threat in any way. And he didn't walk away from him or keep his distance from him. He connected to him. He used the loving power of connection to calm Sage's fears of him. Sage slowly began to calm down. At least to the point of ending the spitting, growling, and hissing fit he was having. He backed into the corner of the carrier and just stared at Mason.

Over the next week, I kept challenging Sage to adapt more and more to Mason. Sage would be his rascally self, playing on my lap on the couch. Mason would be lying on the floor right below us. And every once in a while, I would place Sage on Mason's back. Sage would freak out and scramble back up to the couch onto my lap. Mason, of course, never moved. No matter how many times I placed Sage on top of Mason, he just lay there, allowing it to happen. After doing this a couple of dozen times, Sage began to stay on Mason's back for a few seconds. He was getting curious about this yellow giant that didn't seem to care that he was walking all over his back. Sage finally got brave enough to walk around to his face to check Mason out. Mason picked his big block head up and gently touched Sage with his nose. He connected to him. And although Sage freaked out and ran away, he cautiously turned around and came right back to check Mason out again.

THE WAY OF CONNECTION

Fast-forward about two weeks, and you would see Sage dart across the room, leap into the air, and launch himself onto Mason's thick neck. He'd hang on for dear life by his front two paws. And Mason would just stand there with his big Mason smile, with a kitten hanging from his neck. What a sight to see. In all of these fun ways, I was watching Sage fall in love with Mason. They had such a beautiful connection that developed into a wonderful relationship. Sage would lie across Mason's legs and cuddle with him. Sage would sit next to his head and just lick Mason's face and head and then rub his whole body under his chin. All the while he was purring a purr so loudly it sounded like someone had a motor running. Every time Sage would clean Mason's head, cuddle with him, or rub his little gray head all over Mason's, he was connecting to him. Physically, energetically, emotionally, and spiritually connecting. He was letting Mason know that he loved him in the various ways he'd connect to him. And he began connecting to him after Mason initiated the first connection to Sage. Despite Sage's crazy, fear-based initial reaction to Mason, Mason didn't react in a negative way. Instead, he chose to connect with Sage. And it was his heart-centered Connection that created the safe space for Sage to shift out of his fears of Mason to gain the gift that was Mason.

* * *

We lack a deep Connection in most of our relationships. We see this a lot in romantic relationships. Our partners behave in a way that isn't so loving, and our reaction is often to sever the energetic Connection with them instead of growing it more strongly. This isn't to say that behavioral programs people run such as defensiveness, yelling, or making a nasty comment is justified or acceptable. They're not. There is no making excuses for the ugly ways we can and do show up to our loved ones or to any other. But instead of attacking back, which breaks the Connection between you, you can shift your energy towards creating a Connection that emanates from love instead of woundedness. When people behave unlovingly, it stems from previous times that a loving Connection was severed with them from others. This happens often during childhood when a parent loses his patience and yells at a child. Or when a punishment is too harsh. Abuse of any kind always severs a healthy heart-to-heart Connection between parent and child. Permissive, disengaged, and rigid parenting styles are strong Connection damagers and even destroyers. So a child that's left disconnected from each of those experiences begins to develop behaviors (AKA behavioral programs) that they run in an attempt to make them feel safe or protected. Their behavioral programs form as they grow up in an attempt to prevent them from experiencing the emotional pain from others that they experienced from their parent's treatment of them and interactions with them.

A permissive parenting style breaks the connection of stability, needed guidance, and structure between parent and child. When these connections are damaged or broken, a child often develops the behaviors of irresponsibility, selfish lack of consideration for others' well-being, a lack of follow-through or finishing, and poor accountability or ownership.

A disengaged parenting style breaks the connection of healthy bonding, reliability, and supportiveness between parent and child. With these connections damaged or severed, a child can develop the behavioral programs of neediness, codependence, impulsivity, and a higher risk for drug, alcohol, or sex/porn addiction. They will often also develop emotional programs of anger and rage and can be emotionally withdrawn or shut down, especially when there is conflict. They can also develop and run fears of rejection and/or abandonment.

A rigid parenting style breaks the connection between Harmlessness and Gentleness, emotional safety, acceptance and honoring of the child for her uniqueness or level of development at different ages and stages of childhood. Children with this type of parenting style can develop the behavioral programs of easily being triggered with a "quick temper," aggressive or violent, poor ability to form healthy attachments with others, impulse-control issues, may have a lack of self-discipline, and are at a higher risk for addiction, especially sex or porn addiction. The emotional programs that commonly arise out of this include anxiety, depression, anger, or rage.

An enmeshed parenting style robs a child of developing an individual sense of self. It prevents a healthy divine Connection between the child and their Higher Soul from forming. This blocks one's intuition and extrasensory perceptions from developing. The patterns of overinvolvement in a child's life from enmeshed parenting teaches poor boundary-setting, insecurity, or a lack of faith in oneself. This leads to them developing beliefs that they are generally incapable and unable, often leading to feelings of helplessness. Children who grow up with enmeshed parenting often can't think for themselves, get completely trapped in the delusions of the mind and mental programs, and may not be able to discern between reality and their own egoic mental thought patterns. Further, since this type of child is constantly attended to, a strong sense of entitlement is a very common program that develops. The child is used to being the center of their parents' worlds. So they grow up with a self-absorbed perspective that everyone should pay attention to them and put their wants and needs first. They often grow up to exhibit behavioral programs of extreme selfishness, powerlessness, poor decision-making abilities, a disregard of others' needs, and can become energy vampires, draining the energy of those around them who they spend time with.

It's critical to understand how we've been conditioned to break healthy connections with others and exactly how they've been broken. And most of these disconnections or unhealthy attachments formed in childhood and by the way that you were parented. You can't form strong, loving connections with others when you run the programs of sabotaging those very connections. Well, you may be able to form them temporarily, but you'll inevitably sever them at some point if you fail to understand what programs of destruction you do run. When you're willing to take the time to see how you were parented and piece together how those experiences created the programs that prevent or destroy healthy connections, you automatically open the door to healing those very programs. For, although these programs may be a part of how you show up in your relationships, they are not *who* you actually are. The willingness to open your eyes of how you are actually showing up in your relationships versus how you like to believe you are showing up in your relationships is the first step at learning how to create and form truly intimate, strong, loving connections that can't be broken.

The programs that destroy connection are the programs that destroy your relationships. Especially your romantic ones. When Sage freaked out on Mason, Mason had a divine knowing that this kitty's behavioral performance was based on fear. Mason didn't take it personally. It wasn't about him. It was about Sage's fear. It really had nothing to do with Mason at all. Mason was simply the catalyst that triggered the fear that Sage already had inside. The triggering of his fear was a critical process to allow for the opportunity for Sage to dissolve his fear. Sage had to be shown his fear in order for him to successfully heal his fear. Mason opened his heart to him and connected with him heart to heart, versus mirroring aggression, fear, or any other way that poisons connection. Mason's ability to pierce through Sage's fear and lovingly connect to his heart is what transformed Sage.

So how do you strengthen your Connection to your spouse when they were just unloving to you? You do what Mason did. You open your heart. This is the key to the Way of Connection. You must have an open heart. Humans are so conditioned to shut down and close their hearts to any little thing that doesn't feel good to them. It energetically occurs automatically. We have taught ourselves to live our lives with closed hearts in order to attempt to prevent us from feeling pain. This is a ridiculous way to live. Only a closed heart can break, so it behooves you to learn how to open yours and keep it open. Additionally, one cannot heal old traumas and past hurts when their heart remains closed. Healing can only take place when the heart center is open for business. The power of transformational healing only occurs in the presence of an opened heart. Mason didn't allow Sage's growling, hissing, and spitting to close his heart. His heart remained expansively wide open. So when your spouse or partner is grumpy one day, pay close attention to how quickly (and automatically) your heart closes in reaction to this. When your heart closes, it cinches off your connection to Life Force energy. You wonder why resentments or negative emotions arise in these situations. Because you are not living as a heart-centered human. You immediately give you power away when you allow your heart to close. Mason never gave his power away. Never. He remained powerfully in love with all things at all times. You can too. But you must choose it. Heart-centered living isn't a passive process. Passivity is for the disempowered and, quite frankly, the lazy. Becoming acutely aware of when your heart closes in reactions to people, situations, or life experiences is your responsibility and your responsibility alone. It is then your free will choice to take the action to lovingly and powerfully command your heart chakra to open, open, open in response to what caused your heart to close. So open it. Open it to every person. Open your heart to every single situation that comes your way. This is how you train yourself to become a more loving and more powerful person. It's also how you'll develop the ability to develop deeper, more intimate and authentic connections with others. When we move through life with our hearts closed much of the time, this inhibits our ability to connect with others on anything deeper than a superficial level. Most relationships get started with very superficial connections, if you can call them connections at all. They're more often than not based on sex and wearing masks so the other can't get to know the real you. Our conditioning tells us to put our best foot forward and to hide the parts of us that we're ashamed of, don't like, or are embarrassed about. But this is nonsense. Because that means the other person is getting to know a falsified you. Or, more accurately, a fractured version of you. The other parts of you that you try so hard to hide are the very parts that, at some point, get triggered to the surface only to show those shadow aspects of you at very inconvenient times. This typically happens during conflicts, disagreements, or when life throws challenges at you. You can guess what happens then. Your heart closes, and the conflict or challenge turns into a fight or an overexaggerated ordeal that creates long-term discord or animosity. Or you suffer grave consequences over something that could've just been a simple learning experience or opportunity for growth. These heart-closing reactions weaken the healthy connection between you and your partner or the other person involved and create a distorted, wounded connection. If you instead learn to apply the divine Way of Connection, you would tell your heart to open during conflicts or challenges, and you would create the space for Grace to flow through your opened heart so Grace could then infuse into the situation.

To understand more deeply what the true definition of the Way of Connection is to understand that it isn't actually referring to the link between two people at all. That's our ego's definition of connection. One's ego wants to limit the definition of connection to it being the attachment between two people. The enlightened definition of the Way of Connection refers to the energetic vibrational frequency of Light that connects or links you to your Higher Soul Self.

It's the bridge of Light between you and your soul. And this bridge of divine Light exists among all things. You are meant to always be connected to your Higher or True Self. When you are, it means that you are in fact, energetically connected to Divinity itself. For you are an aspect of the Divine.

The path of enlightenment requires us to detach our wounded, distorted, disempowered connections between ourselves and all others. Those connections that are based on neediness, codependency, or control. Our shadow self aspects connect to others like leeches. And we think we are bonding in healthy ways with others, when in fact we are more accurately energetically attaching to others' woundedness from our own unhealed wounds. We even mistaken this for falling in love. Healthy connections require us to disconnect from others and then to find the true connection between ourselves and our Higher Souls, which is an aspect of the divine Source. Once we establish an energetic connection to our Higher Self, then we are ready to relate to others from a place of loving, divine Connection, which is the Way of Connection itself. So, the Way of Connection is the open and direct energetic connection with your Higher Self. Once you have an open channel to your Higher Self, it is from this place that you can then connect to other people and beings in a healthy and loving way. Relating to all others from that enlightened vibrational frequency of the Way of Connection *is* the method of creating healthy bonds with others. Attaching to others from your programs, traumas, and unhealed inner child poisons and destroys your relationships over time. The reason that people in our world are so desperate for connection with others is because they are disconnected from their divinity. By being disconnected from your divine self, you desperately seek connection from other people, while grasping for a sense of acceptance and love from them. But what most haven't realized is that your disconnection from your holy self is what creates dysfunctional, egoic, unhealthy attachments to other humans. The more you look to others to heal this wound of divine disconnection, the more you sabotage your chance at happiness and harmony with them.

By prioritizing your connection to your divinity, by nurturing that holy connection, and by protecting that sacred union with that Higher aspect of You, you gain the ability to create and foster loving, divine connections with others outside of you. This will not only cultivate deep, healthy unions with other people, but it will heal the current dysfunctional and unhealthy aspects of your current relationship with them. Simply put, creating healthy, loving connections with other people requires you to first create a healthy, loving relationship with your Higher Self.

Remember that the Way of Connection is an aspect of Oneness. Which means you are technically energetically connected to everything and everyone always, whether you realize it or not. Divine connection comes with no strings attached. It comes with conscious awareness and openness. When you walk barefoot on the sand or on the grass, you are connecting to those aspects of Earth spiritually, energetically, and emotionally. If you go outside to watch and listen to the birds sing, and you command your heart to open, you will gain the ability to feel their songs. Their songs have the mystical power to raise the vibrational frequency of your body's cells to "hear" their music at a heavenly level. But this never happens to those who are closed to it. And one way to be closed to it is when you're trapped in your mind's thoughts and mental programs of, "Yeah, right. That can't happen. Prove it." Or "Okay, I've tried it, and it doesn't work like you said." Well, of course it won't work for you when you're closed and living in your mind. You'll never feel a bird's song radiating throughout your body, observing the sensation of your body's frequency elevating to match the frequency of the song, if you're not anchored into your opened heart. You have to be willing to get out of your mind and drop into your heart because thinking ruins everything. If you're trying to figure things out with your mind, you'll never experience the mysticism of what I've described. But if you practice how to drop deeply inside of your heart center and just expansively open as wide as possible, you'll feel the connection being made from your earthly self to your divine Self, which in turn automatically connects you to the birds' beautiful divine melodies. Their songs will now enter and connect to your subtle body energy fields. And it will forever change you. Such mystical experiences are available to us at all times if we are willing to change our ways of separation and instead learn how to sense our connection with all things *from the level of our divine natures.* When you practice connecting to nature or animals from the depth of your Higher Self, you'll experience what true divine Connection is. It's free from all attachments. There's spaciousness to just 'be.' Once you start to master the Way of Connection in this manner, then you are proving to be emotionally healthy enough to connect to other human beings. If you haven't reached this level yet, it's best that you refrain from entanglements with other people, especially romantic ones. Remember, if you're not connecting to others from the level of your divine self, then you're attaching to them from the level of your wounded self. This is the distorted version of you that is blind to your own divine nature. So you'll look to another to fill you up and make you happy. And when they fail, your relationship will also fail. And then you move on to the next one, and the next one, all the while denying that your own woundedness and shadow self programs are the common denominator in each and every relationship that you engage in. What's missing from the equation is your divine Self. Your disconnection from your Higher Self is what makes you seek out connection with others. But again, that relationship is already doomed because you're connecting from a place of divine disconnection. And the vicious cycle goes on and on, until you finally wake up and choose to unite to your spiritual and holy nature first and foremost, before ever joining yourself to another being.

THE WAY OF CONNECTION

* * *

If you stand in front of the mirror and one by one you strip away the surface layers of what you see, what are you left with? Imagine the femaleness or maleness dissolving away. Your skin, gone. The blood and bones disappear. Everything tangible that makes up your physical body fades away, and you're left with the only thing that's real. The only thing that's infinite and never dies. The real You. The divine You. The Light of consciousness that's You. Capital Y. . .You. The Truth of what you are is a formless being that is an extension of the Light that is pure cosmic energy. You are universal wisdom. You are love. You are me, and I am you. We are the same. We are the same consciousness that chose to experience a human form, in order to experience a life on Earth for a brief period of time. Animals are the same as you and me. Rivers, forests, butterflies. . . the same as we are. We are all the same despite our visible manifested differences. We are an extension of Source, of pure Consciousness, that branched off to form a soul, that then chose a particular physical form in order to move through a unique physical experience. We are all having the same macrocosmic experience while living our individual microcosmic lives. We are solely distinctive while simultaneously being one and the same. We are One. And in this way we are all connected. When you give yourself permission to see the Truth of what you and every other being on this planet are, the organic process of energetic expansion will start to take place. The veils of separation will begin to dissipate, and you will start to feel the sensation of authentic Connection between you and others. If you sit at a lake and watch the ducks, you'll feel the power of connection to the ground, the water, to each and every duck. You'll experience the sensation of divine Connection to the surrounding trees, the lizards and squirrels. And, when you get really good at it, even to the air and to the clouds. The identification of yourself as a mere human will begin to dematerialize, and an awakening to the Truth of who you and every other creature on this planet are will start to take its place. This is when you can begin to experience what the Way of Connection really means.

True awakening isn't just awakening to your own divinity. True awakening is awakening to everyone's. We humans really love to listen to our egos tell us how separate and special we are compared to everyone and everything else. This is the illusion that most people still move through life with. This is how most humans still treat the planet, nature, animals and other human beings, as if we are each separate and one is superior compared to the other. We destroy habitats and then project that wild animals are encroaching on "our" territory and then demand that something be done about it. We create political parties that oppose and fight one another. We focus on surface-level variances like gender, race, and sexual orientation in order to strengthen our erroneous beliefs that "we" are separate from "them." In so many ways and on so many levels, we live in separation, completely disconnected from divinity, and then wonder why we get so lonely. And then to make up for our spiritually unconscious ignorance, we attempt to form millions of superficial "connections" through social media, followers, sex partners, friends, an ungodly number of bridesmaids and groomsmen in the wedding party, or with money and materialism. We strive so hard to prove that we matter, all the while living our lives in the deepest ways as if we, and others, don't. Our failure to live in our divinity causes many to seek for the approval from others in order to feel special. Anyone who wants or needs to feel special is a person who has yet to discover their divine nature. No matter how spiritual you may be, if you want or need to feel special, you have yet to awaken to your true spiritual nature. And you are more than likely functioning from false Light. Only the human ego that lives on in a person who has yet to truly awaken thrives on a need to be acknowledged as special. Highly conscious people realize that every being is simultaneously special and also not special at all. Your divine nature is exponentially deeper than the specialness of your incarnated form. The world is filled with these superficial attachments. But true connectedness is divine. And this divine nature flows from Sacred Feminine energy, which doesn't exist if it's not connecting and connected. The power of sacred Connection has all been absent from this planet for centuries due to poisonous patriarchy oppressing and desecrating the feminine. True connectedness comes from heart energy infused with feminine openness, receptivity, and flow. Connection cannot happen if you're closed off or if you contribute to stifling the feminine. And in fact, when you knowingly or unknowingly oppress feminine energy, and therefore stifle connectedness, you are actively manifesting and living in disconnectedness in various forms. Disconnection is a sickness that spreads through people much like the depiction of a virus-borne apocalyptic zombie movie.

One simple example of being plagued with the sickness of disconnection is when you stick your head in the sand and refuse to give up a food or product that is created from spiritual disconnection instead of those created from Oneness. Refusing to give up dairy products is an example. When you continue to drink milk and eat cheese even though you know of the brutal torture that it causes to animals, and the destruction it inflicts onto our precious planet, you are living in and inflating the same patriarchal vanity that produces tyranny, violence, and oppression. You are literally paying for the affliction of oppression and torture onto other sentient beings so that you can live in your arrogant superiority and disconnectedness from those animals, for the sake of the cheese plate you just ordered off of the menu. And then you'll turn right around and call yourself a good human being because you posted a spiritual meme on social media. This type of extreme disconnectedness is so commonplace that the average person has no clue that they regularly participate in such horrific forms of violence. Disconnectedness has been so deeply conditioned in humans that when you're shown the Truth of where our food comes from, and what we are doing to innocent beings in order to caress our taste buds, you actually have the audacity to call vegans and animal rights activists extremists. There is zero difference between this and when so many people and countries turned a blind eye to what Nazi Germany was doing during the era of the Holocaust. The definition of the word holocaust is "the destruction or slaughter on a mass scale." This perfectly sums up our meat and dairy industry. This perfectly sums up the massacre to the rainforests and to the ongoing extinction of animal species after animal species because of human choices rooted in disconnection. It is recorded that six million Jews were murdered in the Holocaust. This four-year massacre lasted from 1941 to 1945. In the first five *months* of 2021 alone, over 19,400,000 animals were murdered. In the concentration camps, Jewish people were forced to live in ghastly conditions, where they were brutally beaten, tortured, starved, and then lined up and herded into the gas chambers and slaughtered. This is almost an identical play-by-play of what's carried on each and every single day in the meat and dairy industry. But because humans are poisoned with and function from the level of disconnection, they disassociate from the Truth of what our food industry has turned into. Not so different from the way a serial killer disassociates from his victims. He sees them as objects to be used for his pleasure. Someone that he can do whatever heinous acts to them that he chooses to, while having no empathy for the fear, pain, and trauma that he inflicts onto them. He's disassociated from the agony he puts them through. He's severed his connection from them so he cannot acknowledge them as sentient beings. Now I ask you, did I just describe Ted Bundy, Jeffrey Dahmer, or a dairy farmer?

Only through the Way of Connection can we heal and end the harm that we cause to others. And I hope you realize by now that when I say others, I am not only referring to humans. Remember that being in Presence allows you to form connections. Forming genuine connections that stem from Presence ignites the ability of clairsentience. This means "clear feeling." This means you can sense what another person, or animal, is feeling. Or, said in another way, you can sense the emotional state of a person or animal. This occurs naturally when you are energetically connected to one another through the connection of yourself to your own divine soul. For those who have a deeper ability and are empathic, they can literally feel exactly what another is feeling, inside of their own bodies, as if it is happening to them. All people have the ability to be clairsentient. It's a basic psychic skill that all of humanity has. Knowing this then, you can choose to drop into Presence and imagine your heart energy connecting to your pet's heart energy and practice feeling what your dog, cat, or pet rabbit is experiencing emotionally. You can practice this with your spouse, children, or with close friends. Once you hone this mystical ability, take a trip to a slaughterhouse and practice feeling what those animals are feeling. When connected, you can't escape the terror or the emotional agony they're being put through.

And in some cases, you'll be able to sense the physical agony as well. If you practice this skill with your pets, you'll be much more sensitive and efficient at meeting their needs because you'll be able to feel when they're lonely or sad. You'll feel when they're bored because they haven't been exercised enough or given enough loving attention or mental stimulation to that day. You'll treat them less and less like objects and more and more like the emotional beings that they are. Imagine if you could do that with people as well. You'd be able to sense the emotional reaction to the way you just treated them or the words you spoke to them. We would naturally be kinder and more sensitive to the well-being of others with the capacity to feel our impact on them. That's the natural side effect of true connection. And once you strengthen your ability to truly connect with your own soul, and to connect to others from your divinity instead of your ego, it will lead you to an even higher aspect of Oneness. . . The Way of Compassion.

CHAPTER 9

UNIVERSAL WAY OF ONENESS № 7:

The Way of Compassion

THE WAY OF COMPASSION

Two textbook definitions of compassion are "the sympathetic consciousness of others' distress, together with a desire to alleviate it," and "a feeling of deep sympathy and sorrow for another who is stricken by misfortune, accompanied by a strong desire to alleviate the suffering." Mason was so incredibly compassionate it was almost like a superpower of his. If I ever got sad and cried about something, there he'd be, licking my tears that were streaming down my face, followed by gluing himself to my side as if to say, "Don't worry. I'm going to press against you for as long as it takes until I no longer feel your suffering." He was such a compassionate boy. It didn't matter what was going on in my life. He was always there, velcroed to my side, compassionately supporting me through every life change, breakup, ups and downs of entrepreneurship, or through the grief of an old friend committing suicide. No matter what life challenge or experience came my way, Mason showered me with compassion every step of the way.

When we're still living in the lower levels of consciousness, it can be easy to mistake compassion for sympathy. They are not one and the same. Feeling sorry for someone is disempowering to them, and it borders on the lines of enabling and codependency. The spiritual definition of compassion means you see and acknowledge their pain, understand that they are in fact, *in* pain, and you have the desire to support them in a loving way while they heal and move through their pain. It is never the desire to remove their pain for them. That is not what true, conscious compassion is on any level. Taking away one's pain is incredibly disempowering to them. This means that you don't see them as powerful enough to love, nurture, or process their own pain. That they are incapable of healing her or himself. This is what patriarchy has taught us. Toxic masculine conditioning has taught us how to be so weak when it comes to emotional duress that, first of all, we can't even handle our own pain, let alone have the emotional capacity to be in the presence of another who is in distress. And worse yet, some will want to do whatever it takes to remove the pain that the person in front of them is feeling. This is insanity! You're preventing that person from learning how to tap into the power of self-love and nurture their own emotional anguish. You're disarming them from their own internal power to process negative emotions. You're keeping them trapped in the emotional state of a helpless child who needs Mommy to kiss his wounds and make him feel better because he can't yet do that for himself. Understand something: toddlers can begin to learn how to process emotions. Toddlers. It takes several years for children to get good at this, but if you teach them in toddlerhood, they can have their internal power mastered by the time they're six. There are grown adults in their fifties, and older, who don't have the slightest clue how to process their emotions, and some who spend their entire lives never learning this skill.

Now, if you can understand how being compassionate is never about disempowering or enabling another person, then you can elevate to the level of divine Compassion and freely offer it. Compassion is the ability to offer Patience, Presence, and Connection synchronously. It's being divinely spacious and understanding. It's not closing your heart, contracting, or shutting down in reaction to your own or to someone else's pain. It's opening yourself up in an expansive way with heart energy. You morph into the beingness of spaciousness, like the cosmos. And in that spaciousness of cosmic Compassion, another person has the space, the freedom, the love, the divine support and patient encouragement to process their own misery. It's freedom while moving through pain.

The Way of Compassion sets the stage for learning about others' struggles and suffering with an opened heart. And since you've already mastered the Way of Connection, Compassion comes easily. It moves you to support, to pray for, to send love to. Compassion reminds you that a person's trauma or life-altering experience could've just as easily been yours. In this aspect of Oneness, we can learn from others' mistakes, choices, and experiences, their triumphs and failures, instead of only learning by experiencing those things firsthand for ourselves. We can be uplifted and become better human beings through compassionate understanding and learning through others' stories and exploits. People in their unconsciousness and limited sensory perceptions refuse to learn from others and stubbornly insist on only learning from direct experience. Many people like this have a "prove it to me" attitude and lack faith. Lacking faith also means they lack openness in their heart centers, which means the characteristic of Compassion for people who function like this tends to be a harder trait for them to come by. Compassion is loving and gentle while simultaneously being empowering. Compassion lets others know that they're not alone. But it never enables. It's not compassionate when you ensue victim consciousness onto others, rendering them helpless and unable to invoke healing or change within themselves or for themselves. Victim consciousness always blames others and points fingers. Compassion allows for loving understanding and support while believing in the person that she or he can rise above what they've experienced and grow into a wiser, more powerful being because of what they are going through. It's offering support of the cosmos by being spaciously Present for another with loving emotional support. It's also understanding that just because a person has the power to heal himself doesn't mean he has the knowledge or the skills. So guidance, coaching, or counseling may be in order. But professional support never means codependency or enabling. It means expert teaching and instruction while simultaneously offering a safe, nurturing space where one can be taught how to heal himself.

The Way of Compassion gives rise to a softer way to interact with others. This Way is infused with the divine feminine trait of nurturing. So, as you become more and more compassionate towards yourself and others, you are naturally becoming more nurturing as well. This 'nurturing' component of the Way of Compassion begins to make its way into your energy fields, which in turn sparks other nurturing aspects, such as the desire to become more gentle and offer harmlessness and patience towards others. Another beautiful energy that is infused with the vibrational frequency of Compassion is divine masculine energy. Divine masculine is the energy of safety and stability. Compassion is a safe and stable energy and therefore glows with the Light of divine masculine while being balanced with the nurturing of the Light of the divine feminine. This is a true reflection of energetic Oneness. So inside of the Way of Compassion is a balance of divine feminine and masculine energy, as well as the previous Ways of Oneness that have been introduced to you thus far.

Understand what is truly happening here. As you focus on the Ways, and they begin to emerge from inside of you and are offered outwardly to others and to the world, you are consciously choosing to release yourself from the suffering that your personality, or your human aspect, has caused you. You are making a shift to align with your soul. When you only know yourself as a human being, you give rise to lower human experiences. You compete instead of support. You dominate instead of lead. You oppress and segregate. You despise. You focus only on superficial things and define yourself in superficial ways. You believe money makes you special or important, and you see those that have less money than you as people who are somehow inferior to you. You judge. You judge. You judge . . . everyone and everything. You become violent, hateful, and unforgiving.

You find ways to ridicule, make fun of, attack, or tear others down. You define yourself as your physical appearance, which is the most superficial, ever-changing and fleeting aspect of you in human form. All of the ways that humans show up in unloving ways are symptoms of spiritual unconsciousness. These characteristics are aspects of the personality who is unaware of their soul and definitely not aligned with it. But when you become aware of how impatient you are, for example, and you begin to see the suffering that you cause yourself and others, due to your extreme impatience, then you make a change by choosing to work at being more patient. Becoming more patient means you are expanding. You are expanding because you are now starting to align with your soul. Patience nudges you to learn the Way of Surrender. Surrendering moves you towards being in Presence. Presence allows you to see Truth. Living Truthfully creates honest Connection. And all of these Ways elevate you to being a more Compassionate person. And every aspect of Oneness that you embrace means that you're letting go of your egoic personality, little by little. You're releasing the aspects of yourself that oppose the enlightened characteristics of Oneness. The shadow aspects that keep you in suffering and in separation, not just from others, but from divinity itself. As those parts of you transcend, there is more spaciousness for these divine traits to expand within you. Your soul is beginning to shine through and Light your journey as you continue to walk through this university called Earth. And the more you shine your soul's Light, the more you release the harsh and rigid aspects of your lower self. This allows you to deepen your awareness and understanding of all the ways that you have caused harm throughout your life thus far. How you've harmed other people, animals, the planet. How you've contributed to the harming of others through indirect choices, purchases, behaviors, and actions. And as the previously mentioned Ways continue to grow within you, you'll transform into a person who embodies an even more elevated way of being: the Way of Harmlessness and Gentleness. A person who makes this shift has undergone a major transformation in her level of consciousness. Many who are practicing the previous seven Ways stay in the lessons of those ways for a very long time. Those Ways alone can not only take a lifetime to learn, but many lifetimes. While learning to master those ways, one can continue to cause much harm. You may be a very patient person who can bring Presence to a situation for example, but also turn a blind eye to the products that you use, even though they may be contributing to the extinction of an animal species. There is a big jump in consciousness to rise to the next level of the Ways of Oneness, beyond Compassion. But it's one that is required if we are to save Planet Earth and all of its inhabitants. Violence, ignorance, and programs of separation will only continue to destroy our beloved planet and everything on it. What's required to save Mother Earth and all of the beings that are incarnated on Her is the next Way of Oneness. . . The Way of Harmlessness and Gentleness.

CHAPTER 10

UNIVERSAL WAY
OF ONENESS № 8:

The Way of Harmlessness & Gentleness

Mason's essence was Harmlessness and Gentleness. His delicate nature always touched my heart so deeply. I always felt so blessed to be the witness of this holy divinity. Of all of Mason's sacred traits, this was probably the one that was the most enlightening. As a master spiritual teacher, he was here to remind people never to be harmful and always to be gentle with others. Be gentle with their feelings. Refrain from causing harm to their bodies. Offer a delicate interaction with all things so all things can feel safe with you. It may sound like an oxymoron, but to be delicate is to be powerful. Unaware, unconscious people bulldoze through life totally unaware of how their behavior or actions impact others. Powerful people are acutely self-aware and therefore manage the way that they move through life so as not to dominate or impede on others.

Mason's dog bed that was in my office was actually an old chaise from a couch that we threw away. It was the perfect size for him, and it was the only bed that allowed him to be cozy-comfortable without aggravating his arthritis no matter how long he slumbered on it. One day, when Chris and I came home from our gym workout, we stood in the hallway to my office to see Mason fast asleep on his "office bed," just where I'd left him before we left in the morning. As Mason woke up to realize his family was back home, he began to thump his big tail on the bed with excitement and love. I always took time in his elder years to wake him up slowly and gently so as not to startle him. Once he was awake enough to realize I was home and he wasn't dreaming, his eyes brightened, and this big huge smile swept across his face. He lay there smiling, watching us, wagging his tail, awaiting for the command of what was to come next. While we were standing there, Chris started to "hit me" with his gym towel. He was just standing next to me, and he faintly and rhythmically began to tap. . .tap. . .tap. . . his towel on my thigh. Almost immediately after he started doing this, he said, "Oh my God, look at Mason." Every time Chris "hit" me with his towel, Mason winced. His smile was wiped off of his face. Mason winced like he was about to be beaten with a newspaper. But we were ten feet away, and nothing was directed at him. And with every "tap" of Chris's towel to my leg, Mason coordinated a wince followed by a look of concern. His eyes followed the towel. Tap. Wince. Look at me, concerned. Look at Chris. Look back at the towel. Repeat. My mouth dropped. I couldn't believe that he was concerned that Chris was hurting me. You could almost hear him saying in his mind, "Hey, that's not what a towel is for. I would prefer it if you stopped touching my mom with that towel of yours. It's making me uncomfortable and a little concerned." Chris and I then both walked over to Mason and loved all over him to reassure him that no one was harming and no one was being harmed. He happily used his huge tongue to shower us with dog kisses to communicate his understanding and approval.

* * *

Mason was a thick, strong dog. If you bumped into him, you'd probably fall backwards or bounce off of him. Meanwhile, he wouldn't even notice that you ran into him. He was also extremely playful. He would get frisky sometimes in the house, and I'd yell to him, "Mason, get that cat!" And Mason would look over at one of the cats sitting on the floor, charge her at full speed, and pounce directly at her, landing about two inches from her face. Staying in that play stance, he would then, ever so softly, nudge his nose onto Lilly's side, enticing her to play with him. Lilly would just look at him and turn her head away from him. She wasn't about to play with, what to her, was this massive giant. But she also never moved away from him. She never got scared and ran. She stayed perfectly still, with Mason's nose gently nudging on her until he gave up trying to get her to play. She intuitively knew that he would never harm her. And he was so incredibly gentle with her that she didn't even get annoyed with him while he was enticing her to play with him. Inevitably, he would at some point look over at me as if to say, "What's wrong with this cat? Is she broken? Why won't she play with me?" It was amazing for me to witness this solid dog, who, if he bumped into me I'd go flying, charge a cat, but stop short enough so as to never, ever harm her. And then to watch how he'd calibrate his force down to Gentleness before he physically touched her with his nose. What a master of Harmlessness and Gentleness.

* * *

THE WAY OF HARMLESSNESS & GENTLENESS

As already discussed, there is quite the elevation in consciousness to move from the previous Ways all the way up to the Way of Harmlessness and Gentleness. Even if you're very compassionate about nature and animals, for example, it doesn't mean you're elevated enough in your level of consciousness to stop buying products that invoke harm on others. For example, if you knowingly purchase products that are made with unsustainable palm oil, you are paying for deforestation and for the near extinction of orangutans. A conscious person who realizes that they are using products that harm completely ceases using and purchasing those products. Period. Rainforests are often cleared to make room for palm oil plantations, causing orangutans to lose their homes. And as orangutans lose their homes, they encroach on farms looking for food sources. Farmers then kill them and treat them as invaders instead of victims of humans destroying their habitats. And the cycle of harming, destroying, and killing for profit and greed continues. And what keeps this cycle going are two things: you continue to purchase these products and the low level of consciousness of the people who engage in unsustainable practices for profit. Both sides of this coin need one another for this to continue. Wake up to the harmful products that you pay for. Stop paying for them. That particular unethical business is forced to then elevate into a higher level of conscious practices, or it dies. Simple.

Becoming the Way of Harmlessness and Gentleness takes tremendous effort. Because most companies on the planet don't yet embody the Way of Truth, the harm that their products cause to wildlife, Planet Earth, or our oceanic brothers and sisters are often hidden from the general public. Which means many of us try to purchase products that don't harm, but have no insight on what we're even purchasing. If we go back to the example of unsustainable palm oil products, it's not like the companies that make them state on the labels: "Made from unsustainable palm oil. Your purchase contributes to deforestation and orangutans becoming endangered and near extinction." No. Instead, it can be nearly impossible to tell exactly what you're buying. Unsustainable palm oil can appear on labels under the following terms: Vegetable Oil, Vegetable Fat, Palm Kernel, Palm Kernel Oil, Palm Fruit Oil, Palmate, Palmitate, Palmolein, Glyceryl, Stearate, Stearic Acid, Elaeis Guineensis, Palmitic Acid, Palm Stearine, Palmitoyl Oxostearamide, Palmitoyl Tetrapeptide-3, Sodium Laureth Sulfate, Sodium Lauryl Sulfate, Sodium Kernelate, Sodium Palm Kernelate, Sodium Lauryl Lactylate/Sulphate, Hydrated Palm Glycerides, Etyl Palmitate, Octyl Palmitate, and Palmityl Alcohol. Now, how many of you know this, first of all? And how many of you carry a list of these terms around with you so you can check the labels on everything that you purchase?

It definitely takes extra effort, but it's vital to choose products that are made from deforestation-free products, and that are responsibly sourcing their materials. Simply choosing to not purchase products that cause harm will force these companies to change their practices, or completely put them out of business. No company should be in business making any profit from harming or killing. The only way to raise the level of consciousness in businesses and companies is to raise the level of consciousness within yourself. Only a highly conscious person who functions in the Way of Harmlessness and Gentleness will end all contributions to a business or product that causes harm... no matter how much they like that product! No matter how delicious it is to your palate. Another example is to refuse to buy anything that isn't organic because it will force all produce-farming practices to make the shift into becoming a certified organic farm. Pesticides poison our food, the soil, animals, and cause cancer and other harmful diseases and side effects. And yet we continue to purchase and eat poisoned foods from our grocery stores and from restaurants, taking no responsibility at all for what we put into our bodies. Believing that the burden of change lies solely on the farmers or restaurant owners is viewing this from a selfish perspective.

As you can see, the practice of Harmlessness and Gentleness is multifaceted. You are causing harm to yourself and on a global scale simply by purchasing and consuming certain products. But you also cause harm by the way you choose to interact with other people and with animals. How harsh are you with your words towards others? How critical are you? Do you constantly make fun of others, making them the focal point of your cruel jokes? Do you point out others' flaws so you can feel superior for a moment? Do you interfere with your adult child's relationship with their spouse? Are you an enmeshed parent and parent by enabling and creating codependency with your children? Do you engage in sexist or racist commentary? Or do you turn the other cheek and ignore it when others do? How gentle are you with your partner's emotions when they're having a bad day? Are you impatient and selfishly make their frustration about you? Or do you sit in Presence and offer them Compassion while they move through their emotional pain? Do you lash out at people on social media, viciously attacking them because you disagree with them? Do you exclude people based on their ethnicity or political views? Do you scream, yell, and bully your new puppy into submission because you lack the Patience and Responsibility to properly teach and train her? Do you imprison a bird in a cage inside of your home, robbing him of his freedom and ability to fly, and call it a pet? Do you keep violence towards women and misogyny alive by continuing to feed your porn addiction? When someone makes a mistake or a poor choice, do you scrutinize and vilify them instead of offering them grace and forgiveness? How much harm are you *actually* causing others that you refuse to see and take responsibility for? Remember the Way of Responsibility? That Way teaches us to take self-inventory and to be radically honest with ourselves about how we're showing up in the world. We must be willing to see the ways that we cause harm that we aren't even aware of in our everyday lives.

For this is the first step to truly awakening and transforming from unconscious, harmful people to people who heal, love, support, and uplift others.

Choosing to believe that you're not someone who causes harm is to live in ignorance and denial of the fact that you do. All unconscious humans cause harm. Most are just unaware of *how* they cause harm. So they continue to repeat patterns that cause harm to others with no motivation to change. And then people even preach that you should find a romantic partner that never wants you to change who you are. *What the absolute fuck*?! The exact *opposite* of that is what is healthy! The only stabilizing constant in your life is the fact that you are here to change from the minute you are born until the minute you die. You are never ever meant to stay the same. Why would you ever want to be as ignorant, immature, and naive at forty-five as you were at fifteen? Or live your life at seventy as though you were still a clueless teenager with no life experience yet to understand how every choice you make contains a karmic responsibility as well as a chain reaction on others' lives? This is the definition of unconsciousness. It's the lack of self-awareness of how you are actually showing up in the world versus how you like to think you're showing up. The more you choose to heal yourself and embrace the Ways of Oneness, the more you see the programs, patterns, and wounds that you project onto others and into the world. As you choose to heal all of these, you are healing your harmfulness. You transform into a person who is harmless and gentle with others. You can also learn from the HSPs of the world. **H**ighly **S**ensitive **P**eople make up approximately 20 percent of the human and animal population. HSPs and empaths are the Light Warriors who are here to lead humanity out of violence and destruction and into the Harmlessness and Gentleness that is expressed in the New Golden Age of Harmony.

* * *

Anyone who is a highly sensitive person (HSP) or an empath shares a common soul purpose in this lifetime. Their global mission is to bring the Way of Harmlessness and Gentleness to our planet and to humanity. If you are a highly sensitive person or an empath and you never knew what your mission was, you know it now. Even if you are not an HSP or an empath, chances are you know one. Your spouse, child, family member or loved one may be one. So it's important to understand what these are, why they are so important, and what it is that you can learn from them. First let's talk about the highly sensitive person, or HSP.

Dr. Elaine Aaron was the pioneer of HSPs who coined the term highly sensitive person back in 1999. HSPs intensely process subtle information from their environment. The depth at which they process all of this information can evoke intense emotions and requires a tremendous amount of energy. They feel *extremely* deeply. HSPs tend to observe new environments before "jumping in" and they need a lot of recovery time after interacting with others in order for their nervous system to reset. HSPs can sense the emotions of others, including stress and anxiety, and then process this detection inside of themselves. You can see how being around others or socializing in general can cause fatigue and exhaustion. Highly sensitive people are continuously processing subtle energies and stimuli in their environment and from other people which makes them keenly aware of the most subtle behaviors in others. They'll notice someone's eyes shift or an attempt to hide their discomfort. They'll detect a subtle change in tone in someone's voice when they're lying. Nothing gets past an HSP. An HSP notices way more than the average person does. Since an HSP notices and deeply processes absolutely everything around them, it's natural for their nervous system to become overstimulated and as a result become energetically drained. HSPs often experience exhaustion or chronic fatigue-like symptoms.

There are varying degrees of one's gifts of sensitivities including the hypersensitive person and the empath. There is even a hypersensitive empath, which tends to be the person with the highest abilities to read subtle energies in their environment and in other beings. Hypersensitive persons are exactly what it sounds like. They have a higher degree of ability to interpret energies in the environment and in other people. Their nervous systems process environmental stimuli extremely deeply whether they are conscious of this or not. They pick up on more subtle emotions of others. For example, a slight increase in anxiety in another expressed by shifting their eyes or the slight change in body position. They may pick up on the multitude of subtle auditory stimuli around them and therefore can be negatively affected by too much noise or loud sounds in their environment. They are often soothed with silence or with gentle, calming sounds or music. These types of people will get overstimulated by chronic and ongoing white noise or music playing nonstop. It will become agitating and even physically painful to hear loud noises, and sudden, loud noise can trigger heightened startle responses. Secondarily, it takes much longer for the nervous system to calm down and come back to healthy homeostasis after being startled. A fight, flight, or freeze response tends to be easily triggered and, once again, will take significantly longer than the average person to readjust out of the stress response. The benefit of all of this is that hypersensitives can pick up on danger faster than lightning, whereas the average person wouldn't even perceive that they are in a potentially dangerous situation. Hypersensitive people are the ones you want to listen to when taking safety and the wellbeing of all others into consideration.

Next let's understand what it means to be an empath. Empaths take the experience of being highly sensitive to infinity and beyond, so to speak. Empaths have the ability to sense and feel emotions and subtle energies of other beings and their surroundings. Empaths actually detect (and often absorb) subtle energies in their environment and from other people and then experience them within their own bodies, in very deep ways. Since everything in the universe is made of energy, empaths can get very overwhelmed and overburdened with the energies around them. Your emotions are different frequencies of energies. Your thoughts are different frequencies of energy. Your physical sensations are frequencies of energy, all of which emit their frequencies continuously. Empaths are receptors to all of this. All empaths are also highly sensitive people. Highly sensitive people are not all empathic. There are various types of empaths and also varying degrees of each type. Before mentioning the main types of empaths, it's important to know that having empathy is not the same as being an empathic person. All humans have the ability to be empathetic towards others. Being empathetic means having or showing the capacity for sharing the feelings of another. You may have experienced something similar, so you know how it feels. This is one way that allows for compassion for others to develop. Empaths actually acutely and efficiently tune into the pain of others and feel it as though it was their own, inside of their own bodies and energetic system. The five main types of empaths are general empaths, physical empaths, emotional empaths, intuitive empaths, universal empaths, and hypersensitive empaths.

General Empaths

To be empathic means that you sense and feel the emotions and subtle energies of others and from the environment as if they are your own. This is a visceral experience inside of your own body, even though the stimulation or energies belong to someone else.

Physical Empaths

Physical empaths feel other people's physical pain and bodily symptoms inside of their own bodies. If someone next to you has pain and tightness in the back of their neck and upper traps, you'll suddenly start to feel pain and tightness there. If someone near you in the airport has a kidney infection, your kidney may start to ache. If your spouse tells you he has a terrible headache, you'll also get a terrible headache. If a client of yours has throat pain because their throat chakra is blocked from fear of speaking up and setting boundaries, your throat will start to hurt during your session with them. If you're in front of someone who is extremely dehydrated, you'll suddenly feel like you're dying of thirst.

Emotional Empaths

These types of empaths feel others' emotions inside of them as if those emotions were their own. Anyone in close proximity or someone you're speaking to over the phone or when on a video conference with others, you feel all of their emotions. If someone has anxiety, you suddenly feel anxious. If someone is depressed, you feel depression as if it were yours. Anger, fear, hopelessness . . . no matter what someone feels, you feel it inside of your own body in exactly the same places this energy shows up in the other person's body. You will feel your in-body chakras, or energy centers, heavy with negative emotions, fear or pain, if the person you're communicating with is experiencing this inside of themselves. You are an emotional mirror experiencing precisely what the other person is experiencing.

Intuitive Empaths

An intuitive empath is directly connected to her or his inner, divine guidance. This allows for discernment between feeling other people's emotions and knowing that those emotions are not your own. An intuitive empath often knows, sees, senses, feels, and understands another's emotions far better than the person does. This is a gift that can guide others into deep transformational healing for a person who strongly suppresses their emotional pain. An intuitive empathic coach or therapist can feel and understand deeply hidden traumas and unhealed suppressed emotions in another person who has buried those traumas and sometimes has no idea that they're even there. Buried, unhealed emotions always manifest themselves as difficulties in life, roadblocks to what one wants to achieve in life, ruined romantic relationships, or health problems such as cancer or chronic physical pain. Guiding a client towards awareness of their repressed or suppressed pain is key to the healing process and becoming emotionally and even physically healthy. You can see how priceless it is to possess such sensitive, divine gifts. Sometimes this is the only chance that a person has to heal themselves. Conventional medicine doesn't take into account suppressed or repressed emotions or traumas when treating cancer, a broken leg, or a spinal injury. They ignorantly focus solely on the physical body, when nine times out of ten, the injury or disease they're suffering from has been caused by mental or emotional anguish.

The main types of intuitive empaths include animal empath, dream empath, earth empath, mediumship empath, plant empath, precognitive empath, telepathic empath, and the universal empath.

An animal empath can sense and feel the emotions and subtle energies of animals. A dream empath often receives communication from spirit guides, their higher soul, or other divine beings in their dreams. An earth empath is someone who is attuned to the energies of our planet and deeply impacted by them. A mediumship empath is someone who can communicate with deceased people and animals. A plant empath can feel the essence of plants and communicate with their souls. A precognitive empath can feel or sense an event before it actually happens, or simply know what's going to happen in the future regarding someone or something. A telepathic empath can intuitively read and interpret what's happening in others in the present moment. No matter what someone is saying or how they are expressing themselves, telepathic empaths can see and know what their true intentions are and what masks someone is wearing.

Universal Empaths

This type of empath is all three: physical, emotional, and intuitive. In addition, they function with at least three of the seven types of intuitive empaths.

Hypersensitive Empaths: HSEs

Finally, let's talk about hypersensitive empaths, or HSEs. These are people with profound psychic gifts. HSEs see, feel, detect, and translate subtle energy bodies of people, animals, and the environment. When observing someone's behavioral programs, or when a person shares with them an unhealed wound or trauma, the HSE has the ability to translate the energetic codes of a person's words, thoughts, and emotions and get to the core of what created those programs or wounds to begin with. Because of this, they can see what's in a person's blind spots. The very patterns and programs in their lives or relationships that are keeping them stuck and stagnant or unable to heal from. HSEs are extremely, extremely sensitive to all energies and to others around them, which makes them the most powerful and effective healers, psychics, and alchemists. Simply put, they can "see" what you can't. They can detect the energy in your mental and emotional bodies, two subtle energy bodies that surround your physical body, and find the "negative energy" frequency there that is causing an illness or problem in your physical body. Your subtle energy bodies that surround your physical body all impact the health and state of wellbeing of your physical vessel. If you're not healthy and whole in your subtle energy fields, this will seep down into your physical body and cause disease or problems. How many of you have experienced problems that you go to your physician about and they can't figure out "what's wrong?" They are unable to find the cause of your weight gain, or high blood pressure, or chronic inflammation or pain. Some will just tell you that they don't know, prescribe you some medications, or even refuse more testing, although testing can never get to the root cause because scientific technology isn't advanced enough yet to detect what's in a person's subtle energy fields. But an HSE can.

When an HSE works with a person, they uncover the energetic programs of shame, for example, that you never knew were even a part of your existence. If you were criticized a lot as a child, or if you experienced abuse or molestation, then one energetic byproduct of that is shame. If your parents shamed sex and you became promiscuous, that promiscuity went against the mental programs that your parents imprinted onto you. So going against those subconscious beliefs that sex is shameful and you should be ashamed of yourself for engaging in it creates a byproduct of shame. So the energetic frequency of shame exists within you. And it exists within you whether you have any awareness of it or not. These shame programs are often floating around in a person's mental and emotional subtle energy bodies, which will eventually seep down into the physical body, wreaking havoc on the physical vessel when it does. A common result of this is the eventual, "unexplained" weight gain in adults. And it often won't even occur until well into someone's thirties or forties (but it can certainly manifest at much younger ages). When your healthy lifestyle, complete with a clean diet and the appropriate amount of exercise, still results in increasing weight gain, it would be best to see an HSE who works at alchemizing the energetic programs that are at the source of your physical problems and symptoms. It's likely that shame is the culprit, and you have absolutely no awareness of it. And you have no awareness of it because you don't necessarily feel shameful for anything you've done. Because you probably haven't even done anything "shameful." But that doesn't matter. The only thing that matters is that the energetic program of shame got created at some point by the way you were parented or by the religious nonsensical upbringing that you were raised in. And energy never dies. Energy can only be alchemized into a different vibrational frequency. So when you go to your doctor and they test you for thyroid problems, and the tests come back reporting that nothing is wrong, you can now understand why. You don't have a problem with your thyroid. You have a problem with the energy of shame that's causing disruption to how your physical body functions. Eventually, if left untreated, the energetic program of shame *could* lead to an actual thyroid problem. But, again, what's the actual source of these physical problems? And no doctor, certainly no traditional western medicine doctor that practices in the United States, could ever be evolved enough to tell you that you are carrying shame programs within you and that you should see an HSE healer immediately to address the problems.

If we stick with the weight gain example, there are many reasons for "unexplained" weight gain. The most common reason is simply unprocessed and unhealed emotions from old traumas. These can be micro-traumas or major traumas. Unhealed emotions, shame being one of those, can wreak havoc on the physical body over time. This leads to many "unexplained" symptoms and physical problems that most traditional physicians that continue to practice outdated medicine based on Newtonian science tend to dismiss or throw pharmaceuticals at the problems and leave it at that. Einsteinian science is far more expansive and utilizes a holistic approach that is inclusive of the entire beingness of a person. Hypersensitive empathic healers and holistic healthcare practitioners make assessments of all four bodies of a person who is unwell. A person's spiritual, mental, emotional, and physical bodies are taken into consideration. All four bodies are evaluated for distortions that create an unbalanced state. If something is causing a distortion of a person's mental body, it will "leak" into the emotional body, which eventually leaks into the physical body. If left unhealed for a long enough period of time, this will manifest into a disease, illness, health problem, or negative physical symptoms. Can you understand why going to your doctor and only having them evaluate your physical body isn't remotely efficient enough? Do you understand the critical importance of holistic care that focuses on health, wellness, and healing on an energetic level is the only *true* form of healing? If the source cause of your cancer is located in your emotional body, one of the subtle energy bodies that surrounds your physical body, but you are only treating your physical body, then you are *not* treating the source-cause of your cancer. You may have your cancer surgically removed. And when you're tested post-surgery, your doctors tell you there's no more cancer. And you feel healed. The problem is you're not actually healed. You are only temporarily relieved of the cancer mass at the physical level. If your cancer stems from unhealed and unprocessed rage that's trapped in your emotional body because of something that happened to you decades ago, that is the root cause of your cancer. And since this hasn't been addressed in your treatment program, then you haven't yet healed at the emotional level. And that means the source of your cancer continues to "leak" into your physical body. And over time, it's highly likely your cancer "will come back." The truth is it never left. If the energy of unhealed anger or rage is still trapped in your emotional body, the energetic source of your cancer continues to re-manifest into the physical body, which will cause the cancer to "recur" at some point in the future. Research the statistics on recurrent cancer in people who have been treated and go into remission. The statistics are scary. Some types of cancer have a 60 percent recurrent rate after one year. Some types of brain cancer have a 100 percent recurrent rate. It has been reported that one in eight women will be diagnosed with breast cancer. One in eight! And there are varying percentages of recurrent breast cancer rates within the first five years of going into remission. Who knows what those statistics will be like ten or twenty years from now if we stay on the same path of spiritually unconscious medicine?

The most common energetic or emotional reason for the development of breast cancer is a lack of nurturing. Nurturing is a divine feminine quality. When there was a lack of divine feminine nurturing from one or both of your parents growing up, that tends to teach a child how to neglect nurturing of her own painful emotions. You didn't learn how to effectively nurture yourself when you got scared or when you experienced something emotionally traumatic. Most likely you grew into adulthood seeking nurturing from others outside of you, including your spouse, but never really received it. You don't receive a divine level of nurturing from others because you run the energetic program of "no nurturing" or a "lack of nurturing" within yourself. What you seek outside of you will be met with what you carry inside of you. So if you lack self-nurturing, you'll marry a partner, for example, that is terrible at nurturing. This is how our unhealed emotional pain and traumas manifest into our life experiences. The other unfortunate part of this is that if you have children, you are very likely to withhold loving, gentle nurturing from them when they really need it. This is because you never learned how to offer it to yourself. You can't give to others what you haven't learned how to give to yourself. Compound a lack of nurturing with the harmful chemicals, fecal matter, and toxins that are dumped into our drinking water and foods that are sold to us, and you now have the perfect concoction to develop breast cancer. Authentic healing is holistic healing. That means that a person diagnosed with breast cancer should be evaluated and treated on the level of all of her subtle energy bodies as well as her physical body. A course of treatment would be based on the results of these assessments. This might look like adding a water filtration system in her home so she can immediately eliminate things like fecal matter, Teflon, mercury, chlorine, microplastics, and numerous other toxic poisons that are commonly found in tap water. She would begin a program with a certified mystical life coach or another holistic practitioner that was highly trained in guiding people through the process of seeing and healing all aspects of her unhealed trauma and lack of self-nurturing on an energetic level. She would be guided and taught how to heal herself from the inside out, spiritually, mentally, and emotionally. Her physicians would handle the process of surgical intervention or emergency interventions if required. Often, these traditional steps are not required when holistic treatment is immediately put into place. The physical body can be monitored closely by her physician for changes in her diagnosis and how quickly her emotional healing is impacting her physical healing. If further intervention would be required, she, of course, would be guided through that by her physician and supported through that by the other holistic practitioners on her healing team.

Can you see the problem when so-called medical experts have only been trained on one of four bodily systems? Three of your bodily systems are subtle energy bodies. Only one of your bodies is physical. The true definition of holistic health is taking a "whole body" approach to bring all four of your bodies into wholeness. Traditional medicine based on the old, outdated Newtonian model lacks the education and expertise in energetic science that is required for thorough evaluations of all aspects of an individual. You are not just your body. And when you are reduced to that, you will never have the proper tools, education, or guidance to truly heal yourself on all levels.

Hypersensitive empathic healers and practitioners are experts in energetic science and have the extrasensory perceptual abilities to detect energetic distortions in one's subtle energy bodies. Once these unhealthy vibrational programs are discovered, the practitioner guides the client through the process of alchemizing the unhealthy or distorted energetic frequencies. By adding these types of holistic, energetic experts to medical teams, we will revolutionize medicine and medical practices. Something that is long overdue. Holistic practitioners and most types of energy healers naturally carry within them the Way of Harmlessness and Gentleness. When that gets infused into our current medical system and medical practices, the field of medicine will be elevated to how enlightened medical treatment should function. This is what the future of healing teams will evolve into.

* * *

A lot of animal activists, especially vegan animal activists, are HSPs and empaths. Most are animal empaths. They are here to bring awareness to the torture and brutal, inhumane treatment of these sentient beings in order to raise the level of consciousness in humanity. HSPs and empaths are the keepers of Harmlessness and Gentleness. They are way-showers of a new way of living that is free from violence and brutality. They are here to evolve humanity out of their aggressive behaviors and violent tendencies that toxic patriarchy has taught us and elevate them to a level of consciousness that no longer causes such harm. Murdering people, fighting one another, raping, and verbally or physically attacking absolutely cannot and will not be a part of the New Golden

Age of Harmony. There is no New Golden Age if humanity's level of consciousness remains low. Attacking of any kind, violence, domination, and aggression are characteristics of toxic masculine energy that became more and more distorted with the absence of sacred feminine energy. The more that people choose to heal themselves, and integrate the Ways of Oneness, the more that sacred feminine energy infuses in and powerfully heals and transforms all of these unhealthy, imbalanced states. Then humanity can be reset into a loving and balanced state of global consciousness that reflects the gentle nature that our divine souls represent. That can then be brought forth into human form. HSPs and empaths already possess the Way of Harmlessness and Gentleness. Because of this, they also possess the Way of Compassion. Everyone else is here to learn the Ways of Harmlessness and Gentleness and the Way of Compassion from them. They are highly gifted and loving individuals. They feel deeply and intensely. Their heightened sensitivities challenge everyone else to stop, reflect, and evaluate where they may be showing up in an insensitive, selfish, or hurtful way. Empaths and hypersensitive empaths can detect hurt feelings at the most subtle level, where most would ignore and have no understanding that what they just did or said was really hurtful or *how* it was hurtful. So many people are completely oblivious to all of the ways that they are causing emotional and mental harm to others. In this way empaths, along with HSPs, are the Leaders of the Light. They are here to show us the way into the Light that creates enlightened societies. Those that learned domination and competition are the ones who must now follow. Your reign has come to an end. To dominate and conquer means to never have the ability to create equality. It's impossible to create Harmlessness and Gentleness or to ever create equality when you are busy competing, conquering, and dominating. Those characteristics of a dysfunctional patriarchy lead to destruction, violence, and harm. Sensitive and empathic people carry the Light within them very strongly. They are the ones standing up to protect the people, animals, our oceanic family members, and aspects of Earth that cannot stand up for themselves. They are the voices of the abused. Of the tortured. Of the slaughtered. Of the raped. Because of their innate, incredible, divine gifts of sensitivities, they are here to heal all. By following their lead, learning from their wisdom, and supporting their causes, you yourself will transform into the Ways of Harmlessness and Gentleness. And when this powerful holy quality integrates itself within you, you will find it to be impossible to ever believe in or participate in belief systems that create separation programs of superior/inferior, AKA inequality, ever again. For the loving and gentle nature of the Way of Harmlessness and Gentleness leads us to this next one. The Way of Equality.

CHAPTER 11

UNIVERSAL WAY
OF ONENESS № 9:

The Way of Equality

Another way that Mason demonstrated Oneness was through his divine knowingness of equality. It didn't matter how young or old, big or small, what ethnicity, gender, religion, or sexual orientation someone was. He loved everyone the same. Whether it be a hummingbird, a flower, a dragonfly, a bunny hopping by, a cat, the grass under his paws, the ocean he was swimming in, another dog of any size, a gay man, a white woman, a black child, an elderly transgender person, Mason loved every being the same. The Being that Mason was understood that every living thing comes from the same Source. Source creates and gives birth to an infinite number of things so She can experience Herself through those creations. A deep understanding of this allows one to see every incredible, unique expression of Source in every living thing.

Living in the Way of Equality means that you realize at a soul level that no other living thing is either inferior or superior to you. Every soul is exactly equal to another soul, no matter what physical form they have incarnated into. Your soul is a divine expression of sameness as another's soul, even though you inhabit different bodies.

This means you can suddenly see past the color of one's skin to the true divinity that they are while incarnated as a particular race. You can suddenly see the divinity in a cow or a chicken. A honeybee or a crane. A man from Kenya or a woman from New Guinea. A dolphin or lizard. A tree or a mountain. An insect or a worm. A child or an elderly person. A boy with autism or a girl with Down Syndrome. There is no creature or being that is superior to another. All lives matter equally. Every Being's life matters. . . period. We are all the same despite our beautiful and unique differences in our various incarnated forms. This is very easy to understand when you've mastered the Way of Harmlessness and Gentleness. The Way of Equality naturally arises out of those traits. Instead of resisting and fighting all of the empaths of the world who speak out, rise up, and promote the end of the torture and massacre of the Earth, animals, rain forests, oceans, nature. . . lay down your defensive guards and follow these teachers. They are here to show you a new way. A way that involves aspects of Oneness that allow for all of the beings of our beloved Mother Earth to live in peace and harmony.

* * *

To truly function in Equality, people need to understand how they substantiate inequality. There are two main ways: 1) To be the perpetrator who creates, speaks, and carries out prejudices against others . . . the person who plays *superior*; and 2) the martyr who drowns in victim consciousness and disempowerment. . . the person who plays *inferior*. There is no true inequality unless both parties play out their chosen role reflecting either a superior position or an inferior one. Two sides of the same inequality coin. When we act out these positions of duality, inequality is manifested into our experienced realities.

Can you begin to understand that even when oppression, sexism, and racism are believed in and acted out by humans, that you can choose to step into your own divine power and break these cycles by taking Responsibility for your contributing part to these expressions? Women and minorities have been oppressed and treated as less than equal in innumerable ways for centuries. People who have been victimized often fall prey to the ego's development of victim consciousness. They blame oppressors for their unhappiness and misery. They blame sexist and racist people for their inability to get ahead or achieve high levels of success. They are playing inferior. They are running programs of inferiority, excuse-making, and victimhood. This does not mean that it isn't a million times harder for a woman or minority to become successful. It most certainly is! But a woman connected to her true divine power, or a person of color connected to his true divine power, refuses to role play as a weak and powerless person. She rises above. He stops at nothing. She makes no excuses. He knows that because he has to work harder, against all odds, that translates to his spiritual growth. She knows that when she's blocked from achieving, she will create a new way. A way that no one has thought of before, and therefore she is carving a new path for those that come after her. Each of these powerful examples are people who refuse to play inferior in a system that claims they are inferior. They demonstrate the power that a divine being does in fact have, to create change and manifest a new and more loving world. A world that sees all as Equal to the next and is treated that way. When you've already integrated the Way of Truth, you see the Truth in all things. Seeing Truth includes a person's delusion that he is more powerful than a woman simply because she is a woman. A person of color can see the Truth that they are never in any way inferior to a white person. They see through the delusions of the other's ego.

It's really quite silly what people choose to believe and engage in. If you are a person of color and your subconscious beliefs and your unhealed traumas tell you that you are a victim because racism exists in our culture, then you are in fact showing up as inferior to those who believe they are superior over you. This is quite ridiculous. Stop acting out disempowerment programs and rise above the level of Truth that is so desperately needed today. Everyone and everything is in fact equal whether others believe it, speak it, see it, or not. Just because racists behave in racist ways does not mean you should resort to behaving as a victim or as inferior. Just because much of the world continues to act out sexist behavior programs and even continue to pass sexist laws that oppress women doesn't mean women need to behave as disempowered victims. It's time to live in the Way of Truth, and as the Way of Harmlessness and Gentleness, so we can show up as the Way of Equality. Living the Way of Equality allows you to show up in your divine power in all situations no matter what. Even if you're protesting against an acted-out injustice, you now come from peace and power... not rage, hate, and resentment. That's not powerful. That's weakness. Hating those that hate you makes you hateful, just like them. You are in fact no different than those that hate you. As a woman, if you hate men because of the tremendous sexism and misogyny that still exists in the world today, you are lowering yourself to the level of those that participate in those ugly, chauvinistic behavior programs. Instead, learn what it means to powerfully stand up to those men who have such low self-worth. And be sure to love and honor the men who live in the Truth that both men and women are equal and are One. Powerful, divine women don't make the men who act out the weakness of sexist/superiority programs inferior to them, so they can feel a false sense of superiority. That's exactly what they do, isn't it? Why would you lower yourself to the status that they choose to live by? Instead, simply live in the Way of Equality and speak out when injustices are directed at you or when you witness it happening to other women. It's no different for a person of color who has experienced racism. If you hate all whites, then you are no better than any white supremacist. In fact, you're a mirror image of them. If you create a social media group that clearly states "no whites allowed," then you are no different from the racists that fought so hard for segregation to continue. Trying to be superior to white people in order to heal your wounds of inferiority will never work. And what's worse, you're running the very same hate and separation programs that racist white people have run for centuries. We don't excuse child molesters just because those offenders were once molested as children. They don't get a pass from being an abuser because they were abused. We expect them to rise up. To heal their traumas and woundedness. And break the cycles of abuse by doing the hard work to self-heal, preventing them from ever turning around and harming a child the same way that they were harmed when they were children. And this is exactly what all women, all minorities, and people who have been oppressed or victimized must learn how to do.

Living in the Way of Equality means to step out of these psychotic games of duality and to do the inner work within oneself to be a loving person of inclusion and acceptance of others. You can't whine and cry about a lack of Equality in others when you yourself don't embrace Equality. This is not limited to people based on race, on gender, or even on sexual orientation. Equality also pertains to the Earth. To rainforests. To water creatures. To all animals across the globe.

The fact that animal testing still exists shows just how far off the mark humanity is from being a loving society that represents Equality. All living creatures experience mental distress and a wide scale of emotions, including emotional pain and suffering. Just like humans do. Living under torment with constant physically painful procedures being done to them and the constant fear of what's going to happen to them is nothing short of savage cruelty. Having no quality of life. Having no freedoms to live and roam in a natural habitat that is intended for that particular animal. We callously rip away their freedoms and test on them like they are objects. Speciesism is objectification in its lowest form. And what's worse is that we then mask this brutality under the label of 'science.' These forms of torture that are inflicted on these poor creatures are somehow justified in our society because the ones who carry out the torture wear white coats and carry the label of a scientist. So, if you're educated and work in a specific field, you are then encouraged to inflict torturous acts of violence onto innocent, precious beings? How is this different from serial killers who torture and abuse their victims before they kill them? Neither one feels empathy for their victims. Both see their victims as objects. Both abuse and torture, then kill innocent beings. The difference? Our spiritually unconscious conditioning brainwashes us to believe that one form of a brutal murder is unacceptable, and the other is perfectly fine. In fact, we're taught that it's necessary. This is the insanity that continues to plague humanity. All of it is torture. All of it is murder. All of it needs to end. *But what about advances in science?* Advancement? Savage torment isn't advancement. It's archaic. Only those with a very low level of consciousness believe that torturing and testing on innocent beings is necessary. Awakening to higher levels of consciousness means that cosmic Wisdom flows through. If more humans became highly conscious beings, who practiced the Ways of Oneness, scientific formulas and breakthroughs would just be given to them. They would become divine channels of Wisdom and would become receivers of information for advancement. No animal testing ever actually needs to be a part of what humans do. But because most people continue to be aligned with their lower selves, aligned only with their egoic personalities versus their souls, they only have access to their conditioned, brainwashed minds. Open channels of communication with the divine require extrasensory perception. This level of evolution requires individual expansion to a higher level of consciousness. To be at an elevated state of consciousness where you would never. . . *could* never . . . intentionally harm another being means you embody the Way of Harmlessness and Gentleness as well as the Way of Equality.

To integrate the Way of Equality requires you to stand up and end your participation as an abuser or victimizer. Stop purchasing products . . .all products . . .that involve animal testing. If the company no longer makes money, they are forced to stop their practices. It's that simple. Stop spending blood money and hiring sadistic barbarians to continue the torture on innocent creatures so that you can have fake eyelashes. Stop buying food that comes from animals being abused and tortured. Stop saying nothing when your friends, family members, or acquaintances say sexist or racist things. Use your voice and your purchasing power to rise up to a higher standard so others, including corporations, will be forced to do the same, and the Way of Equality can reign. Look at yourself with radical honesty and identify what programs you run that continue to manifest the experiences of hate, separation, and inequality in all of its forms. Do you segregate or isolate in any way? Do you exclude others because they're not of the same race, gender, or sexual orientation? Do you continue to objectify women but justify this objectification because at least you're not a rapist? When we fail to carry within ourselves belief systems, and energetic frequencies that make us equal to all others, we don't develop the ability to trust. We see all around us that our cosmetic products can't be trusted because they use animal testing. That food products that are laced with poisonous chemicals that cause cancer are marketed as healthy. If big entities such as corporations and governments saw everyone as equals, they would never market products that were out of alignment with integrity, with Harmlessness and Gentleness, or that lacked the belief in Equality.

When you as an individual don't emulate the Way of Equality, then you won't be capable of living in the Way of Trust. For Trust requires Trust of yourself. Only in the trusting of yourself are you capable of trusting the universe, the intangible, or in the divine guidance of your intuition. How can you trust anyone or anything when you constantly view one of you as inferior to the other one? If you view yourself as inferior, then you can't trust yourself. If you view another as superior, you can't trust that they will treat you with the compassion of Equality. The Way of Equality allows you to see that you are the same as all of the other souls on this Earth journey despite all of your human differences. You're the same but different. You're different and yet the same. This level of awareness deepens your understanding of how the universe functions and why we're all here on Earth to begin with. This deeper understanding allows you to grasp the richness of your Earth experience and to taste that richness by developing this next Way of Oneness. The Way of Trust.

CHAPTER 12

UNIVERSAL WAY
OF ONENESS № 10:

The Way of Trust

When Mason was about two years old, his vet tested his blood to see if he could be a blood donor. Vet personnel said that Mason's demeanor was so calm and easygoing that he'd probably make a good donor if he had the right blood type. The results came back that Mason was a universal blood type. He could donate! We had about a month to wait for the blood donor truck to be scheduled to make a stop at our particular vet's office. When the time came, Mason and I showed up for the appointment. Mason kissed and loved on all of the personnel like he always did. He went with the flow for all of the preparations. Getting him onto the table to lie down. Inserting the needle in preparation for the blood draw. And then the vet techs paused. They explained to me that the machine that drew and collected the blood was very loud. This typically startled most dogs, and some couldn't go through with the procedure because of how scared they became. The plan was to turn the machine on and observe Mason's reaction before drawing any blood. They also reassured me that if Mason became too scared, they would cease everything at once. There was no pressure to continue, and they would certainly never force him to continue. Once they informed me of this, I made a request. I asked them if I could stand right by his head, so he could see me and I could comfort him if he got scared. I wanted time to calm him down before making the decision to terminate the process. They agreed.

The vet tech turned on the machine, and the thing was so loud it startled me! Mason got very scared by this and jumped up from his side-lying position almost in a panic. But I was right there. I immediately placed my hands very gently around his head to massage his ears, and I looked right into his face. Just centimeters from his nose, I looked into his eyes, and his eyes dead-locked right into mine. I telepathically communicated to him that he was okay. There was nothing to be afraid of. He was safe, and I was right here. I gently spoke to him out loud as well in a soft, serene voice, reassuring him that everything was okay and he could lie down and rest. Within a second of Mason's eye-locking gaze into my eyes, his face relaxed. His eyes softened. As I spoke to him mind to mind as well as aloud, he slowly lowered back down and lay on his side. I saw the female vet tech's mouth drop open. She covered her mouth with both hands as she watched us, tears pouring down her face. Mason kept looking at me for a minute or two. The more he relaxed and eased into the acceptance of the loud noise, the more I continued to comfort and nurture him until I felt he was in full Presence to this experience. He trusted me fully with what was happening. Once I felt that trust anchor into his Presence, I stepped away from him, and the male vet tech took my place to complete the blood donor process.

When the procedure was done, Mason got his sticker that said "Blood Donor" on it. Both vet techs loved on Mason, gave him treats, some water, and lots of butt and behind-the-ear scratches. The female vet tech actually got choked up again when she told me, "I have never seen that kind of connection between dog and owner before in my entire life. I've seen extremely obedient dogs. But this was different. He looked into your eyes, and it was like your souls connected. He trusted you so deeply. I think we could've done anything to him at that point. He relaxed and allowed us to put him through this because he trusted you. He trusted us because he trusted *you*. It's one of the most beautiful things I've ever witnessed."

One of the reasons Mason trusted me so absolutely was because I lived in the Way of Equality with him. I never saw him as "just a dog." That because he was a canine, he was somehow inferior to me as a human. I saw him for what he was. Consciousness that incarnated into a manifested tangible form that we label as 'dog' in this life's existence. He is the same as I am, only in a different type of manifested body. I also knew that I had just as much to learn from him as he had to learn from me. Of course, I was ignorant in my thinking back then. Mason was my spiritual master teacher, and I had *way* more to learn from him than he had to learn from me. But I humbly accepted this Truth as it was revealed to me over time.

Trust can be tricky when you don't understand it at its depths or how trust is developed in the first place. When I speak of trust, I'm speaking about the feeling of or the knowing that you are emotionally safe. Trust arises out of emotional safety. Emotional safety is organically present when you are free to simply be you, without any criticism, judgment, attack, or threat offered to you. I didn't scold, punish, or "correct" Mason when he got scared and jumped up from lying on his side when the blood donor machine was turned on. Instead, I connected with him. I became very Present and nurtured him until he felt safe enough to fully relax and allow the procedure to continue. He felt safe with me because I offered to him the Ways of Patience, Presence, Connection, Compassion, and Harmlessness & Gentleness. From this, Trust is born.

All too often we offer judgment and criticism to others: to your children, your spouse, loved ones, or to complete strangers on social media. We scold and punish while closing our hearts to others when they do or say something that we don't like or approve of. These behaviors and ways of interacting with others will always destroy trust or prevent it from even being created to begin with. Humans are going to make mistakes. You've personally made a ton of them so far in your lifetime. You're going to make more. Mistakes are wonderful growth tools that help us to learn from contrast while increasing our self-awareness. Mistakes are never bad. In fact, they are one of the main avenues through which humans learn things so they can grow and expand. But something very twisted has developed in our society. The collective has jumped on so many high horses viciously attacking and slandering anyone who they arrogantly deem as "being wrong," disagree with, or who they misinterpret as being hateful or prejudiced, *even when they're not.* We've lost control of ourselves. There is enough legitimate hate and prejudice in the world. We don't need to make it unsafe for people to express themselves or be themselves without turning them into villains. There are enough of those in the world that we need to focus on without endlessly accusing everyone else in society of also being evildoers.

Part of the problem here is that no one knows how to live in the Way of Trust. People assume that there are vicious ulterior motives from others all of the time. . .AKA they lack trust in others. The only reason why one can't trust others is because he can't trust himself. This doesn't mean all others are automatically trustworthy. Oh good god, don't think that! The definition of Trust is a firm belief in the reliability, truth, ability, or strength of someone or something. It should be obvious to you that many people in the world cannot be trusted. But to live in the Way of Trust isn't about blind Trust of all people all of the time. No. It's about trusting yourself 100 percent of the time. That means to trust in yourself to handle challenges that life throws at you. To trust that you will love, nurture, and process your grief when it comes. That when some trauma occurs, you will take the time to nurture yourself and be responsible for getting additional help when you know you need it. Trusting yourself never means all other humans will magically become trustworthy individuals. It means you trust yourself enough to handle it when you come across someone that violates your trust. It also means that *you* are, in fact, 100 percent trustworthy. That you live by the code of honesty and transparency. Because that's what it takes to be an authentically trustworthy person. It means that all others can unconditionally trust *you*. To live in the Way of Trust means that you don't lie to others or to yourself. It means that you don't make excuses for or justify your ugly behaviors or poor choices. You take radical ownership of them, and you heal the situation with whatever means it takes. It means you make good on your promises. That you are faithful no matter what the temptation is. It means that you accept consequences for your mistakes and actions that were harmful to another. It means that you are trustworthy even if it seems like no one else is. A trustworthy person doesn't make excuses or feel like living in radical honesty is some sort of punishment. Infused in the Way of Trust is the wisdom that being trustworthy sets you free. So a trustworthy person lives with freedom. It's easy to sleep at night when you're an unconditionally honest person. To live in this particular Way means you trust in yourself to always do what is ethically right. It defines you as a person who can trust yourself to heal yourself when someone has betrayed you or lied to you. And that you are powerful enough to move through that self-healing, shift into forgiveness, and move on with no scars of resentment. Trust is power. Trusting yourself means it matters not whether someone is watching or not. Your behavior is no different whether someone is there to bear witness or not. When you trust yourself to handle whatever life throws at you, you'll open up to a more potent form of trust: faith. This is a trust that runs so deeply it touches your soul. It's trust in the universe. It's trust that what you are experiencing right now, no matter what that is, is for your highest good, no matter what. Whether it's something blissful or something filled with pain. It's trusting that this. . .whatever *this* is. . . came into your life laced with gifts for you to unwrap in the form of lessons, growth, and wisdom. This is the true meaning of faith. You trust that everything has a purpose, and you embrace what you get to ascertain from moving through the experience. The Way of Trust always comes back to *you*. It's a level of faith you hold within yourself, for yourself. If you start a new relationship and you find yourself asking if you can trust this person or not, you are not living in the Way of Trust. Time will reveal all about the other person. Through a combination of your own intuition, detached observations, and nonjudgmental patience, you will find out if the person before you is trustworthy or not. Instead, what you should be asking is, "If this person turns out to be an untrustworthy person, *do I trust myself* enough to set boundaries, use my voice, or to walk away?" If that answer is "yes," then you have nothing to fear. If that answer is no, then you should not be dating in the first place. You have too much healing and growth to achieve before getting entangled with another. You'll most likely blame the other person in the end when things go sour and it doesn't work out. Then you'll act out behavioral patterns where you're not trusting of others, and you'll push the next person away while in relationship with them; then you'll believe how they behave is proof that you can't trust anyone; and the cycle will continue. Meanwhile, it's never about the other person. It always comes back to you and how much you can handle the ups and downs of life and relationships. To take this a step further, the Way of Trust isn't asking the universe to bring you your soulmate and then "trusting" that it will happen. The Way of Trust is trusting yourself enough to be in a soulmate relationship without running old programs of inner child wounds and relationship sabotage. It's about trusting yourself to be honest and faithful, to refrain from lying, to move through conflict with grace and patience. It's never about "trusting" that the other person will never make a mistake or hurt you in any way. That's nothing more than a control program running in your subconscious used as a defense mechanism to try to prevent yourself from getting hurt. I can promise you that your partner or spouse will hurt your feelings at some point or will make some mistakes in the relationship. They are human after all. Over and over and over again, it always comes back to you and how much you actually trust yourself. When you trust yourself fully and completely, you'll open more to trusting others who are actually trustworthy and deserve to have your trust. And it will be easier to discern between them and the people that you should never trust. Further, when you fully and completely trust yourself, you slowly become an honorable being and one who learns what it means to honor. For only with unconditional trust of yourself can you elevate to the level of being that is able to honor others, honor yourself, and honor your relationships. And that is the next Way of Oneness. The Way of Honoring.

CHAPTER 13

UNIVERSAL WAY OF ONENESS № 11:

The Way of Honoring

One of the discussions that Chris and I had a few days after Mason's passing was my intention of planting Mason as a tree once we had our forever home. We would transfer his ashes into a tree-urn, plant it, nurture it, and spend the rest of our days on earth watching it grow. Until we found and moved into that home, we would keep his bamboo urn somewhere special, and we would find other ways to honor him. Sunday, May 9, 2021 was Mother's Day. This was ten days after Mason left this Earth plane. Mother's Day was challenging for me. It had been a very difficult decision for me to make to not have children. I have a very strong Sacred Mothering energy. And although I use Sacred Mothering with my clients, with other animals that I give healing to when they're sick, or with friends on occasion, it's not enough of an outlet for me to pour my Sacred Mothering energy into. Clients and students also need the fierce warrior and a giver of Truth for them to move through deep transformation. So a way for me to fulfill part of my purpose as a Sacred Mother is to have fur babies. When I get to nurture, care for, and raise a dog, I get to be their mother. It is extraordinarily fulfilling for me to be a mother in this way. When Mason died, I was instantly stripped of my role as a mommy. Our cats don't need a mommy in the same way. Our little dog, Sasha, was Chris's dog before coming into my life, so he's her number one. She's not bonded to me like she is to him. From morning until night, Mason was my first priority. I was his mommy, and you could tell what an amazing mom I was by how much he trusted me. And just like that, my mommy role and responsibilities completely vanished. Because humans don't yet live in Oneness, no one really recognizes the significance of being an animal's mom. You don't get honored on Mother's Day when you don't have a human child. So in the early stages of grieving the loss of my Mason, on Mother's Day I was also grieving the loss of being a mom. And it's hard not to feel invisible among all the other moms that are being honored on that day, while sitting in front of them as an afterthought. If I had had more time to heal before this day, it wouldn't have been so painful. But the wound of losing Mason was still extremely raw. But after a Mother's Day brunch to honor the other mothers in the family (which of course they deserved and I was happy to celebrate them), Chris and I came home, and I opened my laptop to work on this book. Then Chris came in from checking the mail and handed me a large white envelope. When I opened it and read what was on the 8.5 by 11-inch cardstock, I burst into tears. On the left half of the page was a scenic picture of trees. On the right half it was written:

> alivingtribute.org
>
> **AS A LIVING TRIBUTE
> 5 TREES WILL BE PLANTED
> IN OUR NATION'S FORESTS
> IN MEMORY OF
> *MASON***
>
> *In honor of your dog, your friend ... we plant these trees to remember the pawprints of love that he left on your life :)*
>
> *From,*
> Eric & Nadine

I couldn't even believe it. I never mentioned to Eric or to Nadine about my wishes to one day plant Mason as a tree as a way to honor his life and my love for him. I also hadn't spoken of grieving the loss as my role as a mommy. And here it was. Five trees were to be planted in his honor. And I received the news of this gift from them on Mother's Day. That is divine synchronicity at its finest. Not only was Mason being honored, but I felt like my love for him, as well as the tremendous loss I was grieving, were being honored as well. Eric Goldstein and Nadine Lovret are two of the sweetest, most thoughtful, and wonderful people you could ever be lucky enough to meet. I don't have words that could possibly express how deeply their kindness touched my heart. But at least I can try by extending my appreciation to you, Eric and Nadine. Thank you for shining your loving Light onto me while I was healing in the darkness of grief. You are two very special people that make this world a better place simply by you being in it. I will lovingly be in gratitude for your kindness and generosity for the rest of my life.

* * *

To honor means to hold in high regard with great respect or high esteem. To honor someone or something isn't just using the words. It's a deeply felt, energetic expression that is offered in their favor. One of the deepest ways to offer Honoring is to bow or to prostrate before someone. Nowadays, many people misinterpret the act of prostrating to mean that the one doing the prostrating feels like she is inferior to whom she is prostrating to. This couldn't be further from the truth. First of all, only egoic, unconscious thinking labels any other as either inferior or superior to oneself. When living in Oneness, this is a ridiculous way to view anything. In Truth, only equality exists. Just because people have differences, or there are a variety of different forms of beings that share this planet, never means that any are superior to any others. Of course, most humans lack this level of divine understanding, so they go on and act out the unconscious behaviors of inequality. To bow or to prostrate before someone requires a heavy dose of humility coupled with deep gratitude. I'm sure you've seen disciples prostrate to the saint or guru that they follow. To humbly honor a person for their gifts of Wisdom and teachings that they share is such a noble thing to do. It's an expression of gratitude extended for receiving their divine insights and guidance that they so abundantly and selflessly offer.

The Way of Honoring is incessantly absent from most relationships. Most look to their partners and spouses to make them happy and blame or hold them responsible for when they are not. So-called experts, authors, and even therapists have fervently taught us to set nonnegotiable terms on our partners that stem from selfish greed with the intentions to control, or to masterfully avoid doing the self-work necessary to heal and create a healthy relationship. Trying to control how your partner behaves in order for you to feel safe and happy is destructive to the relationship. Not to mention that you will fail in achieving happiness in this way. Happiness is an internal job. That means that when you can shift to seeing your spouse as a beautiful mirror who is there to trigger absolutely everything inside of you that needs to be healed, you'll shift into Honoring them. Honoring your partner is the evolution from relating to them from codependency and unhealed traumas to sacred unity. Honoring is seeing another as the sacredness that they are and offering your humbled gratitude to their sacredness. No disempowered person has the ability to do this. It means gaining the ability to see that as they trigger you, they're actually triggering within you the potential to heal what just got triggered. Prior to them triggering you, you had no way of knowing that you had something that was unhealed. If something inside of us is unhealed, then it can, and *will*, be triggered. That triggering is to alert us of our unhealed pain, programs, and patterns that are unloving. Instead of blaming your partner for triggering you, you can learn to honor them for triggering you. For it's your best opportunity to heal what you were previously unaware was even there. Self-healing is a required step before gaining the ability to honor another. Only someone who recognizes their own divinity and honors that divine nature within themselves can learn what it means to honor another.

* * *

Most people in general do not know or comprehend what the Way of Honoring is. Their egos automatically make them feel offended or that they're somehow less than the person to honor. To honor is such a sacred gesture that it changes you from within to be more sacred yourself. Now, anyone can superficially bow and offer "namaste" or even prostrate during worship. But it doesn't mean you're being true in your intention or your feelings. When you are in fact in the frequency and act of honoring, the vivacity of your beingness revamps.

Have you ever prostrated in honor of someone? Have you ever honored someone with such deep gratitude that it moved you to tears? If you haven't, I strongly recommend that you try this act of reverence. Such a feeling of profound respect or adoration for someone elevates your entire energetic system. You'll elevate to a much higher level of consciousness. Authentic Honoring is composed of the integration of the energies of humility, gratitude, and respect. All three of those qualities rolled into one is what it is to honor. I told Mason over and over again that it was an honor to get to care for him. That I felt so honored that he chose me to be his mommy in this lifetime. And I meant that. It was such an honor to have him as my spiritual teacher. To receive his unconditional love, even when I was at my worst. The amount of special care and attention that he needed the last years, months, weeks, days, and especially hours of his life were my honor and privilege to be the one that was gifted the opportunity to care for him in those ways. I never saw it as work. I never saw myself as limited because I couldn't leave the house for too long. I never for one second saw Mason as a burden. I saw him for the gift that he was to me. And that holy insight deepened significantly during his last two days on Earth with me. And it deepened because I bowed to him. While he lay on his dog bed, his physical body failing at a faster pace hour by hour, minute by minute, I energetically, verbally, and physically bowed down to the splendor that lay before me. I told him that I realized I was God's favorite person. Because only Her favorite human would have received the most special angel boy that existed on Earth to share fourteen years of her life with. Because that's just how special Mason was. And that's just how lucky I was to have had him touch my life.

When in the deep emotion of honoring, it has the potential to lift you to the level of bliss. I felt an incredible and very intense transformation occurring within me when I was honoring Mason. Even while feeling the ferocity of my grief, I simultaneously moved through a mighty transformation. I was elevating. And I was rising to a higher state of consciousness because of the level of humble honoring that I was in. My spiritual insights, psychic abilities and even the level of Wisdom that has channeled through me since I was a child exploded to much higher levels than ever before. What was extraordinary was that I realized that this explosive elevation in my consciousness occurred because I was in such a tremendous state of Honoring. Not only because I was Honoring Mason. But because I was Honoring my grief. I was Honoring every moment. I was in zero resistance to the experiences that we were moving through. I cherished every last minute I got to have with Mason and felt lucky to have them. I held dear every stroke of his fur and scratch of his ears. I treasured being able to praise him and tell him repeatedly what a good boy he was. I felt beyond blessed that I got to kiss his face and nose over and over again. I was given twenty-four hours to say goodbye to him. And I honored every aspect of those last minutes with him. And although the grief was so excruciatingly palpable that it felt like I was going to be swallowed whole by it, I did nothing but love and nurture that grief. Not for a second did I wish it to go away or diminish. The severity of the level of anguish in my heart was equivalent to the level of love that I had for him. Why would I ever want to minimize that? Grief can be powerfully transformative. But only if you negate resisting it and instead embrace, nurture, and love it. Providing nothing but nurturing love to your negative emotions is one of the most divinely selfless offerings that you can give to yourself. It's also the most powerful. And if you gain the ability to offer this to yourself, it means you're starting to walk the true path of the Way of Selfless Service for others, which is the next Way of Oneness.

CHAPTER 14

UNIVERSAL WAY
OF ONENESS № 12:

The Way of Selfless Service

THE WAY OF SELFLESS SERVICE

Mason so easily demonstrated the Way of Selfless Service by his ongoing outpouring of love, dog kisses, tail wags, and his incessant eagerness to please. He wanted you to be happy and feel loved. What a beautiful way to selflessly serve others. To shower them with joy, affection, and a constant reminder that they are loved. He always selflessly offered his affection in abundance. His way of Selfless Service was seen most prominently through affection and his devotion of reminding me that I was never alone, especially through periods of feeling nothing but loneliness. There he always was. Right by my side, selflessly serving my heart and soul with his.

Many confuse Selfless Service with doing things for free. That, in order for something to qualify as Selfless Service, that it must be offered for free or on a volunteer basis. This is not an accurate or truthful depiction of what the Way of Selfless Service is. There are unlimited ways one can be in Selfless Service to others. Some of those ways are in fact volunteer work, free training, or giving products or services away for free. Other ways of Selfless Service are provided in what others do for a living.

If someone spends many years studying, training, and perfecting a service, investing a lot of money for their schooling or training, they deserve reciprocation for what they offer. They deserve to get paid. One can be a person who offers Selfless Service to others and also be a person who is paid for what they are offering. You would never expect a physician to treat patients for free. How in the world would she earn money to live? Why would you ever expect a coach, a therapist, or an author to do what they do for a living and give all of their services and books away for free in order for them to be considered selfless? That's ludicrous. Actually, that's selfish of those who expect to receive others' expert advice, guidance, healing, or products for free. If you expect that from others, *you* are the selfish one. Not them. You are projecting your program of selfishness onto selfless people who are helping to uplift others and do their part to change the world. Not only have we been taught how to be selfish, we've also been taught a sense of entitlement, the ultimate level of egoic self-centeredness. Many run subconscious belief programs that they deserve things just because. That others should give to them, take care of them, and meet their needs. People tend to function as if the world revolves around them. That you are the center of the universe and everyone around you should watch what they say, how they behave so you don't get triggered or feel uncomfortable about anything. I hardly know a person who doesn't buy into the program that they were born to become a multimillionaire. That you actually feel that you somehow deserve this just because you are alive on this planet. Let's not forget to mention the ridiculous labels people keep coming up with to refer to themselves and then expect entire nations or all of humanity to now call them by a special name or label. This reflects a stronger identification with the ego. The stronger human identity you have, the farther away from divinity you are. To disidentify with any labels is a deeper spiritual path where your consciousness realizes that when born into a physical body that may be a female, male, a goat, or a whale, the Truth is, at the deepest level of who you are, you are not any one of those. Your spirit is not a man or a woman or an animal or insect. Your spirit is genderless and not materialized into form-matter. It's a divine energetic consciousness. Your spirit or soul has chosen to incarnate into a male body to experience what it's like being a male during this incarnation. That doesn't make the 'real you' male. It's a reflection of your soul's choice to move through a temporary experience as a man in human form. This is the same for all physical forms, whether it be insect, animal, plant or otherwise. There is an immature selfishness present when we expect others to fit into a specific category and then reject those that don't fit into the ones that you've defined as acceptable. Have we not yet learned from our unconscious past? Race and the color of one's skin has always been a massive "separator." You were treated differently based on the color of your meatsuit. Gender has almost always been a separator, by treating women as the weaker sex or inferior to men. Being homosexual was put in the spotlight for awhile in our human unconsciousness. More recently, it's been transgender, then non-binary. And the list goes on. Pick a label. Pick a human experience those souls have chosen to experience while on Earth. See how humans continue to label, judge, reject, attack, and remain in the hamster wheel of separation? Whether you're on the side of the coin of separation that represents attacking one or more of these categories of people, or whether you're on the side of the coin that hates and rejects themselves so much that they need all of humanity to recognize them and their specialness with a special label, both sides of the same coin represent nothing but separation. And separation is representative of selfishness. The selfishness of wanting everyone to be like you are, or the selfishness of wanting to be highlighted and treated as special because of who or what you are. Selflessness arises naturally out of the Way of Equality and the Way of Trust. When you see through the egoic illusion of inequality and simply know you're equal to all others, then you're more capable of trusting your inner power to respond in divine ways to those that reflect a lower level of consciousness. This allows you to rise out of the way we've been conditioned to view society: through the selfish lens of me, myself, and I.

Another way humanity manifests selfishness and prevents Selfless Service from arising is seen in romantic relationships. Our culture teaches that when in a relationship, your partner is here to meet your needs. That's selfish. It's a self-centered, disempowered, and childlike expectation. You're not a child anymore, so why create a parent-child relationship with your life mate? What happens when you're single? Who meets your needs then? Believing that your partner is there to meet your needs is you functioning as a baby. Babies require their parents to meet their needs. Mature, independent adults meet their own needs and don't expect their romantic partner to also play the role of their parent.

It's also selfish of you to constantly meet all of your partner's needs. It keeps them incapable, needy, and dependent upon you, never allowing them to grow up and mature. This is a form of codependency. This is a type of disempowerment that you bestow upon others when you do too much for them. Many parents raise their kids this way. They keep them helpless, dependent, and emotionally immature. Then they wonder why they struggle as adults at holding down a job and failing at creating healthy, loving relationships that last. And then, so as to not feel like failures or inadequate, these same people turn around and claim that "we're just not meant to be monogamous." What a copout. They can't create healthy relationships that last because they were never taught how powerful they were while growing up. Changing this starts with selflessness. Selflessness isn't always about others. It starts with yourself. To be selfless means that you focus on your own healing and your own continuous growth. No one can be truly selfless when they carry around their wounding and unloving programs that they project onto others. That's far from selflessness. This self-absorption that you probably aren't even aware of is a part of who you are. Keeping yourself in a perpetual state of an unhealed, wounded, immature child who can't take care of yourself is an incredible act of selfishness to those around you. If you can't even take care of yourself, how will you ever selflessly care for others or contribute to a relationship versus being a burden to one?

* * *

Another thing we need to awaken to that prevents us from being selfless is shame. Let's talk about shame and how selfish it is to carry around shame. Not to mention that shame is something that the majority of humans drown in, and many of those humans are completely unaware of it. Let's say that you victimized somebody. It's bad enough that you chose to harm and cause damage to another person in the first place. But when you are stuck in shame about it, you are continuing to make the situation about you (selfish) instead of your victim (selfless willingness to heal). Carrying wounds of low self-worth and shame means you are choosing a path of unparalleled levels of selfishness. You make everything selfishly about you. Brené Brown defines shame as "an intensely painful feeling or experience of believing that we are flawed and therefore unworthy of love and belonging." What I'm here to tell you is that when you carry that around inside of you, you are choosing to be an insanely selfish person who is incapable of empathizing, supporting or being genuinely compassionate to another person. That when you do things that seem selfless on the surface, you're actually doing them with the agenda to get something in return. You're trying to receive the validation that will somehow magically heal the shame you carry within. You're trying to prove you have nothing to be ashamed of, so the things that you do for others are actually selfishly motivated.

The Way of Selfless Service means you have healed yourself from shame. You have nothing to prove to anyone. You don't need to circumstantiate your "goodness" so others will applaud and validate you. Only people carrying shame and insecurities within themselves need that.

Those that give to charities and then share with social media and the world that they are "givers" are seeking recognition and accolades for their so-called giving. This isn't selfless giving. Those that volunteer at a soup kitchen on a major holiday and post all over social media how selfless they are are egomaniacs. They feel shame deep down inside whether they are aware of it or not, and so try to show the world that they are good. They try to stuff their shame down so deeply so that they'll never have to feel it. But that's not how it works. We can't heal what we don't feel. So burying it with superficial acts of kindness that are laced with agendas to suppress one's shame only anchors the shame and low self-worth in place. And this then gets triggered anytime others don't recognize your "good deeds."

One example can be understood by a woman I'll call Denise. Denise was to attend a gathering for Reiki students at their Reiki teacher's house. It was made very clear to all of the students that this was not a social gathering, or potluck, so not to bring any refreshments or snacks, other than for themselves individually. The teacher wanted to make sure not to make anyone feel uncomfortable for not being financially able to contribute a food dish or beverage. In a complete disregard for her instructor's request, Denise took it upon herself to cook some elaborate hors d'oeuvres and bring them to the Reiki class, despite the instructions not to. At the end of the afternoon, the Reiki master discreetly pulled Denise aside and reminded her that although this was held at her home, that this was a classroom. And in a classroom you wouldn't turn a class into a potluck. She also expressed her disappointment at Denise for blatantly ignoring her rule about bringing food and beverages. Denise was appalled. She complained to everyone who would listen to her for several months after this incident about how insulted she was. That she was so thoughtful and considerate and selfless, and not only did she not get a thank you, she was reprimanded! Now, Denise certainly played the role of Selfless Service on the surface. But how she was *actually* showing up in this situation was of someone who was insanely selfish and disrespectful. Her underlying goal for bringing hors d'oeuvres was to receive the praise and attention that she thought she would get. Her underlying intention was to receive the verbal words of affirmation that she was selfless, thoughtful, and wonderful. When she didn't get that, she became angry and resentful. That's a telltale sign that her intentions were selfishly motivated and not selflessly motivated. Not to mention she completely disregarded her teacher's request, which showed a total lack of respect for her teacher, which is a form of selfishness. People who carry a deeply rooted sense of shame and low self-worth will behave in ways similar to this. They'll perform the surface behaviors of selflessness, but from the deep, internal (often hidden) belief that they are "bad" or flawed, so their behavior is for the selfish purpose to get rid of the deeply rooted feeling of shame that they carry within.

If you carry the program of shame inside of you, you will do shameful things. When you act in harmful, unloving ways towards others, the energetic program of shame gets created as a byproduct inside of you. Once that shame is there, you will act out in shameful ways, creating more shame inside of you, and you are now in the hamster wheel of shame. Shame is often first created in very early childhood when you did something your parents didn't like and they overreacted. If they scolded or yelled at you, they were shaming you. Unconscious parents don't know the difference between teaching their children at a moment when a child is not making a wise choice, and shaming their children because what they're doing "is bad." Many parents with the best intentions in the world teach their children at some point that "they're bad." They shame them without any awareness that that is what they're doing. Young children learn to be ashamed from so many adults in their lives. And they are never taught how to drop into their hearts, process that shame, and alchemize it. So there it stays. Trapped emotions of shame that will find a way to surface later in life. It will manifest through our behaviors and in how we feel. When we focus on healing ourselves at the deepest level, we learn to heal the shame that's been trapped inside of the body, most likely since childhood. When that unhealed pain is alchemized, we have no more urges or temptations to "behave in shameful ways." Our behaviors are shameful because a part of us believes we should be ashamed of ourselves. So we act out in the subconscious beliefs that we carry within. So healing this is never about changing behavior. It's about healing the shame that drives us to show up those selfish ways so we can continue to live in the selfish cycle of shame. Once healed at the energetic level, there is no shameful energy behind the steering wheel of your behaviors. Your shameful behaviors disappear organically because you've spent the time needed to heal shame.

Now this should not be confused with divine shame. Shame is actually a very important emotion to feel. It's necessary at times to feel shame. It's dangerous to teach or think that you should absolutely never under any circumstances feel or experience shame. You absolutely should. Shame is an emotion of energy that is offered to you by your soul. It's your divine communication that you just did something that was selfish, thoughtless, and unloving. The energetic byproduct of that is the emotion of shame. And that is perfect. That feeling of shame in that very moment is your intuition letting you know that you just stepped off of the path of divinity. How do you know? You feel shame. That feeling of shame is your guidance to right your wrong, so to speak. It's your soul nudging you to become aware of the hurtful thing that you just did, and to heal that immediately. That's divine shame. That communication to make you aware of the unloving thing you just did is one of those things that separates you from a sociopath. So the more we ignore our shame, suppress it, deny it, and pretend that it's not there, the more we commit shameful, selfish, unloving acts. Boom. Back in that hamster wheel of shameful unconsciousness.

Towards the end of Mason's life, when his vision was failing and he became afraid to walk on the floors throughout the house, it would take sometimes twenty minutes to convince him to walk down the hall to get to the door to let him out to go potty. Now, one time it might take two to three minutes. One time it could take ten. Occasionally, it could take twenty. So one day, when I was home alone with him, it was getting close to that twenty-minute mark, and I had a coaching client that I started to get nervous that I was going to be late for. Now, the sad thing is that I knew Mason really had to pee and had to pee badly. But I couldn't get him to walk down that hallway. And if I just took him back to the office to wait until my next hour-long client was completed, I knew he'd be lying there in pain with an overly full bladder. So as he stood there, panting with a full bladder and with a ton of anxiety about walking on the floor, I had a moment where I felt the frustration bubble up, turn into anger, and I yelled, "Mason!" And before any other word left my lips, I felt the shame. I saw him flinch from me yelling his name in frustration. He was a hypersensitive being, after all. And his stress skyrocketed. That feeling of shame that washed over me was divine shame. It was an immediate kick in the gut to alert me of how selfish and unloving I became in that moment. This poor baby was scared and stressed out, and in one instant, I made him so much more scared and stressed out because he wouldn't do what I wanted him to do in the time that I wanted him to do it. Shame on me. Shame was my gift from the divine in that moment. The second I felt the shame, it shook me right out of my selfishness. I then dropped to my knees in front of Mason and burst into tears. I told him how sorry I was, and I scratched his ears and massaged his face just the way he liked. My tears of shame poured down my cheeks, and through my humble sobbing, I told him how wrong Mommy was to yell at him. And as I owned my moment of falling from Grace, Mason took it upon himself to lick my tears and press his forehead against mine. It was a moment when an enlightened being offered me Grace instead of judgment for my lack of divinity. And as we exchanged love for each other, my shame alchemized, and his stress disappeared. I stood up, and he simply followed me down the hall, out the door, and pottied.

You see, I was in the selfish energy of rushing and expectation. I expected Mason to get up and take a potty break in the amount of time that I had allotted for him to do so. That was selfish. Because I was in a selfish, expectation energy, that energy caused Mason stress. It made him more fearful to walk across the floor that he was already apprehensive to walk on. Instead of making that potty trip about him and his needs, I made them about my schedule. I was far from offering Mason Selfless Service that day. Selfless Service would have been to scratch his ears and spend time loving him and talking to him first, before ever even getting up. Selfless Service would have been to serve his emotional needs before asking him to walk on a floor that he didn't want to walk across. Selfless Service would have been to help him mentally and emotionally just because. To make him feel joyful, confident, loved, and supported, especially before asking him to do something that he was afraid to do.

Selfless Service is the act of offering something to another for the sole purpose of helping another in some way. Period. It isn't about you. Anytime you make it about you, it's not coming from self*less*ness, but self*ish*ness. Writing this book is for the purpose of spreading the Wisdom about the Ways of Oneness. It's to help heal and raise the consciousness of humanity. It's to provide enlightened laws to create enlightened societies. That's it, and that's all. If one copy sells and helps to elevate one person, the purpose of this text was fulfilled. If one hundred million copies sell, the purpose of this text was fulfilled. There is no expectation. There is no other purpose for allowing these words to channel through and for writing down the Ways that are being provided to me. If you are writing a book in order to become famous or wealthy, you are writing for selfish reasons. If you are writing something with the intention of elevating others, then you are practicing the Way of Selfless Service. As far as recognition goes, or how many copies are sold, the universe will take care of that. It's really not your concern. And it's not selfishly about you. It's about how what was created through you serves humanity, the Earth, and all the beings on this planet. Anything else that comes your way as a result of your work and efforts is a gift from the universe. True Selfless Service activates reciprocity from the universe. You never even have to think about what may come back to you. The Wisdom of the universe knows what you deserve, and so it will provide. Doing anything for what you'll get in return removes you from the bucket of Selfless Service and shifts you into the category of "selfish agenda." So simply refuse to ever do anything with an agenda that has "selfish" attached to it. Selfishness empties your bucket more and more over time until you are so depleted you're no longer able to do anything without a selfish agenda attached to it anymore. This is how evil slowly drips into people and collectively floods onto our planet. Part of the mystical, magical aspects of divinity is what comes into your life or what you are rewarded with when you show up in the Way of Selfless Service. When you're doing it for the 'wrong' reasons, you'll never get to experience this. When you are authentically selfless, whatever forms of abundance flood into your life are experienced with a sense of deservedness. This level of expressed deservedness is gratitude from your very soul.

* * *

In romantic relationships so many people do things for their spouses in order to receive a "thank you," appreciation, or to be able to use that as ammunition to justify a future request. They keep tabs on what they do for others in order to cash in later. All of this is selfish manipulation. When your "giving" comes with an agenda, or a "now you owe me" attitude, you're living as a controlling, manipulative, and very selfish person. Often, these same people will then drown in victim consciousness at a later date when they whine and cry about how much they do for others and how they never seem to be treated with the same "kindness" or "selflessness." Well, you weren't coming from true kindness or selflessness in the first place. You had an agenda. You were doing things for people that on the surface level looked nice, but you had ulterior motives for why you were doing them. You wanted others to recognize how kind or thoughtful you were. And when they didn't, you became upset and projected onto them that they were the selfish ones. Remember that everything is energy. Your true intentions can be felt by others on an energetic level even if they're unaware of what they're feeling at the time. You may be offering something that appears to be thoughtful or sweet, but it activates a feeling of uneasiness or discomfort. It's likely that you're sensing the person's true intentions. The true intention is to use you, manipulate you, or control you. An extension of this is when people put the effort into buying someone's love. And so many people fall into this trap. True love can't be bought. "If I buy you enough stuff, you'll devote yourself to me and love me." This is a reflection of the low opinion you hold for yourself. That you're so flawed and unlovable that you must showboat your wealth and buy someone's devotion to you. On the surface it may appear as though you are a selfless and giving person. But deep within, you don't love yourself. And you believe that you're not worthy of love. Therefore, you try to safeguard against future abandonment by gifting the jewelry, the cars, the house, the lifestyle. The problem is the superficial and meaningless parts of our life experiences fade because they are only temporary to begin with. And they usually fade pretty quickly. So then what? Not showing the part of you that you were trying so hard to hide from the start is a selfish act. You had someone fall in love with a fake version of you. With a version of you that can't possibly be maintained forever. And this version of you is superficial, so at some future point, the awareness of a lack of fulfillment in the relationship will begin to awaken inside of your partner. So once the façade begins to crumble, you're always going to be left with *you*. The you that you were so afraid to show. The you that was so in fear of being rejected, shunned, or abandoned. The part of you that still needs to heal and evolve. The hidden you will come out, and when it does, your partner is left bewildered at what they never saw. Then both of you are left with facing the Truth. The Truth that you were too selfish and scared to elevate yourself to a level where masks aren't worn. To open to what Selfless Service is actually about. And, what's worse, you'll then selfishly expect your partner to suddenly just deal with, accept, and love unconditionally these hidden, dark aspects of you that you masterfully hid from them for however long. This is a very dysfunctional and twisted level of selfishness. And it's one that is sure to destroy the relationship. This level of selfishness projects programs of expectation onto your partner to love and accept you as you are, when *you* don't even love and accept you for who you are. You can't be more hypocritical than that. And then we blame, get angry with, and resentful at our partners when they don't love us unconditionally. You're expecting your partner to give to you what you are unwilling to give to yourself. So, failing relationships have nothing to do with the inability to be monogamous. They have everything to do with the refusal to heal, do the real self-work, and fully open to loving yourself in a divinely selfless way.

I hope it's hitting home that the Way of Selfless Service starts with selflessness towards yourself. Inner selflessness is the devotion to align with your soul. This means that you're willing to heal and transform anything and everything about yourself that is attached to your ego. . . to your little personality that causes all of your suffering. Because if you're causing your own suffering, you're also causing others to suffer. For we are all One. Inner selflessness focuses on aligning the human self, AKA the personality, with the soul self. This allows one's soul to be in the driver's seat of one's life experiences, creations, and relationships. When aligned with your soul instead of your egoic, shadow self, Selfless Service inherently flows from the very essence of who you are. This means that your inspiration for anything that you do is to uplift, heal, elevate, or help in some way. It means you don't buy a pet so that you feel better. This is viewing an animal as an object. You adopt a new animal into your family because you're loving, selfless, and responsible enough to provide the guidance, training, love and support for that animal to thrive and live an incredible life while in your care. How could you not emotionally and energetically benefit from that as a natural side effect? It means that you don't choose to bring a child into this world unless it's purposeful. That you've educated yourself on the mental, emotional, behavioral, and spiritual development of children, and you're willing to do whatever it takes to educate and uplift yourself as this soul's first teacher in the Earth School of life. You don't have kids because that's what you've been brainwashed to do. You don't have kids by accident. And when you bring a child into this world, you devote yourself to that child's soul growth and guide them in their journey of soul evolution until they can do it for themselves. You don't treat them as property, like you own them the way that most parents do. You realize you have no say in what or who they are to become, but your role is to serve as a temporary guide for them while they are too young and helpless to care for themselves. You're here to teach them, not control them. You're not here to trap them in helplessness and codependency by doing everything for them. Toddlers should be helping to cook, to set the table, and to clean up after meals. At this age you include the child in the meal preparation activity by giving them a bowl and a wooden spoon. Whatever scraps you have left over from cutting, you give to them so they can practice putting that into their own bowl and mixing it up. They can easily carry certain lightweight dishes, spoons, napkins, or sippy cups to and from the dinner table to set the table and to clean up. They can throw things in the trash. You can also do this at an age-appropriate level with laundry. Pushing or pulling the laundry basket to the laundry room can be really fun for a toddler! Plus they're gaining a sense of self-worth. And parents, when you come back from a vacation, don't send your kids off to play while you unpack and wash everything. You're teaching your children entitlement, laziness, and irresponsibility if you do this. They should be unpacking, washing, and putting away everything *with* you, together, until they're skilled enough to handle it on their own. When you include them on all of the responsibilities of the house, you've selflessly stepped into the role of their first divine teacher. This *is* your role as a parent. It empowers them. It teaches them the skills of self-care, survival, and responsibility. It teaches them to be independent while also functioning as a great team player. It teaches them selflessness instead of entitlement. This form of inclusion and teaching as a parent is a form of Selfless Service for your children. Doing everything for them does not selflessly serve them. It prevents them from being capable, responsible adults who remain trapped in a perpetual state of immaturity. You're teaching them to become a burden to a future partner instead of an asset.

THE WAY OF SELFLESS SERVICE

The types of conscious choices described above reflect the Way of Selfless Service. It is the ultimate way of giving. Corporations around the globe have a lot to learn when it comes to this. Many continue to pay their employees wages that one can't even survive on, let alone thrive on, while the ones at the top make more money than they could ever spend in a lifetime. When people work for you, in whatever type of business, to function in the Way of Selfless Service means that you have the intention of enhancing your employees' lives in any way that you possibly can. It's never to use them as cheap labor so you can greedily gain financial wealth for yourself. This is also an example of out-of-balance masculine energy. When you function within yourself and within a society that is predominantly masculine, and the feminine is suppressed and not integrated, the result is as described above. It creates domination, competition, and rising to the top with greed and selfishness. Sacred Feminine energy, when present, would never allow this to occur. As a CEO rises to the top, for example, so do all of her employees. They all rise together. Because the CEO didn't get to the top without the help of her employees. Living in Oneness means understanding this. If this CEO's company is making billions of dollars, then those dollars go back to the employees through raises, bonuses, paid education and training, extra vacation time, etc. You don't keep paying an assistant minimum wage just because you can. If that assistant is a great assistant, and has been devoted to you for the past four years, and your business is thriving, you automatically give that assistant a significant raise. They shouldn't even have to ask you for one. They are serving the functional aspects of your company, and you should be serving them in return. This is an example of the innate reciprocal functionality of the Way of Selfless Service.

* * *

We need to mature in our understanding of what Selfless Service is. Many who run the programs of lack, disempowerment, or envy, criticize coaches, healers, or spiritual teachers for not giving their services away for free. Stop projecting your jealousy and resentments onto other gifted, successful people. Charging for your services is a reflection of valuing yourself. It's a form of Selfless Service by the very nature of offering your expertise to the world. And it's a form of selflessness towards yourself when you charge a price that reflects your level of expertise. When you're doing it to help heal people and the planet, this is indeed selfless. It's ignorance and a reflection of your own unhealthy relationship with money that makes you believe that if money is being charged for those services, then it can't be a selfless offering.

When a person can gain a deeper understanding of what Selfless Service truly is, what also arises is a strong devotion to being Selfless. Your priorities change. You'll spend more quality time teaching your children making sure they gain the skills they need to thrive in this world. You'll work harder to ensure the success of your business so that an elevated way to run a business becomes widespread, and you can impact more people, including your employees, in a positive way. You'll no longer do things only for the sake of getting something in return. The nature of devoting yourself to a mission or a purpose that enhances, heals, or elevates people, animals or the planet in some way will activate, and the inner drive to focus on this will become stronger. The devotion to healing and elevating this planet will just become a part of who you are. This devotion to "being better" and "doing better" leads us to the next Way. The Way of Loyalty.

CHAPTER 15

UNIVERSAL WAY OF ONENESS № 13:

The Way of Loyalty

THE WAY OF LOYALTY

I think pretty much everyone knows the level of loyalty that dogs offer to their owners. Even in an entire family, a dog typically chooses that one family member that he is the most loyal to. It's this divine level of devotion that makes you feel like the most important person in the world. It's a devotion to you that is at the soul level. We must not mistake kindness or generosity for loyalty. Mason was loving and kind to everyone that came across his path. But he wasn't loyal to just anyone. He reserved that for me and for me alone. Now, it's slightly different when speaking of humans being loyal. But the point to understand is that Mason was loyal to me in such a profound way because he trusted me so deeply. He was loyal to me because I was loyal to him and his well-being. I put his needs ahead of mine on most occasions, and he knew that at the soul level. Because I honored him and treated him as my equal, he offered to me a level of divine Loyalty that few souls demonstrate on this planet. Mason's Loyalty to me really was at the soul level. He was here for me, to support my life's journey, to teach me, to love me unconditionally, and to support me emotionally through every negative experience and life challenge I had to face. His Loyalty to me made sure that I was never alone. At my loneliness and darkest times, he was by my side. And I knew he was absolutely never going to leave me while he was still alive.

* * *

Humanity's unconscious nature has taught us that Loyalty means never to snitch. To keep secrets of infidelity for a friend. To not speak up or speak out when there is injustice if the person committing the injustice is a family member or someone that you know. And many go beyond that and actually protect those that do harm when that person is a family member or loved one. You're supposed to take these lies and destructive secrets to the grave. You're never supposed to tell the truth if that means the truth will get your loved one in trouble. Most don't speak up against an "old friend" who verbally vomits misogyny because they might not like you or hang out with you anymore once you stand up to them. The government lies about the levels of poison and harmful chemicals that are used to grow and preserve our foods, all the while causing cancer and countless other health conditions in people. They are "loyal" to keeping things the way that they are because of the tremendous cost to change things for the better of humanity and the planet. And we wonder why the world is in the state that it's in. None of this is divine Loyalty. It's disgraceful. It's cowardice. These dysfunctional gestures of "Loyalty" aren't loyal. They are actually forms of separation. They create nothing but separation, pain, suffering, and destruction. Destruction of love and trust, experiences of inferior/superior, disempowerment, hate, resentment, and a multitude of other aspects are the shadow experience from living in loving unity with one another and all things.

THE WAY OF LOYALTY

To what or to whom are you loyal to? Are you loyal to your parents just because they are your parents? What about the ways they still criticize you and abuse you? "But they're my parents." So what! Stop mistaking allegiance to dysfunction as divine Loyalty. You're not being loyal to yourself when you do this. You're abusing yourself by choosing to put up with parental abuse. This shows such a lack of self-love on your part. Someone who truly loves themselves would be loyal to Gentleness and Harmlessness over an abusive parent. Are you loyal to your church even though it preaches misogyny and the oppression of women? Are you loyal to your community even though they preach racism and separation? Are you loyal to your job even though it's slowly killing you from the demanding hours while ripping you away from spending quality time with your loved ones? Are you loyal to your unhealed wounds and self-sabotaging ways? Are you loyal to the many paths of infidelity while selfishly remaining in a supposed committed relationship? Where do your loyalties lie and what disempowering excuses do you make to justify them?

It's really important to understand that codependency is not Loyalty. It's dysfunctional disempowerment. So is being "loyal" to certain people just because they wear a label of 'family member' or 'friend,' as already mentioned above. These are unconscious programs of obligation and blind commitment, two forms of brainwashing that most cultures promote in their family, community, religious, or country units. That learning about other cultures or beliefs and choosing to practice those because you admire them or have been inspired by them is being disloyal to your own roots or is somehow lumped into the label of appropriation. Appropriation contains a lack of Honoring others. Of others' cultures, rituals, practices, etc. When there is a lack of Honoring of others, appropriation takes over. Remember that the definition of cultural appropriation is "the adoption of an element or elements of one culture or identity by members of another culture or identity." It's no different than plagiarizing someone else's original work. This lacks integrity for sure. However, let's also see that people are taking this to such an extreme that all they're doing is continuing to rewrite and repattern programs of separation. That we must all remain separate and different, while never crossing cultural boundaries or blending the beautiful aspects of various cultures. If I read a quote that I regurgitate in my own teachings or writings, to live in the Way of Integrity is to quote that teacher or author when you use or integrate her teachings as your own. To lack Integrity means you act as if you were the one who came up with that nugget of Wisdom or clever phrase. But understand: to be in Integrity never means that you don't use the other person's work, research, Wisdom, or teachings. It means you give credit to that person when you do. Thousands of years or decades after a great teacher has blessed this planet, we still quote and promote those incredible teachings. Jesus, Saint Teresa of Avila, Buddha, Kuan Yin, and Gandhi are only a few examples. But when you teach from their teachings or quote their Wisdom, you also give credit to the original source that they came from. This is not only integrous, but it's a reflection of the Way of Loyalty to them and to what they came to Earth to teach others. Celebrating and learning from other cultures and taking on some of their beliefs, styles, or practices is a beautiful thing to do. As long as you are not "plagiarizing" them. As long as you are honest, in Honoring of, and in Loyalty to where those things originated from. We are *meant* to learn from each other. We're not meant to keep to ourselves and live as separate from everyone who is different than we are. We are meant to compare, not to make one superior and one inferior to the other, but to compare so we can learn and grow from each other. So we can have epiphanies about one's own culture in order to dismantle the aspects of one's culture that are poisonous and unhealthy. To adopt from other cultures ways that are loving, or that function at a higher level of consciousness, is what we are meant to do. We are meant to learn from one another what we are doing that is unloving and fear-based, as well as to embrace those things that are based in love. This is no different than going to a friend's house as a child and seeing and learning from another family new ways of being or new practices that may be healthier or more loving that what your family taught you. You *should* adopt those new ways. This is one way that your eyes open to new things! We are meant to share, to learn, and to grow with each other, from each other.

* * *

THE WAY OF LOYALTY

A further understanding of the Way of Loyalty never means you must stay in a commitment forever, whether it be a job, a relationship, or even volunteer work. It means that while you're fulfilling an obligation or commitment, you do so with impeccable integrity. With honor. With trustworthiness. With faithfulness. You never waver. That's divine Loyalty. You give it your devotedness and your whole heart. It means you never reduce your relationship to lower levels of infidelity and claim that you're not cheating simply because you're not having sex with another. A truly integrous and loyal person engages in flirting and sexual attention towards others only when they're single. Never when they're in a relationship. And never with another person who is in a committed relationship. It means that even though you're working at a job that isn't one you love, you show up and give 100 percent of yourself in that faithful, devoted way while you're employed there. The Way of Loyalty means learning all the time how to be a better, more highly conscious parent so you can break the generational traumas and wounding that came from your parents, and theirs before them. That's the level of divine Loyalty that your child or children deserve from you. Loyalty means when you make a commitment like getting a pet, you know it's for the pet's entire lifetime while she or he is alive on this Earth plane. Loyalty is investing in proper training and veterinary care. It's the time and the devotion to caring for your furry family member when he's elderly and sick. And it's never. . .*never* putting your pet to sleep just because you feel they're too difficult to take care of, especially when they're old. Can you see how mastering the Way of Selfless Service naturally leads you to the Way of Loyalty? Because one who practices the Way of Selfless Service would never consider their loved one, and yes, even their furry loved one, as a burden to care for. Only selfish people project the idea of being a burden when other beings need a person to care for them.

The Way of Loyalty really means being devoted to all of the Ways of Oneness with absolutism. It means to selectively reserve your allegiance to only doing good and loving things. To behave in positive and loving ways. To be impeccable with your word. To dedicate yourself to the process of self-awareness and course correction when you realize you're not in alignment with the Ways. And never to criticize, shame, or judge when you or others are not. But simply to speak the Truth about it so you can readjust whatever needs to be elevated to a higher state until it does align with the universal laws that allow societies to become and remain enlightened. Divine Loyalty is a constant commitment to realigning your human self with your divine self until they merge in unity with one another. It means to align your business, your purchasing power, the foods you put into your body, the ways that you behave or respond, the ways that you care for animals, nature, and the planet, all to the Ways of Oneness. It means to be loyal to truth and to justice and never to be loyal to lies and injustice so that you can remain in power or continue to earn corrupt wages.

THE WAY OF LOYALTY

And finally, the Way of Loyalty means learning how to be Loyal to yourself. . . to your soul. To devote yourself to your own healing and evolution. To break the cycle of Loyalty to your ego and emotional and spiritual unconsciousness and choose the Way of Loyalty to your soul's growth.

If you want to know what the Way of Loyalty looks and feels like, observe dogs. They are loyal in the holiest way. They show you that Loyalty means consideration of the whole. Of all. Of the bigger picture. Being Loyal means never getting a dog and then abandoning him because you decide to have children. This is a selfish act that causes trauma and devastation to an animal. You get a dog for her lifetime, or you don't get a dog at all. If you're concerned about the way the dog may behave or react if you decide to have a child, guess what. . .you don't have children then. Humans evolved enough in their level of consciousness would never bring a child into the world if it meant that their canine companion would suddenly be ripped away from their family and their home. You see, you are first Loyal to your dog. Not some idea of an unborn child. Your dog was your family first. That child's soul can go to any number of billions of people on the planet and be born into their family. But that dog's soul chose you and you her. That's already a working soul contract. You don't breach a soul contract because your selfish, destructive and harmful ego tells you that something better will come along. So, just like you would never get rid of your child if a dog came into your life, the Way of Loyalty says you would never get rid of your dog by bringing a child into your life. You would never get rid of your pets if you met someone who didn't like them. If you enter into a romantic relationship and that person requests for you to get rid of your furry loved one, you should dump that person immediately and never look back. That level of selfish entitlement should be spotted from a thousand miles away and never fed into. And anyone who functions in the Way of Loyalty wouldn't hesitate to end that relationship and move on. It wouldn't even be a question. The real question is what took you so long to see this level of selfishness in that person before you dumped him from your life?

Now, to raise this to an even higher level of divine teaching, the Way of Loyalty also reflects being Loyal to the highest good for all beings. For example, to be Loyal to birds is to never own one and lock it in a little cage in your home. For that robs it of its most fundamental essence. . . to fly. Loyalty to the highest good means you would never take a bird prisoner in this way. The Way of Loyalty is never using pesticides or poisons in your yard, garden, or farm. Nor is it to buy items that do. For being Loyal means being Loyal to the ecosystem and the wellbeing of Earth and all of the species that inhabit this planet. Being Loyal means being devoted to your employees' happiness and ability to thrive by working with you. It means that you genuinely care for their level of balance that they have in their lives. That this job doesn't drain them or make them sick with unrealistic demands. That you offer flexibility to allow them to be successful, happy, and to feel elated by being a part of your company. You don't treat them as less than you, and you certainly don't treat them like it's audacious for them to want to enjoy life outside of work. And although it's their divine responsibility for an employee to offer 100 percent effort from themselves while at work, it's also divinely responsible to completely forget about work and focus their attention on themselves, their loved ones, or anything else outside of work when they are not working. In addition, Loyalty to their wellbeing means no more 40-hour work weeks for a full-time employee. And certainly not 80-hour work weeks! Because that's slavery and abuse. To expect someone to devote that much time of their lives only on work is nothing short of self-serving greed. It's a form of prison. It leaves next to nothing after you factor in hours per night needed for sleep, showering/self-care, doctor's appointments, exercise or fitness, caring for children and/or pets, or maintaining a home with all of the cooking, cleaning, laundry, grocery shopping, and lawn maintenance. When does a person who works the traditional full-time hours have any time to enjoy the other pleasures or adventures of life? The two weeks per year they get a vacation? This is enslavement.

Remember that the Ways of Oneness are the ways that enlightened beings function. That means they are always functioning with the love and consideration of what's best for all. Not just what's best for me. It means being Loyal to the wellbeing of all at all times. To be Loyal to that means reasonable and flexible work schedules for employees with reasonable accommodations for family members and loved ones. How is it that we live in the twenty-first century, and corporate buildings aren't automatically built with child and doggie daycares? How are these things not a part of your benefits package, as a perk for working for any company? How are reasonable hours, flexibility, great benefits, and vacation time not automatically a part of what an employee receives? And for the few percentage of employees that will exploit and take advantage of this, simply fire them. Get rid of them. Because that is a reflection of the Way of Loyalty to yourself and to the selfless business that you're building. One rotten apple can quickly spread rot to all of the other apples. So remove the rotten apple and continue to be Loyal to all of the wonderful employees that you are so lucky to have.

When you learn the universe's definition of Loyalty and apply that to your life, your career, and your relationships, it becomes easier and easier to discover what it means to love. Being loyal to the health and wellness of yourself and to all others places you on a path to learning what Unconditional Love actually is. And that is the next Way of Oneness to explore.

CHAPTER 16

UNIVERSAL WAY
OF ONENESS № 14:

The Way of Unconditional Love

Dogs have their own language of Unconditional Love. I mean, they don't speak human languages like English or Italian, but they do speak an energetic language of love. Dogs say "I love you" in many different ways. One way is that they gaze into your eyes. Japanese researchers have written about this, and one of them, Miho Nagasawa of Azabu University, reports that, "Dogs who gazed into their owners' eyes showed elevated levels of oxytocin. Oxytocin is a hormone that is produced within the brain that's related to nurturing and attachment. Once their owners received this gaze from their dogs, the owners' levels of this same 'cuddle hormone' increased as well."

Another way dogs show their love to you is by listening to your voice when you speak to them. Have you ever noticed when you speak to your dog in that "voice that you only use when you speak to your dog with," he looks at you intently and wags his tail? He's listening to you. He may not understand all of the words you're saying to him, but he's energetically connecting to you while you speak as a way to show his love for you. A neuroscientist, Attila Andics, conducted a study in Budapest using MRI technology to see a dog's brain activity upon hearing voices. This study revealed that what happens in a dog's brain is exactly what also happens in the human brain. A dog's temporal pole, a part of the brain that's known for processing acoustic information, lights up when hearing his owner's happy human voice.

THE WAY OF UNCONDITIONAL LOVE

Look at how happily dogs greet their owners when they come home! They make you feel like you are the most important and special person on the whole planet! They do this because of how much they love you.

Dogs also seek emotional comfort from their owner as a sign of love. Mason was no exception to this. If he observed things that he was unsure about, that made him nervous, or that he felt negative energy around, he would immediately come and sit right next to me and ask for comfort. With some gentle, soothing talking-to and some reassuring scratches, he would calm down and shift back into peace and calm. Receiving comfort from me, and any dog that receives reassurance and comfort from their owner, strengthens the bond between them. Dogs are so in tune with their owners, and they're capable of picking up on the most subtle mood changes. This is partly why dogs bond so closely with their owners. They can read you like a book and energetically decode what's going on with you. Their ability to do this deepens their love for you because it makes them feel so close to you. Understanding this about dogs, and seeing all of this in Mason, allowed me to learn the real definition of what Unconditional Love is.

Most people grow up believing that love is a feeling. It's not. Love is a way of being. Many mistake the feeling of attachment to another as love. Love isn't attached to anything or anyone. Love is free. Love is spacious. Love flows while also being the glue that keeps us together. Love is everywhere always but often missed or even dismissed due to the lack of recognition by humans as to what love really is. To truly understand what Unconditional Love is, you can begin by understanding the infinite forms of manifested expressions of love. So, if Unconditional Love is a state of being, then to experience Unconditional Love is to either be Unconditional Love or to receive Unconditional Love from another. We offer Unconditional Love not just through our Presence, but through countless expressions of that love. An expression of love is the vibrational frequency of Unconditional Love manifested. It's a tangible or semi-tangible form of love. An act of kindness is an expression of love. Holding the door open for someone walking behind you is an expression of love. Sitting in Presence and offering divine spaciousness for someone while they are moving through painful emotions is an expression of love. Active listening. Validating your partner's or your child's emotions. Uplifting, words of encouragement when someone is frustrated. Surprising someone with a gift for absolutely no reason. Notice that these examples are all "ways of being." The vibrational frequency of Unconditional Love manifests itself through us with what we say, how we treat others, how we show up and move through this world, the tender emotions that we feel about someone. These are expressions of love manifested in the countless ways that love can be expressed and experienced.

THE WAY OF UNCONDITIONAL LOVE

It can be pretty easy to offer expressions of love to others when they offer them to you. Where most fall short is the lack of ability to offer expressions of love when others are unable to. This is a direct reflection of one's level of consciousness. People who function at a low level of consciousness are only able to be loving when others are loving towards them, which is conditional love, AKA not real love at all. Most can easily offer kindness in response to kindness. Patience when someone else is patient. Selflessness when another is selfless first. People who are on the path of authentic spiritual awakening are those who can respond versus react. Those that can offer expressions of love in moments where love seems to be absent from the situation. During a conflict, for example. The ability to refrain from pointing fingers, blaming, criticizing or name-calling is an expression of love offered when moving through a conflict. The absence of judgment of another when they made a poor choice. Holding others accountable and setting healthy boundaries while simultaneously freeing oneself of judgment, rage, or hate are other forms of love. Saying "no" when you're too exhausted and need to recharge your own battery is a form of love. . . of self-love. Standing up for yourself. . . love. Speaking out against true injustice. . . love. Refusing to engage in any type of infidelity. . . love. Healing oneself of all forms of objectification of others . . . love. Disengaging from codependency or enmeshment. . . love. Focusing on self-growth . . . love. Holding yourself accountable to the Ways of Oneness. . . love.

If you continue to live in the ignorance that love is a way that you feel towards someone, you are living in an extremely limiting world. You also won't be able to truthfully see how unloving you are actually being to your partner at times, if you only identify love as a feeling that you feel for that person. You can't claim to love someone one minute, then get so easily distracted by an attractive person walking by you the next. That's not love. Remember that love is a way of being. So lusting after another simply because she's trying to get your attention when you claim to be in love with someone else is far from being loving. In fact, if you're *that* easily distracted by another, you have yet to learn anything about the true meaning of love, and quite frankly, you're too immature to be in a commitment to begin with. Any time you objectify another, you have choked off the energy of love from flowing through you or to you. Any time you're open to receiving the temptations from someone else when you're committed to another, you sabotage love. This is one way that people actually withhold love versus offer love. Offering love in these examples is to pay no attention to the one trying to distract you away from your relationship. Withholding love is to give your attention to the one who is trying to lure you away with the energy of lust and objectification. Continuously checking her out means you're giving your energy away to *her*, which means you're unlovingly and unfaithfully sharing your sexual and attentional energy with someone that is not your partner or spouse. These ways of behaving are *not* loving. They are examples of how we close ourselves off from love. And more often than not, how we slowly bleed our relationship dry without ever realizing the ways that we've sabotaged it over time. Then we claim things like, "Well, once the honeymoon period is over, passion naturally dies." This is one of the dumbest beliefs that people continue to believe in. First of all, with romantic love, what attracts people in the beginning is not passion. It's lust. It's sexual attraction. That is not the same thing as passion. Passion is most often completely missing from the equation at the beginning of a relationship. Lust, however, is not. We're so deeply brainwashed to sexually objectify others that that is what drives our desire to spend more time with someone. We allow the sexual attraction and the sex to become the dominant energy. That dominant energy takes over the way we think, how we feel, and it sexually charges us to the point where we're willing to overlook huge red flags and obvious signs that this person is absolutely no good for us. None of this is passion. Passion is not infused with ignorance, a lack of control, sexual objectification, lowering standards, disempowerment, or stupidity. But lust sure is. Passion is infused with divine energies of intimacy, adoration, respect, Honoring, selflessness, and Unconditional Love. Passion requires Presence. One is cut off from being Present when lustful energy is flowing. For those who can detect subtle energies, lust feels disgusting and violating because it's objectifying. Passion, on the other hand, connects two souls together while Unconditional Love, emotional intimacy, and sexual intimacy dance and celebrate each other while becoming intertwined in an expansive way. Passion feels enlightening! When you understand what passion actually is, you can understand that passion is one expression of Unconditional Love. Passion does not and cannot exist without love. If you're lusting over someone you meet and have a one-night stand, this is lust, not passion. You don't love this stranger that you just met an hour ago. So passion has no ability to be brought into the equation. Passion can only arise in a relationship when there is Loyalty, Trust, and Honoring between two partners. This is what forms passion. Because of these qualities that create what passion is, passion is an expression of Unconditional Love.

One must become universal spaciousness in order to allow Unconditional Love to flow into their lives and relationships. Examples of what this looks like helps us to comprehend what this means. If a loved one lashes out in a negative way, Unconditional Love means there is no lashing back. There is no judgment because of their behavior. Unconditional Love being present never means you fail to set a healthy boundary or to respond in a powerful way. No. In fact, if you allow yourself to be a doormat, then Love is missing from the equation. Because it means that you don't love yourself enough to stand up for yourself. Part of the challenge in understanding what Unconditional Love really is is that most people's level of consciousness is stuck in duality. So your mind may tell you that if you don't lash back at your partner for lashing out at you, that automatically means you're being passive, submissive, and are allowing your partner to mistreat you. The egoic mind can only think in black-and-white terms at the lower realms of consciousness. The egoic mind has no ability to think in terms of balance and Harmony. So, your partner snapped at you and treated you unkindly. To meet your partner's negative behavior program with love means to see the *behavior* as unloving, not the *person*. Maybe the behavior was unkind and harsh. But that doesn't mean the *person* is unkind and harsh.

I know, I know. Some of your minds just exploded. This concept can be a difficult one to grasp. But hang in there and tell your heart to open so you can receive the teaching. Also, you may want to tell your mind to "shut it" for a while so it doesn't block you from receiving this.

Anyway, when you begin to separate the behavior programs (literally what the person's specific behavior is) from who the person is on the inside (their soul consciousness), you begin to shift towards becoming more loving. This occurs because judgment begins to dissolve. Separating the behavior from the person automatically begins the process of healing judgment that you tend to offer to others. So if your partner bites your head off because he's frustrated with something, then it's your job to bring love into the equation since he is incapable of that at the moment. This means love for him by no longer defining him as his crappy behavior. The behavior is what's crappy, not *him*. More love enters when you love yourself enough to set a boundary with his crappy, unkind behavior. So you tell him, "Hey, I know you're frustrated, and that's okay, but what's not okay is that you take that frustration out on me. I'm really sorry that you're frustrated. But it's not okay for you to speak to me that way when you are." By treating this scenario in this manner, you've stood up for yourself, AKA set a boundary, against unkind treatment. This is an act of self-love. You've validated his emotional state by telling him it's okay that he's frustrated. Because it *is* okay that he's frustrated. Demonizing another's emotions is never loving. It is absolutely fine that someone feels frustrated. Validating his frustration is an act of love. You've also seen and acknowledged the negative behavior of his personality as being different from who he is at a deeper level, or soul level. This begins to heal the programs of separation that we all run.

Becoming a person capable of Unconditional Love is a person who truly loves themselves. When you truly love yourself, there is no more seeking outside of yourself for approval, validation, or love. You believe in yourself. You love yourself enough to say no and to set appropriate boundaries when necessary. Because you've truly learned what it means and what it feels like to express self-love, you are also capable of truly loving others. Authentic self-love means that every single time a negative emotion gets activated inside of you, you pause, connect to your heart space, grow your Light throughout your entire body into your energy fields surrounding your body, and you offer those emotions the Love that you just activated. That Love is your Light. Never again do you shame your emotions. There's no more avoiding emotional pain. Only weak people try to avoid pain, and therefore, weak people never heal. Only warriors have the ability to heal themselves. Warriors of the Light offer the power of divine Love, the Unconditional Love that is the Truth of who you are, to your emotional pain when it arises. And you sit in the Presence of this Love, embracing your emotions until those painful energies entrain into the very Unconditional Love that you are infusing it with. *This* is what it really means to Love yourself. This is the Beingness of Love. To embrace and infuse yourself from the inside out with your Divine Light, which is the vibrational frequency of Unconditional Love, is true Power. True Love. Now you can better understand that Love is not an emotion. It's not a spa treatment or covering yourself with materialistic fakeness so others will be impressed with you and shower you with attention. It's not a feeling. It's the essence of the Divine Light that you are. And the more you respond to your emotions and pain in this way, the more powerful you strengthen your ability to self-love. The more self-love you offer in your times of darkness or pain, the more capable you are at offering this to others in their time of darkness or pain. This is what allows the true definition of what Love is to actually grow in power. The more powerful you become in the Light and Love that you are, the more your egoic programs of fear and separation will dissolve within you. The more you heal yourself from the inside out. The more things like confidence and courage will build, and things like pride, jealousy, and selfishness will dissolve. Your emotional IQ will rise higher and higher the more you meet your emotional pain with Unconditional Love, and even higher still when you meet others' emotional pain with the Unconditional Love that you are. And as you raise your emotional IQ, and as characteristics such as greed or pride dissolve, you're more able to shift into the next Way of Oneness. The Way of Humility.

CHAPTER 17

UNIVERSAL WAY OF ONENESS № 15:

The Way of Humility

THE WAY OF HUMILITY

I think dogs are the best way-showers of Humility. And Mason was no exception. Dogs have a way to pull people out of their self-absorbed selves and challenge their level of Humility. How? Because a dog on a walk will suddenly stop, hunch over, and drop a deuce no matter where you are. And it's your job to slide your hand inside of that little poo-bag and pick up a canine's feces, wrap it up, and tie the knot without getting poop on your hand. Then you must carry their poop in your free hand for the rest of the way home. You also have to clean up their vomit on the carpet. Or their dribble spots if they're messy drinkers. Have you ever had to pull a long, thick piece of grass out of your dog's butthole because it was stuck, halfway in, halfway out? If that doesn't light the fire of humility within you, not much will. Dogs also show you just how poor your communication skills are. Try to train a puppy, or any age dog for that matter. You'll be quick to realize that *you* are the one offering inconsistent and unclear instructions. That you don't come across very clearly at all. And then you get frustrated with your dog. How often do you do this in your relationships and then blame your partner for not understanding you? If you live in the Way of Humility, you'd realize how often you communicate poorly and how frequently you have an arrogant expectation of the other person that they should just somehow understand all the frazzled thoughts that float around in your head.

Mason was a constant reminder that anything you were upset about probably didn't really matter, or at least wasn't the life and death situations that you were making them out to be. You see, a humble person never thinks he's the only one in pain or who experiences suffering or challenges. A person that emanates Humility knows that this is simply a part of the human experience, and your job is to learn what you can from it so you can grow. Mason never got depressed because his body aged and his arthritis caused him pain. On his bad days, he would grimace on his way down to the ground. But once lying down, he smiled, put his happy ears on, and wagged his tail like, "Now that those few seconds of pain are over, it's happy time again, everyone!" He never cared when he lost the ability to accurately catch a ball. He would try his hardest, but inevitably, it would bounce awkwardly off of his face and fly in some direction where he had a hard time visually tracking. He'd look around in a goofy, determined way until he eventually found it. Then he'd grab that ball with such excitement and bring it back to you just like when he was two years old. His body certainly didn't work in his elderly years the way it did when he was young. But it didn't faze Mason one bit. It was part of aging and part of living as a being while moving through this Earth School. It was part of the deal. Mason was humble enough to live in the Way of Surrender and the Way of Humility to these life experiences without ever losing his joyous nature and his zest for life. He was no different in his expression of Humility at one year old or at fourteen.

* * *

THE WAY OF HUMILITY

Once a person really begins to experience the beingness of what Unconditional Love actually is, Humility tends to become part of who they are as well. This doesn't mean there aren't people in the world who already possess the beautiful characteristic of Humility or that one must become unconditionally loving first before they can become humble. But the more you can show up for yourself and others as an unconditionally loving person, Humility will easily become who you are as well.

To earn the Way of Humility requires you to stop trying to be special and certainly to stop trying to be right about everything. This can be a tremendous challenge for many since we all have been pushed to believe and promote "our specialness." When you try to prove that you're special, your ego is the one in charge of running your life and your behaviors. Only ego carries the incompetence and low self-worth vibes that pushes him to try to prove to everyone how special he is. A person who is aligned with her soul knows that she is no more special than any other person on the planet, and in that, she is also very special in her uniquely manifested form, gifts, talents, and journey of lessons that she must learn and master in this lifetime. Specialness comes from the illusion of the superior-inferior program. You either believe you are so special that that makes you somehow better than others (superior program), or you feel that you're not good enough and so try very hard to prove to others how special you are (inferior program). Both sides of this dualistic coin are ridiculous. To function in Humility is to no longer function in the ego. It requires releasing the wounded aspects of yourself that believe you are inadequate, can never change, or will never be good enough, *or* that you will never be seen as special. Many also unknowingly carry the subconscious belief that if they are truly humble, and live in the Way of Unconditional Love, that this somehow means that they've reached perfection and can or will never make another mistake ever again. First of all, you are not perfect, and you never will be. The human part of your existence is not here to be perfect. And this striving for perfection (a program that is common for a lot of people) is nothing more than a mask to attempt to hide from others the utter disgust and low opinion that you have of yourself. Ego strives for perfection. Your soul strives to live in the Ways of Oneness with all. Your soul strives to learn, grow, and expand. It chose to have a human experience of imperfection in order to ignite soul expansion. Stop setting your human self up for absolute failure by thinking that you'll ever be perfect, when that is literally and utterly impossible to achieve. Instead, allow your ever-expanding soul to guide your human experience so you can learn how to live as an enlightened being while on Earth. This means learning what Humility truly is.

When we lack Humility, the universe will humble us so we may gain the characteristic of Humility. If we run the mental programs of a know-it-all—close-mindedness, self-righteousness, arrogance, constantly pointing out how "wrong" others are, or any strong trait that is far from being modest—the universe will find a way to have your ass handed to you so you can learn how to shift into a humbler version of yourself.

Remember, to be conceited or arrogant is more often than not a reflection of your own feelings of inadequacy. You act like a know-it-all so no one will question you, in order to hide that you don't know much. Or you show off the knowledge that you regurgitate from others in order to show how smart and superior you are, to cover up the fact that you actually feel inferior to others. When you carry the belief that you are inferior to others, then you are likely also filled with shame. Therefore, in order to hide those parts of you to the rest of the world, you walk around with a cocky attitude. The more conceited you are, the more you buy into the delusion that you're somehow fooling others and hiding the fact that you feel so inadequate or incompetent. A lack of Humility in someone simply is a reflection of insecurity that someone has for themselves. When I am secure in myself and who I am as a person, there is no need to be conceited or a showoff. Do not mistake this for a lack of confidence. Living in the Way of Humility never means confidence is absent from the way you carry yourself. These characteristics do not oppose each other. In fact, they are two sides of the same coin. Confidence actually evokes Humility. Genuine confidence is never absent from the presence of Humility. Fake confidence lacks Humility and presents itself as cockiness or arrogance. Fake Humility, or wearing the mask of modesty in order to be liked by others, lacks confidence. The Way of Humility is to be fully confident within yourself. When you are this, there is no need to brag or show off, for those are behaviors that stem from those that feel inadequate or not good enough in some way. Can you understand that to live in the Way of Humility requires that you have confidence in yourself?

To take this a step further is to understand that confidence doesn't mean you're perfect or that you'll never make a mistake or a poor choice. You're attending Earth University to experience those very things and learn from them. To have confidence in yourself means that you believe in yourself. You know in your heart of hearts that when you make a poor choice, or when you royally screw up, you'll drop into your heart space and love and nurture yourself through it. You'll also focus on what lesson you need to learn from the experience because you understand that you're moving through another Cycle of Wisdom (a Way of Oneness that will be addressed later in this book). You also know that no matter what, you'll commit to repairing the harm that you may have caused others due to your mistake or poor choice. Self-confidence is a reflection of self-love. And when one truly loves himself, he has no reason to brag to others about his accomplishments, to show off in order to feel important, or to place himself as superior to anyone else. These types of behaviors are silly and immature and are a reflection of a lack of confidence. So when you truly believe in yourself, that you are conscientiously showing up as the best human you can be in this moment, the Way of Humility will easily emanate from you.

Humans have developed an aversion to being held accountable for their choices and actions because they lack Humility. And to lack Humility, you now understand, is to also lack confidence within yourself. If you were truly confident in who you were as a person, you wouldn't make so many unloving choices that result in various levels of harm to others. In addition, the mistakes and errors that you make would be immediately owned by you, and you would move towards correcting those errors. This is the gift of Humility. But no, many humans do terrible things, and then, when caught or confronted by what they did, they get defensive, go on the attack, deny, minimize, or downplay the harm that they caused. This is seen over and over in our world on so many levels. When "caught," shame is often activated. When a person is filled with shame versus Humility, they will fight, defend, and downplay their role or the level of harmfulness that they caused to another. They'll go to extremes to further attack the person that has reported them or brought their harmful deeds to the Light. They'll slander their victim's name and do everything to destroy their reputation so they are the ones that are seen as the liar. This is further abuse and victimization of whom they've already victimized. These are the behaviors of abusers, not of humble persons who are willing to right their wrongs.

On the flipside, if someone falsely accuses you of something, for example, a person who is confident and powerful within themselves would never apologize for something that they did not in fact do. The culture that is arising that expects people to apologize for things that they are accused of, whether they are "guilty" or not, is absurd. It's nothing but a collective form of bullying. Being humble never means powerlessness so that you allow yourself to be bullied into submission when falsely accused. The Way of Humility means not being prideful. For pride is a negative, lower emotion. Entire countries go to war over pride. Pride is arrogance and righteousness. This is very different from having confidence in oneself. And remember that having Humility means you also have self-confidence. So if you are truly confident in yourself, then you will stand up for yourself in your innocence. And this *is* an aspect of Humility. But if you "stand up for yourself" when you have in fact committed a crime, or harmed another, then this is arrogant pride. If you own your harmful actions and take radical Responsibility for them, this is someone who is learning what it means to live in the Way of Humility.

Living your life as the Way of Humility also leads to the next Way. Being a humble person, a person that lacks arrogance, cockiness, entitlement, or superiority, means that it's easier to also develop a level of morality and honesty at the highest level. This level of moral uprightness is a reflection of living in the Way of Integrity.

CHAPTER 18

UNIVERSAL WAY OF ONENESS № 16:

The Way of Integrity

In ethics, integrity is regarded as the honesty and truthfulness or accuracy of one's actions. It is also defined as the state of being whole and undivided. Mason was certainly whole and undivided. He just moved through his life as this being of light. You can't be of the Light and lack integrity. Mason exemplified integrity in the canine sense in that he just was always going to show up in this loving, trusting, gentle, and harmless way. There was never a surprise shift in his temperament or personality. He never snuck into the other room so he could chew on things that weren't his toys. He never climbed onto the furniture that he wasn't allowed on. He never stole food from the countertops or tables. You could always depend on him to do what he was supposed to do, to behave in the ways he was supposed to behave. He was consistently honest in his actions. He was always there for you in the highest way. You could always trust him. You knew he was never going to snap or growl or bite. This boy's bladder would burst open before he'd allow himself to have an accident in the house. He was just 'good.' He was good in his personality. He was good in his heart. He was good in his soul. That's how he showed up as the Way of Integrity.

How integrous are you? This question doesn't ask, "Have you ever made mistakes?" It means, "How 'good' are you to yourself and to others?" Having Integrity means that you are reliable and dependable. But it also means that if you don't have the bandwidth to take on another project, or to help your friend this weekend, that you don't pretend like you do and then bail at the last minute. That lacks integrity. It's not honest to them, and you're wearing a mask of agreeability. If you can't be depended upon this weekend, be honest about it. Honesty and transparency equal Integrity.

How integrous are you? If you quit smoking and your partner asks you if you smoked when you were out with your friends, and you lie about it, this is a lack of Integrity. If you're out with your friends and you speak poorly about your partner behind her or his back, this is lacking in Integrity. If you're flirting with someone because your spouse or partner isn't around to witness it, you are far from integrous. If you hide the truth or lie by omission, there is no Integrity.

If someone was abusing a position of power, that would mean they have little to no Integrity. Whether the position is a police officer, CEO, world leader, yoga teacher, healer, physician, or anyone that holds power over any other, if they use their position to control, suppress, take advantage of, or manipulate others, then they lack Integrity. When people come together and elect officials that actively treat women or minorities as less than equal, then society as a whole lacks the Way of Integrity. When beliefs and acts of sexism and racism are completely disregarded as a prerequisite to dismiss anyone from running for any kind of office or position of power, then we all lack Integrity. What you are willing to dismiss or overlook because something serves your agenda is directly equivalent to the amount of Integrity that you do or do not have. Continuing to work for a person or an organization that lacks Integrity means that you also lack Integrity. If you look the other way, turn a blind eye, all of these behaviors occur because you lack Integrity. And a person lacks Integrity because they lack power. A lack of Integrity means a lack of Divine Power. No one who is connected to their true, Divine Power can ever be absent from living in the Way of Integrity.

When your true Divine Power flows through you, you *can't* lie. You *can't* steal. You *can't* cheat. There's no way a Divinely Powerful person would ever lower the bar on themselves and settle for showing up in these ways. When you learn exactly how to connect to your true and holy essence, connect to your heart space and grow your inner, Divine Light as described previously, this means that you are making the free-will choice to connect to your Power over your mental programs, emotional pain, fear, habits of lying, or anything else that represents your shadow self. You learn over time what it feels like to be Powerful. And you learn the difference between Power over force. When you are filled with the Power of your Light, you transform into a person of Integrity. A person who has the Way of Integrity flowing through them is a person who is absent from the temptations and attractions to anything or anyone who doesn't also have Integrity flowing through them. You will energetically be repelled by those who lack Integrity. You won't even be sexually attracted to another, no matter how sexy their physical vessel is, if they lack Integrity. Lacking Integrity actually makes that person extremely unattractive to a person who lives in the Way of Integrity. So ultimately you will only choose to unite with those that demonstrate the Way of Integrity. Those that are the Way of Integrity are the most trustworthy and dependable people around. You can rely on them to always get the job done. They are true to their impeccable word. Lies never form on the lips of integrous people. If a relationship is going south, they'll never... ever... use it as an excuse to practice infidelity. They'll cut ties and have full closure on the current relationship before ever even considering glancing at another outside of it. Remaining 100 percent faithful while committed is the Way of Integrity. Even if their partner was unfaithful, an integrous person would never turn around and cheat because their partner cheated. They simply would never lower themselves to those types of behaviors. And it's not because they believe they're superior. It's because in their own hearts, no matter how anybody else shows up, they themselves are not dishonest like that. They hold themselves, their choices, and their actions to the level of the divine. That's what it means to be in the Way of Integrity.

Integrous people are very selfless people. If they have symptoms of an illness, they will quarantine themselves and practice the necessary precautions to make sure they don't get others sick as well. No way would a person of Integrity have symptoms of a virus all week and then invite friends and family over for a barbecue on Sunday, as that would be out of integrity. They would never risk the chance of anyone else getting sick because of them.

If the human race actually functioned in the Way of Integrity, and a pandemic broke out, it would never be that big of a deal. Why? Because every single person would naturally be so extra cautious for the care and consideration of others. They would put others first. They would be honest if they had even subtle symptoms of any illness so they wouldn't expose anyone. If they thought there was even a fraction of a chance that wearing a mask in public actually helped to prevent the spread of a virus or illness, they'd wear a mask without ever having to be asked. And if wearing a mask actually did not prevent the spread of a particular illness, those in positions of authority would never lie and claim that wearing a mask was beneficial in order to invoke fear so the fearful could be controlled. Integrous people never exert control over others or manipulate them with fear tactics. People who have Integrity don't need to control others because they don't lack confidence or true internal power. Manipulation to control others is a behavior from those that lack power, which is why they use attributes of force to exert control over others. People are much easier to control when they are filled with fear. So if a person, entity, or a government lacks Integrity, they will use dishonesty to create division and separation among those that they want to control. They want to control to feel a false sense of power to make up for their powerlessness that they, themselves, are.

* * *

Someone living in the Way of Integrity is someone with divine incorruptibility and therefore never wavers their sense of morality. They don't fall for temptations. They stay true to their code of honor not so that others will like them, love them, or approve of them. They do this so that *they* like, approve of, and love who they are. Now we're getting to a deeper meaning of Integrity. The Way of Integrity is a deep reflection of self-love. People that lack Integrity lack self-love. Which also means that they lack true power. A divinely powerful person that loves herself doesn't waver because of others' disapproval, criticism, or negativity. She never makes choices in order to fit in. She makes choices that keep her in alignment with her soul. To be in Integrity means to be in alignment with your soul.

Imagine loving yourself so deeply that you would never settle again. You would never settle for two people of the same caliber getting paid different wages because one of them was a man and one was a woman or one was of a different race. You would never lower yourself to sexual objectification from others. You would only participate in loving sexual experiences where both partners felt cherished and would never again settle for less than being sexually honored.

You would never settle by suppressing your voice when a situation calls for someone to rise up against injustice. You would never settle for keeping friends that continue to live in the old paradigm of prejudices and inequalities. You would release them and only spend time with people who were healing, evolving, and demonstrated kindness and fairness towards others. You would never settle by tolerating abuse towards any animal, no matter what type of animal it was. You would never again settle for the passing on of generations of unconsciousness by tolerating your parents' or family's dysfunction, hate, or disempowerment programs. Instead, you would stand up, speak up, rise up, and even cut them out of your life if they continue to refuse to participate in their own healing and growth for themselves. Integrity means that you love yourself enough to set boundaries and set yourself free from the entanglements from others' dysfunctional patterns. And you'll never again make the powerless excuse that you remain connected to people like this because they are family or longtime friends. This is a pathetic excuse that stems from your own internal weakness. You are the power that can end generational trauma, but not if you choose to remain in patterns of dysfunctional connections or allow yourself to be brainwashed or controlled by your unconscious family members for one moment longer.

Do not make the mistake of interpreting this in the incorrect way. You're not empowered or in the Way of Integrity if you cut loose any person who has a different perspective or level of consciousness than you do. It means that people who are truly trapped in the malaise of unconsciousness need to no longer be a part of your life. Let them go. Rise above. If you're rising higher and higher, if they really want to be a part of your life, they'll choose at some point to rise higher as well and will meet you at the top. But if you "settle" by staying with them, at their level, you're actually holding them at their low level of consciousness. Letting them go gives them the space to choose growth. And it prevents them from holding you back from your personal growth and evolution.

When you're able to shift into an authentic level of Integrity, you are living as a powerful being that truly loves himself. The Way of Integrity means that you simply never waver when it comes to choosing between your shadow aspect of self or your Light aspect of Self. You choose the Light that is You every single time. This allows you to go to sleep at night feeling 100 percent peaceful about who you are as a person. You feel peace that your soul is moving through this Earth experience, and no matter how challenging it gets, no matter how many mistakes you make, no matter how many times you fall down and bleed, you never lower your ethical code of what it means to be a divine being. You are the Light. Being in the Way of Integrity means you finally *know* you are the Light, and therefore, in the billions of ways that darkness shows up to challenge you, to tempt you, and to manipulate you into showing up as your shadow, you'll never fall for it again. Living in the Way of Integrity means you choose to show up as the Light in every aspect of life now and forevermore.

When it becomes easier to show up as the Light, with deep self-love, AKA as the Way of Integrity, it also becomes easier and easier to dissolve the shadow aspects of yourself that hold onto resentments and unforgiveness. Embracing Integrity means you no longer make excuses for your lot in life. You don't blame your childhood abuse for your current cynicism. You don't justify why you won't heal your mental and emotional problems. You love yourself too much to settle for excuses, remember? This also means that you're becoming spiritually mature enough to shift into the next Way of Oneness: The Way of Forgiveness.

CHAPTER 19

UNIVERSAL WAY OF ONENESS № 17:

The Way of Forgiveness

There were moments over the course of Mason's life when I certainly wasn't reflecting the Ways of Oneness. I had moments of frustration and of getting angry with him, especially when he was a rambunctious puppy who was resisting learning how to walk on a leash. I would lose my patience and yell at him at times. And then immediately, I would feel guilty and regret losing control. After all, he was just a baby. *I* was the adult. I was ashamed that I raised my voice and got angry with such a sweet, gentle soul. But Mason, as sensitive as he was, never once failed to show me the true meaning of The Way of Forgiveness. I misinterpreted it at first. I thought that he was forgiving me when I lost my patience with him and he would come over wagging his tail and lick my face. But over time, I realized what he was offering to me was something so much deeper than that. He was demonstrating to me over and over again that he wasn't forgiving me at all. He was simply loving me unconditionally because there was nothing about me that he needed to forgive.

To live in the Way of Forgiveness means to have the epiphany that there is no one to forgive and absolutely nothing to forgive. Needing to forgive means that you hold yourself superior to the person who harmed or wronged you. You're living in separation from them. You're in judgment, which means you're in alignment with your unhealed human self. The part of you who believes you are a victim. And this shadow aspect of you that hides in your subconscious mind believes that you are superior to the person who caused you harm. You believe you are superior because "you would never do what they did." And even if you would never do what they did, it's only your subconscious belief of superiority that blocks you from forgiveness of their act of unconsciousness. Because the truth is you're human. And you've done harmful things to others to varying degrees. You have. You have hurt and harmed others, so to never forgive another person for the harm that they've caused to you means you are somehow exempt from taking responsibility for the harm that you have caused to others in the past. To refuse to forgive is to see yourself up on a pedestal to those who have harmed you, which means to see yourself as someone who has never harmed. This is a delusional and very untrue lens to see yourself through. Do you really believe that you are the one and only human exception to the rule of being human? Are you so self-righteous that you believe that you have never hurt another human being, or an animal, or Planet Earth herself? That you don't cause harm with the chemicals that you purchase and destroy the planet with? That you don't cause harm when you verbally attack those with differing opinions than you on social media? That you haven't caused harm when you led someone on just so you could use them for sex and then abandon them after the fact? But you refuse to forgive the person who caused harm to *you*? Unforgiveness is the disease of hypocrisy. The only cure is to awaken to the true meaning of the Way of Forgiveness. And again, it's the realization that there is absolutely nothing to forgive.

The concept of "there is nothing to forgive" may seem foreign or very far from the truth. It is definitely not what's been taught in our society, or in our world, so it may be very difficult to wrap your mind around it at first. But humans have yet to live by the spiritual laws of enlightenment, AKA the Universal Ways of Oneness, remember? So with so many spiritual teachers over the decades writing about and teaching the concept of Forgiveness (which has been very appropriate for the level of consciousness that humanity displayed at the time), it might seem like this is a powerful way to heal and to live. That, if you forgive, this is how you heal yourself. But it actually works in reverse than what most have been taught. To take the focus away from forgiving and place it on your own inner pain is what actually leads to forgiveness.

A deeper understanding of this can be understood by reiterating that focusing your attention on forgiving someone keeps you locked into a pattern of unforgiveness. Trying to force yourself to forgive or convince yourself to forgive someone who hurt you traps you in the unhealed trauma that was created by that person or situation in the first place. Why? Because you're not Honoring your pain. Remember the Way of Honoring? Part of Honoring means to honor yourself. To honor your unhealed pain. To honor how you feel about something. In order to process emotional pain or trauma, and authentically heal it permanently, you must honor your pain. This means go deeply inside of the pain when it gets triggered and bring validation, love, compassion, gentleness, patience, and nurturing to the pain that you feel. It makes no difference if the pain arises in the form of anger, resentment, frustration, sadness, loneliness, grief, or any other subtle energy called emotion. It doesn't matter what the pain is. It only matters that you spend time honoring it. Validating the pain that you feel, bringing unconditional love and compassion to it, is what transmutes the old trauma or pain into a higher vibration. This is the secret to true transformational-healing, of what it means to alchemize and become an alchemist. Saturate your pain with the vibrational frequency of unconditional love, and that divine frequency will transmute the pain frequency into a love frequency. So when you feel guilty about not forgiving your parents, for example, and you tell yourself things like, "They did the best that they could with the knowledge that they had at the time," you are not honoring your pain. There is an unhealed, traumatized inner child who that type of rationalization doesn't make sense to. Until you give the space, the freedom, the encouragement, and the validation for that aspect of you to be angry with your parents, that unhealed aspect of you will never heal. Understand that what you're doing to that inner child is what your parents did to you back then. You're not validating, understanding, or creating space for you to acknowledge your feelings and move through the emotional pain in order to heal the emotional pain. You continue to abandon your inner child over and over again when you do this. You force him to continue to suppress instead of express his pain. And because of this, you never allow that aspect of yourself to heal. What you feel in response to an unloving or harmful situation is simply what you feel. And those emotions are never wrong or bad. Never. Those emotions are variations of pain that need some love, validation, and compassion in order for you to move through them, fully process them, and ultimately dissolve them. This is how one builds emotional resilience. By actually embracing and loving your pain. Nurturing your pain when it happens means it will never turn into a wound. And loving compassion for your own pain is not just a reflection of self-love, but it's a reflection of divine power. Powerful people feel their pain and lovingly process it in real time. When you master what it means to honor your pain, your vibrational frequency rises to the level of Forgiveness. It rises so high that there is nothing left to forgive. People only feel they need to forgive, or that they can't forgive, because they've never taken the time nor created the emotional space for themselves to compassionately honor their own pain.

I had a client who shared with me one of his traumas as an adult that he "knew he was unhealed from because he harbored unforgiveness and resentment" towards the people that hurt him. When he decided to divorce his ex-wife, all of his and their mutual friends turned on him. The ex-wife told lies and stories, claiming that he had been abusive to her, even though he never once had been. And all of those people, dozens of them, believed her and abandoned him. He did not have even one person or loved one to support him or be by his side. He was at the lowest point of his entire life. He was devastated by the experience. Nearly ten years later, going through one of my coaching programs, Jason offered the self-awareness that he was stuck and unhealed from that scenario. In this session I offered Jason a teaching regarding the divine reason why some of us go through the experience of extreme abandonment. It can be seen as a sort of spiritual test of initiation. Having no one to rely on. Having no one to talk to you, connect with you, or emotionally support you when you're going through a devastating experience is so that you'll learn to turn inwards for your source of healing, processing, and comfort. It may even seem like everyone is against you. This is so that you'll stop looking for a source of comfort and healing from others outside of yourself, which is complete disempowerment. It's so you learn what it means to connect to your true source of divine power by going deep within the self. Moving through true abandonment, when you're at your lowest of the low, with no one around to step up to comfort or support you, is the golden opportunity to, once and for all, fall in love with yourself and connect with your internal divine power. Your life experiences are filled with lessons and gifts. You are meant to experience certain things in life so your soul can grow from that experience and from the lesson that you learned from that experience.

During this discussion and spiritual teaching, Jason suddenly fell very silent. His mouth slowly opened very widely, his eyes got big, and large, fat tears started to roll down his face. And he said to me with a shaken voice, "Oh my God, there is nothing to forgive. I have no one to forgive for anything." After he spent several minutes sobbing in his hands, we had an enlightened conversation about how if those people from his past hadn't abandoned him and treated him so unfairly and cruelly, he wouldn't have moved through the experiences of resentment and unforgiveness. Experiencing those emotions, those negative, disempowering energies in his body, brought him to this very moment. And this present moment was a moment of an enlightened epiphany of what true Forgiveness is. No longer wanting to be disempowered and trapped in angry resentment, he saw the valuable lessons of that period of time in his life. And he very quickly shifted into deep gratitude for that experience. He realized that he needed to go through all of that to learn what it means to shift into his true power. A person who isn't needy of support, but supports and loves himself. A person who realizes he is never actually alone, ever, because when he is connected to divinity, to his higher soul, he can't possibly be alone. For when connected to your higher soul, you are connected to all of the universe. You are connected to the Truth of Oneness. There is no such thing as being alone. There *is* such a thing as moving independently through an experience for your soul's evolution, all by your human self without other humans for support. Independently moving through a life experience so you can learn how to connect to your true, divine power is never the same thing as being alone. Source and the powers of the universe are always with you. But to grow and mature emotionally and spiritually, you must move through tough experiences that force you to go more deeply within yourself, versus always searching for someone or something to support you or uplift you. Spiritual maturation is learning how to uplift yourself. No one reaches that level of enlightenment by having others hold their hand. It's a solo journey. It's the journey of the divine warrior. And a divine warrior has nothing and no one to forgive. They do, however, need to heal themselves. Once you reach this level of spiritual maturity, you tend to move through a cleansing process. A cleansing of everything left of you that is a reflection of the ego. Any aspect that is still a part of you that is wounded or of the shadow self gets purified. There is too much Light within you at this point for any darkness to remain. So the spiritual purification process really begins at this point. And this process is a reflection of the next Way of Oneness: The Way of Purity.

CHAPTER 20

UNIVERSAL WAY OF ONENESS № 18:

The Way of Purity

THE WAY OF PURITY

The purest of souls was Mason Fiori. He was such a shining Light on this Earth for fourteen short years. Divinity flowed through Mason so effortlessly it felt magical just to be in his presence. Mason's energy purified the energy of any room he was in. He also purified people's energies that were around him. Similarly to an air purifier that purifies the air in your living room, Mason could energetically purify all of the energies within a given space that he occupied. He could do this because his heart and soul were so pure.

Most religions have dirtied the meaning of Purity, teaching that you were born a sinner. That you are impure and you need to confess your sins and blah, blah, blah. We're going to cut through the religious nonsense and dive into an understanding of the holy definition of Purity. First, to be "pure" never means to be perfect. It is not perfectionism. To be pure doesn't mean that you don't make or haven't made mistakes. It's not possible to never make mistakes. In fact, mistakes are necessary and important teachers that offer us contrast and experiences to learn and grow from. To live in the Way of Purity means you've reached a level of potent self-awareness. You are keenly aware of the words you choose to say to people and their impact that those words have on others. So you choose to speak with conscious awareness and use your voice to express Light, love, and divine power. Your intentions are pure. Meaning you are living in Integrity always so that not even an inkling to manipulate or control

THE WAY OF PURITY

is a part of who you are. You are honest and transparent, whether it's with your spouse, friends, or the marketing you use for your business. You've released all of the masks you used to wear. No more showboating or pretending to be something you're not to others or on social media. You have no heightened, grandiose sense of who you are. Humility is infused in everything you do, and you don't mistake confidence and loving yourself or acknowledging your gifts for a lack of Humility. Purity is laced with Gentleness and Harmlessness. . . always. These qualities are ever-present in the quality of Purity. Purity means you solely intend to offer only good, positive, loving things, that you have the self-discernment when you show up as less than loving in any situation, and that you actively course-correct and take radical Responsibility for the times that you show up as anything less than that. When you make mistakes, you own them and you repent for the harm that you caused to others because of them. Shame no longer exists. For shame disintegrates when you take divine Responsibility for the way that you show up in life. When you have virtuous, innocent intentions, coupled with radical ownership of all of your choices and actions, the conscious self-awareness to see your mistakes or when you fall from grace, and offer loving forgiveness for yourself when you do, as well as do whatever it takes to heal the harm you may have caused to others . . . then you're living in the Way of Purity.

The Way of Purity can be very tricky to comprehend. But it can be easier to grasp the essence of divine Purity by giving contrasting examples. To give a person a compliment may stem from Purity, or it may be laced with manipulation. If you offer false compliments to butter someone up so that they'll say yes to your request, that's not pure. So if your intention is to offer compliments so that the person will feel really good because you know that if you make them feel good, there's a better chance that they'll meet your request of them, the compliments are not pure. They are false compliments infused with manipulation. You're complimenting them in an effort to control and use them. The Way of Purity means that you compliment someone simply to compliment them. That's it and that's all. If someone did a good job, give them the compliment or validation, simply to acknowledge the "good job" they did. There are no strings attached.

An example of what isn't pure is telling someone you love them because you know there's a better chance they'll give in and have sex with you if you say that to them. This is dishonest and manipulative. So saying "I love you" in this case lacks Purity. Only being physically affectionate with your partner when you want it to lead to sex means the physical affection you are offering lacks Purity. Buying flowers or a gift for someone you're interested in so that they'll like you more and say yes to a date with you lacks Purity. If you buy flowers or a gift simply to make the other person happy or smile, that is an action that is pure. If you're doing it just so they'll like you, it's not pure. If you call your elderly parent every week to check in because you feel obligated to, that lacks Purity. If you call because you love them and want to check in, that phone call to them is graced with Purity. If you expect your date to have sex with you because you bought her dinner, you are an objectifier and are actually treating her as if she was a prostitute. She owes you nothing because you paid for her. This is far from acting in the way that reflects a heart of Purity. If you do selfless or thoughtful things for your friends so that they'll validate how wonderful you are, that lacks Purity. If you do genuinely selfless things simply to be selfless, that's the Way of Purity. Having a different intention than the intention that you make known to another lacks the Way of Purity. What are your true intentions behind your choices and your actions? Are your intentions Pure? Are they infused with Integrity, or with subtle manipulation? Or are your true intentions hidden from you in your blind spots because you lack the self-responsibility it takes to admit the shadow aspects within your egoic personality that are tainting your intentions?

You can see that the more you master the previous Ways of Oneness, the more you simply become the Way of Purity. Being radically responsible, truthful, loyal, selfless, compassionate, offering harmlessness and gentleness, living in equality, having integrity, and being someone that is forgiving are all reflections of a pure, divine soul. These attributes of Oneness cleanse a person until they are pure. Living and showing up in the world as your shadow self, as a spiritually unconscious person, contaminates our intentions. It contaminates and poisons our reasons for doing things and the choices that we make, whether we are consciously aware of that or not. When we are impure, we run sabotaging programs that shatter trust and destroy emotional bonds between us and others. When we are impure, we lie and steal and even steal money from our spouse and cover up the debt that we have accumulated. When the car gets repossessed and your spouse finds out you've spent over a million dollars and you may lose the house next, here is your chance to clean and cleanse your soul of impurities. When you put forth the effort to "right your wrongs," clean up all the damage from your unloving choices, atone for the harm that you've caused to others, and heal your own inner wounds so your wounded inner child can finally be set free, you're functioning in the Way of Purity. The Way of Purity allows your priorities to be those that align with the Light of the Divine. It means you're walking on the path of the Light.

A further extension of the Way of Purity includes how you care for your physical vessel. To be physically "pure" means that you love yourself enough to consume the hydration and nutrients that best nourish and fuel your body and to detoxify from anything that isn't purely for your health and wellbeing. The Way of Purity means that you actively seek out organic, whole foods. Your body is cleansed from the chemicals and toxins that are sold to you and masked as food. You refrain from fast foods, chemically laced products, or genetically modified ones. You put an end to eating junk, sugar, and garbage that trash and destroy your body and you terminate all excuse-making and justifications for why you make such terrible food and beverage choices. You heal the addictive part of you that binges. And that means binging on anything: food, alcohol, drugs, porn, playing video games, being on your devices, or any other form that addiction and binging take.

The Way of Purity means to cleanse yourself of all toxins: toxic behaviors, toxic food, energetic toxins, toxic thoughts, etc. If you still play out aspects of toxic masculinity, either as the victimizer or as the victim, it's time to clean out those programs so you can fully learn the Ways of Equality and Harmlessness and Gentleness. It means purifying your own behaviors, beliefs, and generational traumas in your family and societal systems so their lineages can no longer live on through you. It means healing and clearing your mental programs of separation. It means dissolving all of the labels that keep us separated from the Oneness that we all are, continuing to live in the false reality that we are separate.

Purity means expansiveness. It means the power of Divine Light flows through you. In order for the Light to flow through you and integrate with your Beingness, you must actively clean, clear, and cleanse your mental, emotional, spiritual, and physical bodies on a regular basis. The Way of Purity never means that you'll never again experience negativity. It means that when you do, you'll embrace it so powerfully with your Light that the negativity, in whatever form it took or showed itself to you, transcends into Light itself because of the presence of *your* Light. You are now the Light that transcends any and all forms of evil and darkness into the Light that you are. This is how you become a Warrior of the Light. But no human truly achieves the status of Warrior of the Light until they've reached and live in the Way of Purity. And no one can live in the Way of Purity until they fully dive into their own darkness, no matter how ugly and scary this may be. Every shadow aspect of you must be seen and acknowledged by you. It must be brought to the Light for transmutation. You must see it. . . own it . . . pay off karmic debts when you caused harm to others because of that darkness . . . and you must become so powerful in the Unconditional Love for your own darkness that you expand into a Light being that can unconditionally love others' darkness too. For it is only in loving one's own darkness, truly . . . deeply . . . and unconditionally . . .that you gain the power to love others' darkness. And only in the Light of Unconditional Love and Oneness does darkness transcend. This is the path where many have been called, some have been chosen, and even fewer still have succeeded in transcending their darkness in order to elevate into a true Warrior of the Light.

THE WAY OF PURITY

The Way of Purity simplified means that you wake up every day and make the conscious choice to increase your level of self-awareness so that you can transcend within yourself every aspect of you that is less than the vibrational frequency of Unconditional Love and all other Ways of Oneness. Your focus is to elevate yourself to an enlightened being. This requires ego to be removed from the equation that is your life. You willingly release biases and personal opinions and focus solely on Truth. You actively clear and cleanse your energy fields and your four-body system so that when you interact with others, you interact with clear energy. You no longer contaminate others with your negativity, harmful programs, or unhealed wounds. Healing and elevating yourself becomes your number-one priority in life because when healed and whole, everything you touch, offer, or create is energized with pure divine energy. You no longer contaminate this planet while you're on it. You become someone who purifies this planet.

Once you've reached such a vibrationally elevated state, it means that you've realized that everything you experience in this lifetime has a meaning and a purpose. Even the experiences of darkness. Victim consciousness falls by the wayside. You're awakening to the universal truth that your soul is a part of this Earth University in order for you to learn, grow, and expand. This level of understanding is a reflection of the level of consciousness that challenges you to leave the world of mental knowledge behind and open up to embrace the universal, energetic world of Wisdom. Cleansing your soul and living in the Way of Purity removes the veils of illusion that block a person from becoming a wise being. When you can see through the veils of egoic illusion, you're ready to receive guidance directly from the universe. You're ready for your life to be guided by the Way of Wisdom. One cannot be guided by Wisdom if he continues to embrace the ignorance and misdirections of his own ego. Pure souls listen to their intuition, their higher souls, and the Wisdom of the universe over their own minds and egos. Pure souls heal themselves of anxiety, depression, worry and fear. For these are mental disorders of disempowerment. They are what keep people weak and drowning in darkness and in a state that is easily influenced and controlled by others. To bathe in the Light isn't some phenomenon that occurs outside of yourself. It's the choice to go into the depths of your own darkness and transform every aspect of it with the Light that you already are. This is the process of purifying. It's the death of who you used to be and the rebirth of who you're willing to become. A pure soul is a wise soul. So the more devoted you are to processing and healing your own pain and darkness, to living in the Way of Purity, the more you open yourself up to becoming the next Way of Oneness: The Way of Wisdom.

CHAPTER 21

UNIVERSAL WAY OF ONENESS № 19:

The Way of Wisdom

Mason demonstrated the Way of Wisdom simply because he *was* all of the other Ways. That's a master teacher for you, one who doesn't just preach what to do, but one who actually lives it himself. This is walking your talk. And Mason certainly lived with Wisdom flowing through him. For he always seemed to know what to do. When to be extra gentle, when to get rambunctious and bring playfulness into the picture, and when to just rest, relax, and recuperate. No matter what any situation needed, Mason seemed to know what to do and how to do it. That is an example of a being who flows with divine Wisdom.

If you're drowning in victim consciousness because of how unfair the world is, you'll never be capable of learning the invaluable lessons that come with every life experience. If you fail to learn the lesson, you'll never receive the gift of wisdom that's hidden within each and every life lesson. Maybe someone treated you horribly so you could learn what cruelty feels like. If you learn what cruelty feels like by being treated cruelly, you'll learn the lesson of kindness. This leads to living in the Way of Gentleness and Harmlessness. So the life experience was cruelty. The lesson you were meant to learn was kindness. The Wisdom that you're here to gain is Gentleness and Harmlessness. When you move through these, what I call the 'cycles of wisdom,' without resistance, you'll spend a lifetime easily elevating your level of consciousness higher and higher, and you'll live as a self-realized human being. A cycle of wisdom™ is a cycle or span of growth for your own personal evolution. **A Cycle of Wisdom™ occurs as Life experience → lesson learned → gift of wisdom gained → elevation to living in a Way of Oneness.** Each life experience you have is either to initiate a new cycle of wisdom or to offer you practice integrating a newfound level of wisdom so you can live in one of the Ways of Oneness.

When you have a new realization, epiphany, or gain a deeper understanding of something, it takes practice and integration over time for this to become second nature. For example, you look back and see that the verbal abuse you experienced as a child **(Life experience)** → was so that you could learn to powerfully use your voice to stand up for yourself **(Lesson learned)**. → Now, the more you practice to master this skill for yourself, the more easily you learn to speak up and speak out on others' behalf → **(Gift of wisdom gained)**. The more you do that, the more healthy, loving connections you make with others, and maybe you even become a coach or an inspirational speaker. → You're now living in the Way of Connection, in order to help others find their voices and their power → **(Living in a Way of Oneness)**.

Another example of a cycle of wisdom is: Your spouse divorced you **(Life experience)**. → You learned that your refusal to heal your old wounds and grow up emotionally leads to the demise of a healthy relationship **(Lesson learned)**. → You throw yourself into self-growth and self-healing and are starting to relate to others with truthfulness, patience and healthy connection **(Gifts of wisdom gained)**. → As you continue to mature and take responsibility for yourself, and as you integrate these new ways of relating to others, you are starting to walk the path of a master, since you are now living in the Ways of Truth, Patience, and Connection → **(Living in Ways of Oneness)**.

Let's look at another example of a cycle of wisdom. You were laid off from your job **(Life experience)**. → Although freaked out and scared at first, you let go and realize the universe has been nudging you to quit your job for years now. You realize that worry isn't going to help, so you fully surrender to this life experience **(Lesson learned)**. → Because you reached a level of divine surrender, you were able to shift into and experience full Presence → **(Gift of wisdom gained)**. Being in Presence allowed your intuition to show you that being an entrepreneur is your life path, and you now took action to build your own business from a place of peaceful Presence aided by your own intuition. You are now living in the Way of Presence → **(Living in a Way of Oneness)**.

Remember, **A Cycle of Wisdom**™ occurs as **Life experience → lesson learned → gift of wisdom gained → elevation to living in a Way of Oneness.**

Let's look at one more example. Say you dated a narcissist **(Life experience)**. → Through this painful experience, you started to realize the importance of setting boundaries, saying no, putting yourself first, and shifting into your power **(Lessons learned)**. → Through this, you've realized that to be powerful doesn't mean to allow yourself to be controlled or manipulated. Your very freedom depends on your ability to wake up and separate yourself from control and manipulation by another **(Gift of wisdom gained)**. → You no longer play inferior to any other, which means you now live in the Way of Equality. You also have learned to take radical responsibility for how you show up in your relationships and in the world. You realized you were running a program of inferiority and disempowerment. Fully owning that instead of taking the irresponsible way out by blaming the narcissist for mistreating you is living in the Way of Responsibility **(Elevation to living in Ways of Oneness)**.

When you see things from this 30,000-foot perspective, it should be easier for you to embrace the honoring of each and every one of your life experiences, as well as each person that showed up at exactly the right time to offer you the opportunity to become wiser. One misconception that many people make is to mistake knowledge for Wisdom. Knowledge is not the same as Wisdom. Knowledge gained and then integrated into the beingness of who you are is the definition of Wisdom. The old, overused saying that "knowledge is power" is the farthest thing from the truth. Knowledge is not power. Knowledge is an accumulation of information recorded in your mind. It's not until you implement, integrate, and move through the practice of living that knowledge and/or becoming that knowledge that it evolves into Wisdom. Wisdom is the true form of power. You reading this book is gaining knowledge. But if you place this book on a shelf somewhere when you're done and never actually implement any of the Ways, then you've basically wasted your time. A wise being walks her talk, and she does so easily because she's become what she preaches. A person who spews a bunch of knowledge, facts, and figures but doesn't live in that Truth himself is spreading knowledge rooted in ignorance.

One of the most beautiful things about Mason was that he simply *was* the Ways. Divine Wisdom flowed through him as he lived and moved through life. His interactions with everything and everyone was the miracle of Wisdom expressing itself through his ability to connect with others, be in presence, unconditionally love, and even to forgive. Or, more accurately, his never having the need to forgive at all. Wisdom flowed through him as he lived in the Ways of Oneness. Oneness is Wisdom. Wisdom means being in Oneness. A wise being has nothing to prove. A wise being shares her wisdom with no attachment to who embraces the lessons or who rejects or denies them. Living in ignorance or in the practices of separation are lessons within themselves. Wisdom is hidden inside of everything for each to find as they move through the experience. Wisdom is the Light.

But it is also hidden within the darkness. One need only to shine the light of Oneness onto the darkness to see the Wisdom infused throughout it. Realizing this, that the Way of Wisdom can be found in every life experience, should encourage you to lovingly embrace the darkness. Darkness is only perceived as negative because you see it as separate from you. When you learn to embrace darkness with love, with the Wisdom of Oneness, the evil that hides in darkness no longer has anywhere to hide. When you turn a blind eye to the evil that uses darkness as a mask, you are allowing evil to continue to reign on this planet, within governments and organizations, within yourself. But when you face the darkness with your Light, use the Ways of Truth to command that transparency as the method that governments, organizations, and you as an individual live by, then there are no longer dark places for evil to hide within. Once this happens, once evil is transcended from darkness, darkness can take back its rightful purpose in the universe. As the place of creation and birth. Evil only exists within darkness, using it as a cover, because we allow it to be there by individually choosing to live in separation; to live in ignorance instead of Wisdom. Darkness itself is not evil. Evil uses darkness to hide. We create the wickedness that resides in the darkness because of our unconsciousness that we continue to perpetuate on Earth. Once we awaken and live our lives as wise beings, embracing the truth of Oneness, darkness can be set free. It will resume its rightful place as an honored space of new ideas birthing into manifested creation, a place of healing and transformation, the home of the fearless Sacred Feminine. The Way of Wisdom knows this truth, and when you embody the Way of Wisdom, you will awaken to the internal power of love that transmutes the evil that uses darkness to hide itself. Being wise enough to live in the Ways of Oneness is the key to eliminating all of the evil that resides on this planet. And that means eliminating the evil that resides within you. There is not really such a thing as evil in the sense that it is some entity outside of you. No. Evil referred to in this text is the programs that each human runs that are programs of separation. It's the harm that humans have chosen to cause to others in their unconsciousness. Human characteristics such as objectification, misogyny, racism, bullying, judgment, lying, infidelity, lust, manipulation, violence, oppression, and, of course, the list could go on and on, is what evil is made of. Evil is not some entity outside of yourself. Evil is made up of various energies and behaviors created in human unconsciousness, by humans. Those energies live on and move through people's homes, their relationships, communities, governments, and even countries. They also get passed down generation to generation through DNA and how you were raised and parented. The more people that hate those that hate them, the more hateful energy plagues the planet. That's the evil that this book is referring to. Many people's definition of "evil" refers to some negative energy outside of oneself that people fall victim to. Belief systems that are rooted in inequality and the actions that people choose to carry out are examples of evil. Anchoring entire systems in place that continue to be run to keep certain groups of people oppressed is an example of evil. All of these examples are based in fear, and fear is the only true evil that plagues this planet. The fear to speak up and use your voice when someone you know just said something blatantly sexist. The fear of standing up for yourself when someone tries to intimidate you into submission. Evil is when you know your fraternity brothers are drugging and raping women, and you do nothing to report them and nothing to keep women safe from them. Doing nothing in the face of injustice is evil. Cowardice is a form of evil that controls you to the point of silence. Falsely accusing someone or slandering one's reputation when they did nothing wrong are also examples of evil. Evil is an unconscious person's ego that wants revenge or wants to harm another, even if it's just by gossiping about them. Your ego makes others inferior to you, so you can gain a false sense of superiority. This is the evil that flows through each and every aspect of one's shadow self. Knowing this and embracing this is what begins the shift from "evil" and ignorance to Truth and, eventually, Wisdom.

When you are living in the Way of Wisdom, you understand the real reason why you are here, incarnated on Earth. You realize your "purpose" is never about a job you have, a position that you hold, or how much money you can earn in a lifetime. Your purpose is to learn what your soul wants you to learn via tangible experiences while you're here on Earth. Labels are not your identity. Your job is not your identity. How much money you have is not your identity. These things are just temporary Earth experiences that you have while you are alive. When you come to realize these aspects of Wisdom, detachment becomes more easily attainable. When you're detached from your experiences, suffering doesn't have to be a part of your life anymore. When you realize that your true identity is a formless being of consciousness . . . a soul . . . which is an extension of Source, and that soul would like to move through the experience of {fill in the blank}, it helps you to not take things so personally. It helps you to drop your ego identity and attachment to your experiences and live from a place of true energetic detachment. This level of Wisdom brings freedom. Energetic detachment releases your grip on everything, including your delusion that you have control over everything and everyone. . . or over anything or anyone. Living from a detached state of being means living in flow with what life brings to you. It means surrendering, learning, growing, and shifting into a perpetual state of expansion. It means living as who you were last year isn't appropriate anymore because an ever-expanding being should never be stagnant. Humans have come up with the ridiculous term of "midlife crises." All this means is that you've been stagnant for way too long. You're in a strong resistant pattern to growing and evolving. You love to blame your job or your relationship for how stuck you feel. But it has nothing to do with that. It has to do with the fact that you've chosen to be stagnant and you're digging your heels in the sand of growth. You've placed all of your attention and energy on a ludicrous delusion that having a certain job title, or making a certain amount of money, or getting married were going to be the things that brought you peace and happiness. Believing in these falsities pulls your attention away from Truth. The Truth is that you undergo endless situations in order to have a human life experience filled with ongoing growth. When you forget that this is why you're here, why you are incarnated as a person in the first place, you live denying the fact that you are an infinite being. Infinite beings cannot ever stop expanding. What you misinterpret as suffering is simply your resistance to growing through whatever experience has been offered to you that is meant to activate the next level of your personal growth. Of course you're going to suffer when you try to cram the infinite nature of who you are into a tiny little box with a label on it. When you identify your whole self as any label, that's what you're doing. When you proudly identify yourself as a mother, for example, what happens when your kids grow up and move out of the house? Well, when you mistake this as your identity instead of a temporary experience of being 'mother,' you hold on too tightly to your children. You don't teach them what they need to be taught to be independent. You create codependency. You encourage emotional immaturity so they'll always rely on you. You selfishly do your children a disservice. When your egoic attachment is to the label of billionaire CEO, instead of a divine soul who accomplished these roles while in human form, you make choices like refusing to give your employees a livable wage or health insurance. And then you go fly off into space just to say that you can. Meanwhile, your employees suffer in scarcity because you're too selfish to live in Oneness with all. You lack the Wisdom of Oneness when you live as these examples. If you've reached the status of billionaire, it's not your responsibility to take care of the humans of the entire world like they're helpless, incapable children. But as a being who remembers the Wisdom of the divine, you realize that taking radical Responsibility for every aspect of your life is part of how you are meant to live, as well as to be a role model for living in the Ways of Oneness. When you've reached a status where other people will follow you and mimic you, why demonstrate selfish greed when you can show what true divine power is? There is nothing wrong with spending the money you've earned in fun ways. . .whatever you define as "fun." But when you do it while your own employees that work for you can barely afford food and shelter, you're living as an unconscious being who has sold his soul to the devil, so to speak. And that devil is your own ego. When your company or business flourishes, so should the people that work with you. "We all rise together" is a reflection of the Way of Wisdom. This is wise because it recognizes that we are One. It doesn't mean that everyone needs to earn the exact same salary. It does mean that every person who shows up and reflects the hard work and dedication to make your company or business successful should be taken care of. Otherwise you're just using others so you can get to the top. And get to the top of what? To reach the level of the king of greed? Why strive so hard to become entitled royalty that is gluttonous with superiority? All this does is deny your divinity and create suffering for you and for everyone you come into contact with.

The Way of Wisdom is an aspect of Sacred Feminine energy. She is the golden compass that guides, teaches, directs, and leads. The divine Wisdom that flows through everything is the very energy that has been oppressed, objectified, and desecrated on this planet by humanity for so many centuries. Sacred Feminine energy is the Wisdom of the Universe, and She is the true leader and teacher of Oneness. When She guides, it's the role of divine masculine energy to carry forth Her instructions, bringing Her plans to fruition. The end goal is always achieved because of divine masculine energy, which is linear in nature. Divine masculine is what carries Her vision and instructions to completion. Divine masculine energy is what protects this sacred Feminine Wisdom. Anyone still living in the toxic illusion that masculine energy leads is in no way in touch with the universal Wisdom that flows from Source. For this Sacred Wisdom is Sacred Feminine. She leads, and He follows from the front. She instructs from behind using her global, divine Sight, psychic powers of intuition, transformational healing powers, and divine Wisdom to lead and direct, and He follows from the front, listening to her commands of direction that stem from the Purity of Her Wisdom. He guards. He protects. While in front, he takes the brunt of the wind and of the forces who mean harm to ensure She is safe. He helps to create the spaciousness around Her to prevent others from doing Her harm. He uses strength and linear focus, for these are the divine masculine characteristics needed to carry out the guidance of the Purely Divine. Sacred Feminine and the Way of Wisdom are one and the same. Sacred Feminine Wisdom incarnated in human form as woman needs no brute strength, for her other half, the Divine Masculine, when incarnated in human form as man, was made to be physically bigger and stronger in order to serve as the protector of the Divine Wisdom... of the Sacred Feminine. Her divine power is Her mysticism and psychic healing abilities that flow from the Purity of Her Wisdom. She can be soft, nurturing, and gentle because He was meant to be strong in His support and servitude. Together, they are One. This Wisdom and Way of Oneness has been lost for centuries because as humans devolved in their levels of consciousness, they began to live their lives with closed hearts instead of opened ones. Because of this, the roles of feminine and masculine lost their divinity. Losing divinity means losing the Wisdom behind the creation of each.

To further your understanding regarding healthy feminine and masculine energies is to understand that no human and no man is meant to live predominantly in masculine energy. It automatically becomes toxic when this occurs. It also leads to anxiety. The number-one reason that people have anxiety is because they are predominantly living in masculine energy. This linear energy only knows "one way." It drives. It forces. It doesn't stop until it reaches the endgame where all goals have been accomplished. Can you see how if you're residing in too much of this type of energy for too long, you'll experience burnout? Anxiety? Overwhelm? Stress? Not to mention this energy becomes more and more distorted over time, which causes characteristics like domination, conquering, and unhealthy competition. Why? Because this energy is linearly focused and charges forth without stopping. A one-track mind, so to speak. This type of energy can never be the leading energy in charge. There is no balance. No rest. No equality. No wisdom. It's the "worker" or "completion" energy. Not the creative, wise, Beingness energy. The energy that creates, that births, that leads with the Purity of Divine Wisdom, is the Sacred Feminine. Feminine energy is the Creator energy because She is the Creator of All That Is. She births creations with her Wisdom and powers, and the Divine Masculine sees it through to the end. Can you begin to understand that to be balanced is not to be 50 percent feminine and 50 percent masculine? To be in balance with your own divine feminine and masculine energies is more of an 80/20 split. It's living in the Beingness of the stillness of Presence, while remaining open and receptive to the Wisdom and guidance of the Universe, while seeing with divine Sight and leading from this divine centeredness, about 80 percent of the time. All of that is Sacred Feminine energy. And when it is time to grind. . . to get the heavy lifting done. . . to take action and bring something to fruition, that's when the magnificence of the Divine Masculine steps in and gets things done. He is reliable, dependable, and strong. He is the one who completes. We need His narrow, focused tunnel vision. When it's appropriate, that's the perfect energy to complete a task successfully. But you can see why this type of energy is also the worst energy to lead from. It's too narrowly focused. It can't think expansively. It was never created to do that. Masculine energy has a very narrow focus because when that narrow focus is needed, it's vital perfection. When the divine masculine is needed, and is nowhere to be found, your tasks, goals, or projects will fall by the wayside. It's the perfect energy when used appropriately and in small quantities. It's also the energy needed to fight or protect oneself or others. Do you understand how you couldn't possibly be in balance if you remained in fight mode 80, 90, or 100 percent of the time? The only way to rebalance, recalibrate, and create peace in your physical body and energetic system is to shift back into the feminine Presence of peace, stillness, and calmness. A very masculine man who is balanced in his divine nature, AKA close to achieving enlightenment, functions from that 80/20 split that was previously described. Those that function in the Way of Wisdom understand this and are healing themselves so they no longer demonstrate characteristics of unbalanced, distorted, or toxic masculine energies. It creates sickness, not only within oneself, but it spreads like a plague to others because they are then forced to be too much in their masculine to fight off all of the out-of-balance, distorted masculine energy in others.

* * *

THE WAY OF WISDOM

The Way of Wisdom only flows through the heart center, AKA heart chakra, of humans. If your heart is closed, you are also closed off to divine Wisdom, which means you are closed off to Sacred Feminine energy. She is the energy that heals. Masculine energy doesn't heal. Maybe now you can put two and two together to understand why the entire world is one big, unhealed wound. Nothing heals without the divinity of Feminine Wisdom. And we've lived in an unconscious patriarchal world for many centuries now. No wonder our planet and everything on it is dying. Transformational healing only takes place in the Presence of the Feminine. Jesus knew this better than anyone. Well, outside of all of the enlightened women throughout history that you don't know about or will never hear about. Jesus is one of the only humans to date that achieved the full integration of Sacred Feminine Energy. Or, more accurately stated, he is the only man in history who achieved full integration of his sacred feminine and sacred masculine nature. He embodied Oneness within himself. That's why he was able to achieve the miracles that he achieved. He evolved into the full embodiment of Christ Consciousness because he lived in the Ways of Oneness and taught with the Sacred Feminine energy of divine Wisdom. Because he opened his heart fully to the Sacred Feminine, She offered him Wisdom and transformational healing powers that come from Her and only Her. She flowed through him because he Honored Her. They became One. The Wisdom of the roles of feminine and masculine is a large part of what Jesus taught while he was alive on Earth. Why do you think he was murdered? And why do you think the Truth of the Wisdom of the feminine was taken out, fragmented, and rewritten by unconscious men who lived with closed hearts despite Jesus's teachings of heart-centered living and the Wisdom of Oneness?

The more open your heart center is, the more that Wisdom can flow through you, offering you divine guidance in every aspect of your life. The more open your heart is, the more you heal because you're opening to the Wisdom of the Feminine. Wisdom doesn't come from the mind. Knowledge and chaos come from the mind. Being trapped in the knowledge of your mind keeps you trapped in mental programs and ego. Knowledge is not Wisdom. When knowledge is integrated and it becomes who you are or how you show up in the world, that knowledge has been transformed into Wisdom. Wisdom is what is powerful. Wisdom is free from judgment and is unbiased. It's a feminine, intuitive Knowing, not an intellectual one. Wisdom is the ability to see the lesson in a life challenge. It's the ability to detach from the labels that describe who you are. It's the Knowing that you are no more and no less divine than fish that swim in the sea or than the trees that grow in a rainforest. Wisdom is Knowing not to take anything personally, for the universe is intimately impersonal. It's also realizing that you are not in fact the center of the universe. Therefore, you terminate your selfish ways of living where you act like you are, as well as the belief that life owes you something simply for being alive as a human. Further, knowledge can be infused with conceitedness and self-righteousness. Wisdom is infused with Humility. In fact, it's infused with all of the previously described Ways of Oneness.

You can see that someone who has Wisdom flowing through them is someone who is in harmony with life. Living in the Way of Wisdom organically harmonizes your life and your relationships. True divine, feminine Wisdom is what leads all who are ready to the final Way of Oneness: the Way of Harmony.

CHAPTER 22

UNIVERSAL WAY
OF ONENESS №️ 20:

The Way of Harmony

Mason's very essence sang a song that was harmoniously in tune with all. He harmonized with wild animals that he came across, with other dogs, and with every person he met. Mason reverberated Harmony. He lived as enlightened beings are meant to live. In Harmony with one another. Never opposing, harming, or fighting against. To be in Harmony means to be free. To be in Harmony means to stop fighting the circumstances of life and instead embrace everything. Mason's spirit was free. He freely offered affection. He freely played. He freely accepted all, loving unconditionally everything and everyone he came across. I learned the value of living my life in Harmony because Mason showed me what the divine definition of what Harmony was.

To be in Harmony starts from within. You must be willing to heal yourself and elevate yourself to a high enough level of consciousness so that you are in Harmony. That means Harmony within yourself. You must be free from stress and anxiety and free from blaming anyone else for your stress and anxiety. You must be free from negative mental programs that plague your mind and cause you emotional suffering. You must be in Harmony with your own emotional body and learn what it means to love your emotions as they arise, no matter how painful or uncomfortable they are. For this is not just an aspect of self-love, but an aspect of divine power. You must be free from attacking others and projecting your own experiences of suffering onto them. You must be in Harmony with the Earth. With nature. With animals. With other humans. An age of Harmony cannot be created or experienced by some force outside of you that's going to create it for you while you then get to reap the benefits of someone else's creation. To live in the New Golden Age of Harmony means that you must choose to do the work to dissolve all of the ways that you show up in this world as disharmony . . . as disempowered, and deep dive into the inner work that's necessary to become a divinely empowered being. Only then can you become heart-centered enough and powerful enough to contribute to creating Harmony outside of yourself. Only then can it spread to your family members and loved ones. Your communities. The corporations and businesses you work in. The world.

By now, you should understand that the Way of Wisdom leads to the Way of Harmony because you realize that everything is for you. Every experience, every challenge, every win, every loss. When you gain this level of Wisdom, it's hard not to be in Harmony with everything that crosses your path. You realize the abundance of life experiences are all there for your divine benefit. You've learned how to fully surrender and refrain from offering resistance. You embrace what comes to you with love, grace, and nurturing. The power of this isn't simply that you are then in Harmony with whatever flows into your life. The real power is that you become someone who *harmonizes* what flows into your life. So let's say that something is out of Harmony. Let's say it lacks the Ways of Truth and Purity. An example of this could simply be a plan to market your product or service, and your marketing team presented a plan that isn't honest and transparent to potential consumers. Instead of using the traditional manipulative marketing techniques that are typically used, you veto that and refuse to do it. Instead, you work with the team to come up with a marketing plan that reflects the Way of Purity. That means it's free from any manipulation or dishonesty. It's transparent and straightforward. There are no lies, hidden agendas, or gimmicks. By living in the other Ways of Oneness and remaining in the Way of Loyalty to them, you are not just in the Way of Harmony with Oneness, but you become a beacon of Light that actually harmonizes other things that are out of alignment with the Ways. You become a divine harmonizer to bring people, situations, and potentials into alignment with the Ways of Oneness. You are now someone who is contributing to creating enlightened societies.

To be in Harmony is to be in flow, to be a receiver, and to be one who follows intuitive guidance to take heart-centered action, all at the same time. To be in flow requires full Surrender and Patience. To be a receiver is to take notice of the signs, messages, and synchronicities that the universe sends to you while being completely free from any resistance, judgment, or egoic need to understand everything you're receiving. To live from your heart-space means you lack being reactionary and only take spirit-guided action from a place of peace, love, and power. And you follow the guidance of your intuition, never from your mind.

Harmony doesn't mean there are no differences among people. It means those differences don't matter. To be in Harmony doesn't mean you never disagree. It does mean that when you do, you don't make the other person wrong, inferior, or judge them for their stance on things. You never criticize. And you never take things personally. If your boss went with someone else's idea, it's not personal. The Way of Wisdom reminds you of that, and the Way of Harmony reminds you to fully support and flow with the idea that was chosen and with the colleague that had the idea that was chosen over yours. This is living with detachment. Detachment is necessary to be in Harmony with all. The Way of Harmony never means we are suddenly all the same. Trying to be the same as everyone else or only accepting people of the same race or culture into your circle are actions of hate and separation.

The Way of Harmony is the act of embracing and integrating all of the Ways of Oneness, of living the Ways in your everyday life, throughout your lifetime, and of having no more willingness to show up as anything less than those Ways. This is what it will take to create the New Golden Age of Harmony. The new age is not a passive creation. It's a warrior's creation. Divine warriors, or Warriors of the Light, are those who are willing to plunge into the darkness of their shadow selves and rise above the teachings of their egos and the brainwashing beliefs and conditioning of unenlightened people that came before us. They are ready to dismantle and shatter every aspect of toxic patriarchy, selfish greed, hate, systems of sexism and racism, and every aspect of programs of separation and inequality that exist. They are willing to exhaustively spend their lives becoming better people than the people that our unconscious society has taught them to become or that their spiritually unconscious parents raised them to be. Divine warriors don't settle for living in the ways that people with low levels of consciousness choose to live. They are always rising above, coming closer and closer to the beingness of the Ways of Oneness. They gain the feminine Wisdom that the only way to change the world is to first change themselves. And that the only way to heal themselves is to open to the Sacred Feminine energy that knows how to heal. They understand that the macro, what they see in the external world, is nothing but a reflection of the micro, who *they* are as individuals. This knowingness is a reflection of Oneness. No more separation. No more refusing to take responsibility for the wellbeing of the world we live in.

Living in the Way of Harmony also includes the understanding that each soul that incarnates into the Earth University has chosen to be here and has chosen what she or he needs in order to elevate their soul growth. No more living in victim consciousness of your circumstances. You consciously choose to step into your divine power and harmonize with your life circumstances. This is how you learn the lessons that your higher soul chose to learn by having these specific circumstances to live through. It's also how you rise above those circumstances instead of allowing them to define who you are. It's about growth. It's *always* about growth.

Why do you continue to live in the ignorance of the concept of unfairness? The belief that life is so unfair. This is disharmonization. It's only in small-mindedness that one believes life is unfair. Life is what it is. It's not fair, and it's not unfair. It's not personal. The universe will always seek to be in balance. If life seems unfair to you, you're likely drowning in self-victimization, superficiality, and selfishness. You have no idea what another person's karma or soul lessons are. Each human is living out the balancing of their karma as well as moving through the experiences they need to move through for their own soul's expansion. To be specific regarding one's karma, let's look at a few examples to gain a deeper understanding. Let's say you were mean, made fun of, or bullied others when you were in high school. Now, two or three decades later, you feel really singled out and picked on by someone of authority. Maybe it's your boss or person you must answer to at work. They might seem like they don't like you and they're out to get you. And maybe they really are. How are they making you feel? The feelings of anger, embarrassment, shame, helplessness, the feeling of having no control or say over what's happening to you, these are the exact same feelings that you caused in those others that you picked on, made fun of, and bullied when you were younger. Welcome to being force-fed slices of your karmic pie. If you cheated on a previous romantic partner and destroyed your relationship because of it, you now understand why your business partner, who happened to be a longtime friend of yours, betrayed you and left you in debt.

If you were rigid, selfish, and controlling in your previous romantic relationships or friendships, you'll move through an experience where someone treats you in the same way. Most cannot connect the dots between what is occurring now in their lives with how they have previously treated others in the past. You may be more evolved now. Maybe right now you would never treat someone with harmful intentions. But if you haven't yet paid off your karmic debt for the times that you *did* treat people unkindly or when you *did* cause harm to another, you still must move through the karmic consequences of those previous choices and actions.

Maybe you were loyal to a company for nearly two decades. Then all of a sudden, you made a very minor mistake, and you find yourself suddenly fired. The consequence seems radically unfair. After all, humans make mistakes sometimes. And this was not a mistake to be fired over. It's daunting to imagine nearly twenty years of devotion as an excellent employee, to suddenly find yourself fired over almost nothing. But did you ever consider that this is the karmic payback for the fact that you cheated on your partner? That although happily married now, she was devoted to you early on, and you betrayed her by cheating on her? It makes no difference if she ever found out or not, by the way. And although you have a healthy and great relationship and you would never betray her now, you did betray her early on. You have earned the karmic experience of being treated with betrayal in response to showing up as devoted and loyal. This is how karma works.

Karma simply means what goes around comes around. What you put out into the world is going to come back to you. It's just that simple. What can be confusing about karma is that looking at the harmful thing you did to another person isn't necessarily going to come back in exactly the same way. If you cheated, you might not be cheated on, for example. If you stole, you might not be stolen from. If you betrayed your spouse by cheating, the harm that you caused to your spouse is what's going to come back to you. The emotional devastation. The shattering of trust. The anger or rage. The heart broken into a million pieces. Whatever harm that your choices and actions caused in the other person is what is going to come back to you. Or betrayal in some form is going to come back to you. That may come back in the form of a future lover cheating on you, or it may come back to you in a million different ways that don't even seem to be related. Let's say a teacher or a selfless neighbor helped you out when you were a child. If they stepped up and cared for you and went above and beyond because they saw you were having a rough time, and you didn't appreciate what they did for you, then that is going to come back to you. It may show itself by having an ungrateful employee even though you are the most generous boss. You may do a thousand "small" acts of kindness like hold doors for people or let someone go ahead of you in line and never be thanked or smiled at. Well, this will continue until you've paid off your karmic debt of the lack of appreciation or acknowledgment that you offered to that adult that helped you when you were younger. Once that karmic debt is paid, you've come back to balance. You've come back to Harmony.

So, to understand Harmony you must understand both sides of the coin of the Way of Harmony. Harmony has karma infused into it. Karma is the way to ensure Harmony because Harmony means balance. And karma is the universe's way to harmonize things that are energetically out of balance back into balance. If you cause harm in others by way of your beliefs, the laws you make, the way you govern, the way you treat your employees, or how you treat your spouse, children, or your neighbor, the universe will provide to you the experiences, people, or situations that reflect that back to you. It comes back in the form of "harm." Simply put, when you cause harm to others, you will experience being harmed. That's how the universe harmonizes the unloving imbalances of your hurtful choices. If you cause love, in the form of showing up in the Ways of Oneness, you are harmonizing the world from the harm that people cause. You are creating Harmony.

Karma has been the foundation of the Way of Harmony because we needed it as unconscious humans. But now. . . now that humanity is beginning to transform into spiritually awakened humans and raise their levels of consciousness, Harmony can be achieved through conscientious choices and radical self-awareness. It can be consciously achieved by living in the Ways of Oneness. Your vibrational frequency can harmonize people and situations just by you walking into a room or by being a part of the situation. How? By transforming yourself into the beingness of the Ways. When you vibrate as Patience, Surrender, Truth, Harmlessness and Gentleness, for example, you are positively transforming the negative consequences of karma. When you show Unconditional Love in response to hate, you are transmuting that hate, instead of getting entangled into the negative karmic web of hate that the other person or group of people are enticing you to join them in. You're living in the Way of Wisdom when you choose to powerfully love over sinking to the level of hate, the way that others get ignorantly tricked into doing. When you are transparently honest in every aspect of every relationship you are engaged in, including the relationship with yourself, then you are not only in Harmony, but you've reached the level of one who harmonizes. And don't allow your ego to jump in here to try to feel special about being "a harmonizer." To feel special at reaching this level means you haven't really reached this level yet. It means you are still trapped in ego because you lack the Way of Humility. Becoming a harmonizer by living in the Way of Harmony with all things everywhere is something that you *are*. It's not something that you do. Your vibrational frequency at this point has become so pure (the Way of Purity) that all other frequencies in your presence will entrain to yours. This is part of what it means to live in the Way of Harmony. It's an energetic raising of vibrational frequencies in order to always offer each and every Way of Oneness.

Do not make the mistake of believing that you can dissolve other people's karma that they have earned. You cannot. This would be removing them of the obligation of self-responsibility. You cannot remove the Way of Responsibility for another person. This renders them weak, powerless, and incapable. Which they are not. They may be showing up in the world as if they are incapable and weak, but that just means they haven't yet discovered their internal power and aren't yet choosing to take Responsibility or pay off their karmic debts with Grace.

Simply put, the Way of Harmony is the ease, honest, abundant flow of life, completely free from the shadowy aspects of low levels of consciousness. It's being in tune with the joy of life, with the Grace needed during challenges and conflicts, and with your own intuitive guidance so you can make the most of your soul's time here on Earth. Being in Harmony doesn't mean you won't feel pain. It means you mature into a being that is powerful enough to embrace their pain and love and nurture their pain while it's there.

There was no lack of Harmony in Mason's final days. Just because he was dying doesn't mean it wasn't harmonious. His soul's time here on Earth was complete. It was time to end our companionship together during this incarnation and say goodbye to one another. What allows for Harmony in a situation such as this is one's ability to live in the Ways of Surrender, Unconditional Love, Compassion, Selfless Service, and any other Way that is needed to create harmonious balance of what is being experienced. The Ways of Oneness are what nurture, process, and support your soul while you experience the pain of being human. The Ways of Oneness were my saving Grace during those final days with my Mason-baby. The pain of saying goodbye to him was unbearably agonizing. If I didn't have the Universal Ways of Oneness to support me through that, I don't know how I would've been able to endure that level of grief. Living in the Way of Harmony means living with a profound sense of peace. Even in the agony of emotional pain, there was also a divine sense of peace. That nothing is "wrong." That this experience is nothing but an experience and all is well and perfect. Peacefulness is in the background and at the center of the experience. Peace is the spaciousness for all other energies to manifest into. What enters into the energetic field of peace are the energetic experiences of sadness, pain, grief, or any other "negative" emotion. They move through the human experience as a temporary experience only, when divine peace is at the core of who you are. This is what it means to be living in the Way of Harmony. Harmony with all . . . with every energy that manifests as a temporary life experience. I was in Harmony with the experience of Mason dying and with the pain of that experience. The energies of sadness and grief arise and float around the energetic soup of peace . . . of Harmony . . . and those lower, painful energies get harmonized. Painful emotions serve as reminders to live in the Ways of Oneness. To cherish every moment with those that we love because in the very next moment they could no longer be there. When you become the peacefulness that you seek, you are living as a spiritually awakened being. You realize you are the peace. . . the Harmony that you've been searching for. That living in peacefulness doesn't mean never experiencing pain. It means to not identify with that pain or allow it to become who you are. Instead, you are in Harmony with it because the core of who you are is peace. And as peace, a painful experience, a life challenge, or painful emotions can temporarily arise and swim around your peaceful energy fields for a little while and be met with zero resistance. To live in the Way of Harmony is to live all of the Ways at one time, as well as to show up in whatever Ways that the situation or beings involved need the most from you. The constant, ever-steady, unchanging, underlying Presence at the core of every experience you have had and will ever have is the formless you that is energetically nothing but the Light of peace. To live at this level of awareness, to be the peaceful Presence that embraces all experiences and all things, is to live in the Way of Harmony.

CHAPTER 23

Mason's Final Days

Knowing that Mason's health was declining, I called to schedule a vet appointment for him. When I called, they told me they had one the very next morning, but it was a drop-off appointment only. This means I would have to drop him off in the morning, and they would evaluate him and complete necessary diagnostics as they could throughout the day. Then I would pick him up at the end of the day. I told them absolutely not. That this would be harmful to Mason's emotional and mental health. He was too sick at this point to be separated from me. He needed me by his side. Going through anything alone would be devastating to him. So she scheduled me for the following week on a Tuesday so I could be there with him.

Tuesday

Tuesday morning came, and Chris and I took Mason and Sasha for their daily morning walk. We didn't know it at the time, but this ended up being Mason's very last walk he went on. He was happy and vibrant. He sniffed, walked, peed on things. He absolutely loved his walks, and this day was no different. Shortly after we got home from his walk, we left for the vet's office. Because of COVID protocol, we had to wait outside of the building. A tech came out, asked questions, and wrote down some information about Mason. The whole time, Mason kept wagging his tail and heading for the door as if to say, "What are we waiting for?! Let's go inside!" Mason never in his entire life was afraid or nervous when going to the vet. He greeted everyone happily and went with the flow the whole time he was there. Throughout his life, I used to joke with vet staff that they could probably do open heart surgery with no anesthesia on Mason, and he'd probably just lick them the entire time to encourage them to hurry up. This was how carefree and in flow he was. Even when he didn't like something, he just offered this attitude of love and gentleness until it was over. So as it was, it was time for the tech to take Mason inside for the doctor to examine him. Chris and I had to wait outside. Mason never looked back as the door was opened, and he went right in with the tech. I knew he was going to be upset at the point when he realized I was missing from the equation. But I also understood the new COVID protocols that were in place and that Mason wouldn't be left without me for too long. About half an hour later, the doctor came out to discuss Mason's result and recommendations. He felt a large mass in his spleen so recommended X-rays and blood work. Oh, and that he would have to remain there all day with them to get all of the diagnostics completed. I froze. My heart sank so fast and so low into my intestines I thought I was going to poop it out in front of the doctor. I knew this wasn't good. Mason truly needed the diagnostics, but I knew my dog. I *knew* what he needed for his mental and emotional well-being. And being there to get tested all day without me there to comfort him and guide him through it would be bad. I was stuck. He *needed* these tests without question to determine what we were facing and what course of action to take for him. So I made the painstaking decision to leave him there to get the testing done. Six hours later, Chris and I went back to talk about the results of the diagnostics and to pick up our beloved boy. The vet discussed the possibility of a splenectomy to remove the enlarged, tumor-filled spleen that was pushing on his stomach and lungs. His lungs and heart looked clear according to the X-rays. However, the doctor would need to send them to the radiologist for a conclusive reading, as well as to get his opinion on whether the mass in the spleen was a benign tumor versus malignant carcinoma. We discussed possible plans of action but would hold off on anything definitive until the final results came back in a couple of days. We didn't have good news, but we certainly didn't have horrifying news. It was time to get our boy back and take him home to love on him while we pondered the possibilities of treatment moving forward.

A vet tech brought Mason out a couple of minutes later, commenting on how sweet he was and what a good boy he was. When Chris and I greeted our baby, my body began to go numb. He didn't even look at Chris. And when he looked at me, he was almost empty. No tail wags. His jovial nature was gone. He was just there. Energetically, he felt awful, like he was emotionally broken. We got him home as fast as we could. Once inside the house, Chris and I did everything we could to comfort him, reassure him, and love him. But the fact is, he had been traumatized. It was devastating for him to be put through all of that testing without me by his side as his emotional support system. And he was too old and too sick at this point to recover from that.

Mason refused all food that night. My baby had already lost nearly fifteen pounds from the difficulty with eating because of the splenic tumor pushing on his stomach, and now he was refusing to eat anything at all. He was rapidly getting weaker by the hour, and it was hard for him to walk or hold himself up for very long. It was painful to see this. Just that very morning, he went on his daily walk with us and loved it. Now he was refusing all attempts to feed him and had a hard time getting up and walking. We hoped that maybe if he slept for the night, he'd feel well enough to eat in the morning, and we could get him back on track emotionally. But the next morning, he was worse.

Wednesday

I called our vet, but he wasn't in the office that day. I began to call around to vet ERs, but each one told me the same thing. I'd have to drop him off and leave him for diagnostics and treatment. I wasn't permitted to be by his side. I absolutely refused. I knew if I did that he would die alone in an ER without me there. I finally called VEG: Veterinary Emergency Group in Encinitas, CA. They had a very different protocol. I could be there by his side for every single second no matter what they needed to do. On the way to the car, Mason turned around and didn't want to go. First time in fourteen years. We got him in the car and headed to VEG. We were greeted so warmly, and they welcomed the three of us right into the emergency treatment room. They got Mason a huge, brown, doggy couch bed to lay on. I sat next to him on the floor. Unfortunately, Chris had a work thing to attend to for a brief time and couldn't stay with us. But I petted Mason and talked to him the entire time. This was the only vet appointment he had ever been to in his fourteen years of life that he was scared and shaking. I knew the previous day's vet stay had just destroyed him. And let me be clear—the vet and the vet staff from that facility are absolutely wonderful. They treated Mason very well and with a lot of care. I think the vet himself is a very special and compassionate person who treats humans with patience and non-judgment. He is wonderful. But our traditional practices of separating our animals from their humans is detrimental to their emotional and mental health. So I want to be clear that that's what I'm addressing here. Now, at VEG, I was able to be right next to Mason's side the entire time. This is how every vet practice should be.

So my biggest concern at this point was that Mason was malnourished and growing much weaker. And after the previous day's experience, he was getting weaker by the hour. I was interested in getting Mason an NG (nasogastric) tube placed for feedings. After an extensive conversation with the ER doctor, where she sat on the floor with Mason and me, I understood that Mason had been eating less and less because of the enlarged spleen pushing on his stomach. To get him to eat again, he would need a splenectomy. But to survive the surgery, he would need to be eating and much stronger. This was a catch-22. Surgery to remove the spleen would make it easy for him to eat again. But he needed to eat and get stronger to withstand the surgery. At that point I knew we were at a dead end. There was no hope for Mason to recover. At this point an NG tube would be cruel and unusual punishment because the whole purpose of a temporary NG tube would be to assist Mason nutritionally until he ate on his own. If he got strong enough, we could consider the surgery. But that would never happen because of the splenic mass, making it impossible for him to eat enough on his own. And around in circles we go.

I knew Mason wanted nothing to do with any more hospital visits, testing, treatments, or doctors. The emotional trauma he suffered from the day before changed his willingness to participate in the healing of his body. He felt like he had given up. His body was failing at an extremely rapid pace. Prior to this, Mason's magical spirit gave him the emotional power to get through anything that his old body was putting him through. But since the devastation of spending the day without me by his side, he lost his emotional power. The very power that his fragile body fed off of to sustain itself. This is why his decline happened so fast. I decided the only thing I could do was schedule an at-home euthanasia appointment for the next day and to shower him with love and affection until that moment came to pass. The doctor from VEG was incredibly gracious, as was the entire staff there. We discussed making Mason as comfortable as possible with some pain medication. He got IV pain meds, and they sent me home with some oral pain medications. They gave him an appetite stimulant and some free urgent care canned food that he would hopefully eat to be able to take the pain meds with. Chris picked us up, and Mason couldn't walk. So Holly, a VEG staff member, wheeled over an electric gurney, and we put the dog bed with Mason in it on top. The three of us wheeled him out to the car and opened the back of the Jeep to put him inside. Then Chris and I thought out loud about how exactly we were going to get him from the bed to the inside of the car. Holly suddenly said, "You can just take the bed. Pick the whole bed up with him in it and take the bed. You can throw the bed away when you're done with it. He's so cozy in it, and it will be too hard on him to transfer him out of it. Just take it. It's yours." Talk about putting the patient's comfort and what's best for him first. I burst into tears with her kind gesture. She asked if she could give me a hug, and I, of course, accepted a hug from this wonderful, thoughtful woman. She wished us the best, and we set off to spend our last night together with Mason. As soon as we got home and got Mason settled, I called and arranged for the at-home euthanasia to take place the next day, Thursday at 3:00 PM. It was done. We had almost exactly twenty-four hours left with our baby before he was going to be gone from our lives forever. A very surreal realization as I hung up from scheduling the appointment.

To say that our last night with Mason was emotionally challenging would be like saying that 9/11 turned out to be a rough day. Down to about 75 pounds at this point, Mason could barely hold his fragile body up. Chris and I had to lift him and assist him in walking so he could drink water and go out to go potty. When he was guided to the grass in the front yard, he stood there and took it all in. He sniffed the air. He smelled the grass. He smelled the leaves on the plant next to the palm tree. He peed. He managed to walk around the palm tree further into the front yard. And then he just stood in the grass. His head held high, looking off yonder, his nose twitching, breathing it all in. He stood, grounded to Mother Earth, connected to Father Sky, enjoying the slight breeze on his handsome face, energetically intertwined with the grass, trees and plants like only Mason could masterfully do. Chris and I sat down on the sidewalk and watched this beautiful sight. It took my breath away to see him, in his fragile, dying state, being so Present with all of Life that surrounded him. He was once again role modeling to us what being in Oneness is. What being fully surrendered looks like, feels like, *is* like. He was a master spiritual teacher, and he was continuing to teach us even in his final hours.

Mason had been given an appetite stimulant while at the ER. The reason for this? Because quality of life means everything to me and is my top priority. Starving to death must be an extremely uncomfortable feeling, and my assumption is that it decreases quality of life. The rumbles from his empty tummy were loud and yelled of discomfort. I was hoping Mason would eat enough food that evening to fill his tummy and decrease the feeling of starving. So once we got him inside and settled, we attempted to feed him. Chris cooked ribeye steaks, and we crossed our fingers. Now before any animal rights activists throw this book across the room, I am on your side. I am completely against the meat and dairy industry. But I will also be honest with you when I say if I had to slaughter a cow myself to give Mason some relief in the final hours of his life, I would have found a way to do it. I was willing to do anything and give him anything if it meant even the slightest bit of increase with his comfort level. We couldn't believe it. He ate! And he was *perky* and enjoying every bite! Feeding him very small pieces that he could basically swallow whole without choking allowed him to enjoy food again and fill his grumbling, empty belly. He ate about half a steak. And he didn't stop there. I offered him the can of urgent care wet food that the ER doctor had offered to me, and he ate that up as well. He was eager to eat it, and he enjoyed it. I cried tears of joy for him. I knew he could rest more easily that night being satiated.

MASON'S FINAL DAYS

Mason was unable to walk through the house on his own, and we knew it would be too hard on him to guide him all the way back to the bedroom to go to sleep that night. And since leaving his side wasn't an option, we did the only rational thing. We had a slumber party in our living room. With three large dog beds lined up on the floor against our couch, another large round dog bed in the corner of the room, another pillow for Sasha to sleep on, and pillows and blankets...well...everywhere, it looked like a first-grade classroom came over for a sleepover. Mason was placed on the center dog bed in front of the couch, and I lay on the dog bed next to him with a blanket and two pillows. I didn't fit on that dog bed. It was incredibly uncomfortable. But what did that matter? These were my last moments with my baby, and I was going to make the most of every second I had left with him. Chris was on the couch. The cats were. . .well, they're cats. They were wherever the hell they wanted to be at any given moment. And Sasha decided to cuddle into the small of my back like we were on a California King instead of a dog bed that only fit half of my body on it. But that's how we settled in for the night. Several times throughout the night, Mason would sit up with wide eyes, looking for me. As soon as he saw me, he relaxed and would lie peacefully back down. I would scratch him and pet him and softly speak to him, reassuring him that I wasn't going to leave his side. And he would fall back asleep. Once during the night, I suddenly awakened because he was trying to get up. I knew he had to pee. So I jumped up and lifted up his back end for him. Chris woke up and jumped up to join me. Together, we escorted him outside to the front yard, moving him forward towards the door in sync with one another, demonstrating a loving type of teamwork. Managing a 75-pound dog in the gentlest and most delicate nature isn't the easiest of tasks. Once outside, we repeated the same basic routine as last time. Get Mason stable enough on his feet. Wait with bated breath hooping that he can pee without collapsing and praise the hell out of him when he's done. Then just sit in peace and watch this angel boy take in his last starry sky with full Presence and appreciation for life. My heart was filled with gratitude, bliss, and excruciating pain. After he enjoyed his last moments of a cool California nighttime, we helped him back inside, where he slept the rest of the night until morning.

Thursday

Waking up on Thursday morning was daunting. It was hours before his scheduled demise, and this was the last day I'd ever be with my baby boy. Mason was much weaker this morning. Unable to stand and too weak to walk at all, we picked our special boy up and used towels to assist in walking him outside to go potty. He wasn't able to move his legs much to help. Once outside, there were a few moments that he was able to stand on his own, so we removed the towels. He attempted to squat to pee, and his back legs collapsed. We stood him up again so he could try to pee again. I wanted his bladder to be as empty as possible. Mason has always been such a good boy. He'd never pee or have an accident in the house. He'd hold it to the point of suffering in order not to have an accident in the house. That's just how he was. So I was worried that a full bladder would only add to his discomfort. Of course, if he had an accident on his bed, Chris and I wouldn't have cared in the least. He could've had twenty accidents those last days, and we never would've been the slightest bit upset with him. How could anyone be so selfish as to be upset with a dying dog having an accident? Mason was able to relieve himself outside, but this time was different. He wasn't able to sniff the air, squinting his eyes while connecting energetically to everything around him. He was so weak that he was just bracing himself to try to prevent collapse again. We quickly put a towel under his belly, and Chris and I walked him back inside to lay him down on his bed. Surprisingly, he perked up for a food offering, and he ate a little more ribeye, so we were able to sneak a pain pill inside of the meat for him. Anything to make him more comfortable. I asked Chris to remain by his side so I could take a quick shower. I didn't want him to be alone even for a minute. That morning, we put on his favorite Pandora station that played only piano music. This used to soothe Mason and allow him to lie down and rest when I wasn't in the room with him, versus him stressing out and heading off to go look for me. So the piano music played, and after my shower, I velcroed myself next to him. The way he had velcroed himself to me for the last fourteen years. Stroking his ears. Petting his back and belly. And I talked to him. I told him what a special boy he was. That I felt like the luckiest human in the whole world because he chose me to be his companion. That he taught me what selfless acts of service meant at a Divine level. That no matter how much care he needed from me throughout every day, that he was never, ever a burden. That it was my honor to serve him and take care of him in every way that he needed me to. I also told him that I realized that I was God's favorite human. I realized this because She wouldn't offer a being that was so special, so magical, the most incredible Divine spiritual teacher to just anyone. No. She would only offer that to her favorite human. That's how special Mason was. And I was lucky enough to be picked. I thanked Mason for picking me. Over and over and over again, I offered my profound gratitude for him picking me to share his life with. And the talking to him, the massages, the ear rubs, never stopped.

Mason was extremely lethargic at this point and could barely move. His physical body was shutting down. But he was hanging on. He was fighting falling asleep. He just kept fighting. He was hanging on for me. He couldn't understand why I wasn't going with him and why he had to go on without me. For the last year or so of his life, Mason did nothing without me right next to him telling him it was okay. His fragile physical body was letting him down. But emotionally, he knew he could count on me to keep him safe and reassure him that he'd be okay. He would get up from one dog bed and head to another dog bed and just stand there looking at it. He patiently waited until I got up, walked over, waved my arm at the bed like I was a model on a gameshow presenting the prize that he could win. And I would tell him, "It's okay. Go on." And he would lie down. When he'd get stuck in the hallway and was too scared to walk over part of the floor that his old eyes played tricks on him, he would stand there and remain frozen. Until, of course, I went to him and encouraged him to go. But I always walked with him. Touching him physically and telling him, "It's okay. Go on," so he knew I was right there, and he didn't have to face his fears alone. I used to rub his ears, look into his eyes, and gently speak to him to tell him, "Mason, you have the power, my love. You can do it without Mommy. You just have to choose to face your fears and do it without me." I realized as I watched his dying body, unable to move on that dog bed, that all of those months of those experiences were the Universe preparing us for this moment. So I talked to him and told him repeatedly that I couldn't go with him this time. That he was okay, and he could go. "It's okay, my special baby boy. It's okay to go on. You're not alone. Your angels are here, and it's okay to go with them. Mommy is right here by your side. I'm right here, my baby. I'm with you. I just can't go into the Light with you right now. You have the power within yourself to go on without Momma."

It was gut-wrenching to see him holding on. Chris cried and hugged him and loved him while making a promise to him. "Mason, I promise to take care of Mommy. You did such a good job taking care of her for all of these years. It's my turn now, and I promise I won't let you down. I'm going to make you proud of me. And I'm going to live up to all of the things you tried to teach me. If I become the man that you were trying to teach me to become, I hope I will earn my right to see you again one day." This went on for hours. It felt like years. Mason couldn't move any part of his body at this point except for his eyes. But every second was spent in connection with him. Physically, mentally, emotionally, and spiritually. And then, almost on the dot, at 3:00 PM PST, the vet arrived for his scheduled euthanasia appointment.

I had already described the steps to the procedure to Chris so he knew what to expect. The doctor didn't need to prepare us very much. We didn't want to drag anything on because we wanted to free Mason from the pain that he was in. I took his big, beautiful head in my left arm and rested my forehead on his. Chris was right next to me. The doctor administered the first injection to help Mason to fall asleep. She left the room to give us privacy while waiting for the medicine to take effect. I kissed his nose, his forehead, his face probably a hundred times. . . maybe even a thousand. . . in those ten minutes. We continued to talk to him and reassure him. We made sure he knew he wasn't alone. Then the doctor came back in to administer the second injection. And within several minutes, we felt him slip away.

As his soul left his body, his body suddenly felt empty. . . hollow. He was gone. The Life Force was no longer inside of this vessel, and you could tell. The doctor stepped out to give us privacy to grieve. Chris sat behind me, hugging me, while I never let go of Mason. And I wailed. The pain poured out of me through my voice, the shaking of my body, my Niagara Falls of tears. The pain was so extreme, it felt as if it was going to swallow me whole, and I was going to disappear into nothingness. As I wailed, I could feel Chris shaking in his embrace of me. Hearing him cry loudly along with me was cathartic. Through his crying, he managed to force out, "Let it out, baby. Let it all out." We wept with our entire bodies, our whole hearts, the beingness of our souls for our beloved Mason boy. Chris and I were connected with one another, but also with Mason's soul. This connection of Oneness is what nurtured our pain and also what was simultaneously healing it as it was arising from within us. After several minutes of intense crying and emotional release, I began to feel calm. It was time to say goodbye to his physical body and shift into nurturing and loving our grief from the reality that he was really gone.

As the doctor and her assistant gently placed Mason's body on the gurney, covered him up, and carried him outside to load him into the truck, I noticed the feeling of emptiness in our living room. We followed them out. They gave us the space to say goodbye one last time. I must've kissed his nose and face fifteen or more times before

I had the courage to step away from him. Chris and I graciously thanked the two wonderful women who selflessly helped Mason with his transition and for the gentle care they were taking in the handling of his body. Then we turned around to head back inside to begin the painful process of learning how to live life without him.

CHAPTER 24

Grief

GRIEF

After nearly three weeks since Mason's passing, the grief is still potently raw. I still get hit with waves of sadness, and I just sit in the pain while it's there, openly crying, and nurture the tears as they fall. During the last year of Mason's life, he needed more and more from me. More reassurance. More time spent right by his side. Any time I wasn't in the same room as him or if he couldn't see me, he got very stressed out. The anxiety would ignite; he would pant, start drooling, and then get up and bravely walk across the floors that he became so afraid to walk on to look for me. Some of the time, it was just impossible to get Mason up and do all that it would take to get him from the kitchen or living room back to the bedroom where I would shower in the master bathroom. I just didn't have enough time to do all of that every single time I left the room. But through trial and error, Chris and I figured out that after the whole morning routine—take the dogs for a walk and then feed them breakfast—we could bring Mason's dog bed into the kitchen, get him settled and comfortable, and then tell our virtual assistant device to "play piano music." Piano music would play, and within a couple of minutes, Mason just relaxed like he'd been dosed with morphine. The piano music soothed him so dramatically, I could walk in and out of the room, even leave and go take a shower, and he was perfectly fine resting in the room alone. Sometimes he would fall asleep, sometimes he wouldn't, but he was relaxed and calm. We ended up playing piano music for him every time we left the house and basically every time I left the room he was in for more than a minute or two.

I woke up one morning and felt wonderful. My spirits were high. I felt light and joyful. I was sipping my morning coffee, with one of our cats cuddling on my lap, when Chris suddenly loudly said, "Hey, Google, play piano music." The piano music came on, and it hit my nervous system like a bolt of lightning. I hadn't heard that music playing since we played it all day long for Mason on the day of his transition. The grief gripped my body and held on so tightly I almost lost my breath. But that's the funny thing about grief. It comes. It goes. It gets activated by an obvious trigger. It gets triggered by seemingly nothing. But what's critical to understand is that there is always a reason for it. Always. And the response that should be offered to grief is love . . . gentleness . . . nurturing. Nothing but Sacred Feminine energy is appropriate during these times. Sacred Feminine energy is what heals . . . transforms. So I sat there, heart wide open, loving and nurturing the sad tears dripping down my cheeks, embracing the almost crippling pain in my heart, while my cat, Lilly, purred on my lap. It's critical during these times to never wish your pain to go away. That's not loving the pain. It's shaming the pain. It's also important that you don't resort to seeking out another to remove your pain for you. When you're experiencing emotional pain and you desperately want someone to be there for you for emotional support, really what you're asking for is for someone to take your pain away. We have learned to exist in complete powerlessness. Like the pain is going to swallow you up and kill you. Except that it's not. It just hurts. What makes humans so weak that we can't handle some emotional pain? Inside of the pain is *you*. . . your consciousness observing the experience that hurts. And that consciousness is powerful beyond what the little human mind can fathom. All that's required is for you, the consciousness that is the real you, to take over and saturate that pain with the power of its Unconditional Love, its golden, white Light, the Light of Source, the Light that is the divine aspect of you. No one and nothing outside of you can offer the same level of power towards your pain than you can. That power is located inside of you. And it's waiting for you to tap into its source so that it can flow. You are not powerful when all you ever want to feel is joy. This is a childish immaturity that isn't grown enough or strong enough yet to handle the many aspects of life. Emotional maturity requires you to gain the ability to dive into the core of your pain when it gets triggered and to wholeheartedly embrace it with the nurturing power of your love. This ensures that the pain processes and that it becomes nothing more than a temporary experience. People without the ability to tap into their true source of power move through painful or traumatic experiences and then never get over those experiences, develop conditions like PTSD, anxiety, or harbor anger, resentment, or blame . . . sometimes for the rest of their lives. The other side of this coin is for those that have traditionally taught from their ignorant perspective that we should never feel pain or should just "suck it up" and muscle through it. Denying your true emotions cements them in and creates energetic disturbances that will not only get triggered throughout the rest of your life (the universe's way to show you what you hold inside), but it eventually causes diseases, illnesses, and/or injuries (another way the universe is showing you what you're holding onto).

Emotional pain is your access point to your true divine power. It's when you're at your most vulnerable that you'll find out to what degree you're living in weakness or you're living as a powerful divine being. Denying, ignoring, suppressing, or coping with pain is pure weakness. Diving all the way into the depths of your pain, and transforming it with the nurturing essence of your Unconditional Love is pure power. This is what pure, raw, Sacred Feminine energy is. The ability to be in the presence of another while they are in pain and while you sit in the energy of your love, not trying to fix it, change it, enable them . . .and *never* trying to take their pain away for them is also pure power. This is the power of divinity showing itself through human form.

* * *

On the evening of August 29, 2021, I went to sleep and almost immediately started to dream. It wasn't a dream so much as a song that flowed through my mind in my sleep over and over again all night long. When I woke up in the middle of the night to go to the bathroom, the song was *loud*, echoing through my brain. When I woke up the next morning, this song kept playing repeatedly through my mind. When I would get distracted and take my mind off of the song, by brushing my teeth or eating breakfast, for example, the song got louder, so I couldn't ignore it. The song was "I'll Remember" by Madonna. There were two verses of the song that kept replaying the most consistently in my head.

"And I'll remember
The strength that you gave me
Now that I'm standing on my own
I'll remember
The way that you saved me"

"And I'll remember
The love that you gave me
Now that I'm standing on my own
I'll remember
The way that you changed me . . ."

I could remember that this song was a theme song to a popular movie from a very long time ago. I knew that this song was about a main character in the movie who died. But I couldn't remember for the life of me what the movie was. When I looked it up, I discovered that the movie was *With Honors*. This movie starred Joe Pesci, Brendan Fraser, Moira Kelly, Patrick Dempsey, and Josh Hamilton. I also saw the release date of the movie: April 29, 1994. April 29th. I knew in that second that Mason was sending me the message. April 29th was the day that Mason died. So when I saw the release date of that movie, I knew it was him. Of course, I started to cry. What was strange was that his energy was different. It's why I didn't recognize what spirit was trying to communicate with me from the other side at first. I missed him so much, and to be receiving a strong, continuous message that he wouldn't let me ignore, I knew that the message must be important for me to hear and understand. And he started sending me the message on the four-month anniversary of his passing. So I sat down and meditated on the message... on the words of the song, which made me cry harder. And at first, I felt a deep ache in my heart because I missed him so much. Then came a tremendous wave of love and gratitude for Mason and for all of his love, and for my life being so touched by the gift that was him. I spent time remembering him. And one line of the song that I could hear Madonna singing repeatedly to me was "And I'll remember happiness." At first, I just thought that the message to me was to remember all of the things that Mason taught me. To remember what the Ways of Oneness are and to do my best to live in those Ways and to master them before my time to die comes. I also thought that I was being reminded to write more, so I could finish this manuscript and get these teachings out to the world. Feeling raw, with eyes swollen and red from a lot of crying, I cut my meditation short and continued through my morning routine so I could get ready for my coaching clients scheduled for that day.

While I was taking my shower, I had a deeper realization. Mason had received and completed his Life Review. This is why his energy felt different to me, and I didn't recognize him at first. His soul contacted me to communicate what he had learned from this lifetime and from me. Typically, after a being (any living form) on Earth dies, the soul goes into a realm that can be understood as a "resting place." It's a resting place for the soul to recover from the transition from physical body back to formless being. It's also a realm where that soul can easily visit and communicate with its loved ones that it left behind. This is also the place where, when the soul is ready, it completes its Life Review. When the physical version of you dies, and the soul moves through its Life Review, a new, expanded soul-self evolves as it gains the Wisdom of its Earth life after such deep reflection. A Life Review is when your soul revisits your life on Earth with crystal-clear, pure divine sight. You see your entire life through the lenses of the Way of Wisdom, Truth, and Purity . . . no filters. You revisit every single encounter with other people, situations, and experiences, and you can now see the role that other souls played for you, on your behalf, and why they "did what they did." There is no bias. No negativity. No ego. Only the epiphanies birthed from divine Wisdom. This is the gift that divine sight brings. You can now see the deeper meaning of everything. You now understand what lessons you were meant to learn, and how well you did or did not learn them. You remember what goals your soul had for you to achieve in this particular lifetime, and you see how close you came to achieving them. You See everything. All of the egoic veils you had as a human are completely removed, and you see now how unloving you really were in any and all situations that you were unloving. You see the "good." You see the "bad." You see the Truth that every experience you had is filled with gifts hidden inside of the pain you experienced. You see all. And you see it all with the clarity of divinity.

I ended my shower so I could focus on the messages that were coming through. It wasn't just the song that was communicating to me at this point. Mason was communicating with me directly. And I noticed something immediately after he began his communication. He was different. His soul was significantly more evolved. He no longer had a canine energy to him, and he didn't communicate in pictures the way most animals communicate with me. He was speaking to me directly as his soul self. And he had a lot to share with me. He was telling me that he sees all of the lessons and the gifts from his life on Earth and from his relationship with me. He could clearly see the gifts that we were here to offer one another by being in each other's lives. He saw how we both grew and benefited from our relationship. He was expressing the precious realizations that he had and how his relationship with me, through the love and bond that we shared together, had changed his soul. And after this experience of his Life Review, he came to me to tell me "thank you." He spent that entire morning with me, communicating with me. . . guiding my keystrokes to write all of this down.

Mason used the lyrics to the song that he had been sending to me throughout the night and into the morning to speak to me. What he explained to me, verse by verse, was essentially this:

Say Goodbye
Not knowing when
The truth in my whole life began

This refers to "saying goodbye" to the life you know as a formless being of consciousness as you are incarnated into tangible form on Earth. We are born forgetting the truth of how and when our lives actually began. They don't begin when birthed as infants. We are infinite but choose to forget that each time we incarnate on Earth. So Mason of course was incarnated into the form of a puppy when he came to Earth and then came into my life when I adopted him at two months old.

Say goodbye
Not knowing how to cry
You taught me that

As a hypersensitive empath, I was always told growing up that I was way too sensitive. I felt emotions so intensely and so deeply, not to mention I would cry at the drop of a hat. I was so different from anyone else I knew growing up that I hated my sensitivities. I felt very isolated and alone and completely misunderstood. I hated even more that I cried so easily. With Mason, I cried openly. When I was sad, I could just cry and feel my intense emotions without judgment or shame. And Mason always licked my tears and then would lay next to me for as long as I was processing emotions. His Presence taught me that it was okay to cry. That feeling so deeply and compassionately was a gift of Unconditional Love. I eventually learned from him not to be ashamed of my sensitivities or of my crying. He taught me how to cry the way that I simply must do at times as an empath. And he taught me not to hide it or be embarrassed about it. When I said goodbye to Mason in the moments that he passed away, I wailed with pain so loudly I can't believe the neighbors didn't come knocking on the door. And I wailed like that with Chris right next to me and with two strangers who were there to euthanize Mason and take his earthly body away. I had three witnesses, two of them complete strangers, listening to my intense grief vocalize itself. And I didn't for one second suppress any aspect of my grief. I didn't shame, minimize, or feel embarrassed by my intense emotions. I simply allowed them to be there, fully expressing them as they needed to be expressed in order to process such a deep level of pain. Being able to show up with that level of power from Unconditional Love for my own pain was one of the things I learned from my beloved Mason boy.

Now I'll never be afraid to cry
Now I finally have a reason why

I'm not afraid to cry anymore in front of people or in any situation that triggers my sensitive tears. Whether it's a movie, a commercial, a client of mine that just had a big breakthrough, happy tears, or sad tears. And I certainly broke the habit of apologizing for my tears when my attempts at suppressing my crying failed in front of others. Thank you, Mason, for helping me to heal my fear of crying in the presence of others. I'll never be afraid to cry again because of you.

And I'll remember
The strength that you gave me
Now that I'm standing on my own

At the end of Mason's life, he held on for a long time because he didn't want to leave me. And in the hours before his passing, he *really* held on and just wouldn't let go. He just couldn't understand why I wasn't going with him and didn't want to make his transition on his own without me going with him, side by side as he had always lived his life with me. As I described in previous chapters, I always encouraged Mason to be able to "stand on his own." He stuck to me like glue. But I always worked on his confidence level . . . his strength to be okay whether I was by his side or not. His resistance to pass on without me in those last moments made me feel anguish like I've never felt before. It took everything in my power to remain in my heart space and continue to encourage him to be strong and go on without me. Mason was now telling me that all of those times throughout his life, including at the end, taught him to be strong and confident within himself. That now, after his Life Review, his soul expanded. That he's "stronger" now because I always encouraged him in a loving, nurturing way not to depend on me for his source of strength or power. And now that he's no longer with me, and now that he's "standing on his own," he's okay. He wanted me to know that he's 100 percent okay and that I don't need to worry about him being without me. Anytime I left Mason with dog sitters when I would travel, I would worry so much about him. I worried because I knew that he was never okay being away from me. It was always extremely stressful for him to be away from me. His stress usually manifested in the form of an upset stomach and intestinal issues like diarrhea. But the second I came back, they would instantly clear up. He was never really okay when I was away from him. And that's why he held on so tightly when he was dying. He was holding on to me. But now, his soul expanded from that experience, from the experience of me lovingly encouraging him to make the transition without me. He understands now that those experiences allowed his soul to become stronger and more confident. That having someone who was always there for him and loved him enough to encourage the growth of his confidence and internal power allowed his soul to become more powerful.

I'll remember the way that you saved me
I'll remember

Mason feels "saved" by me because he was a highly sensitive being, and I cherished and honored his sensitivities. When we are too harsh on highly sensitive people or animals, we can cause a tremendous amount of damage and even deep trauma to them and to their souls. It's more often traumatizing to them than not. Healing from this damage can take lifetimes. A highly sensitive dog in the wrong owner's hands can be detrimental in ways that the average person can't yet comprehend. He feels saved by me because I offered him the Way of Harmlessness and Gentleness, and I knew intuitively just how delicate to be with him without stunting his soul's ability to grow.

I, too, was saved. I was definitely saved by Mason because I am a highly sensitive person and an extremely sensitive empath. His powerful healing abilities reset and calmed my nervous system, bringing it back to balance for me literally twenty-four hours a day, seven days a week. In the years where I hadn't yet mastered how to nurture and balance myself from the negative impact of being so sensitive while living in a very harsh world, Mason saved my life over and over again. Being completely misunderstood by others, I was never misunderstood by Mason. He just loved me unconditionally the only way a divine soul knows how to. He saved me from the terrible isolation that I felt from being drastically different from others with my psychic gifts, sensitivities, and my level of consciousness. I always felt that Mason was sent from the heavens as my guardian angel and savior to love and support me until I was powerful enough in my own healing to move through this world unapologetically of my gifts, my wisdom, and my sacred feminine power. Once I reached that level, Mason's mission on this planet was over. Once his mission of "saving me" was over, it was time for him to leave Earth.

Inside I was a child
That could not mend a broken wing
Outside I looked for a way
To teach my heart to sing

When Mason came into my life, I was drowning in inner child wounds. I was diving deeper and desperately trying to master what I teach people today. I was still looking mostly outside of myself to heal myself, overlooking my own internal divine power. I wanted to heal my heart but struggled with not quite knowing how to. During my years of combining and integrating advanced education with spiritual and mystical tools, Mason was by my side offering his healing powers and unconditional love to me at all times. I had no idea how to heal myself at the deepest core levels, but I was determined to figure it out and achieve it. Mason came into my life as I was going much deeper into figuring all of this out. I was able to achieve all that I have achieved and now teach and guide others to do this for themselves as well because of his love and support along the way. He truly was my guardian angel incarnated into physical form. He was my soul companion dog. His mission was to love and support me while I healed myself and mastered what I was meant to evolve into before offering these elevated Ways of enlightenment to the world.

And I'll remember
The love that you gave me
Now that I'm standing on my own
I'll remember
The way that you changed me
I'll remember

Mason kept telling me that he "changed," meaning his soul was able to learn what it was meant to learn and expand with growth because of the love and nurturing that I offered to him throughout his life on Earth. I certainly know that I am forever changed, as a human being, and at the soul level because of the Love, the Harmlessness and Gentleness, Presence, Purity, and *all* of the aspects of Oneness that Mason blessed me with. Mason was trying to make me understand that as his soul goes on . . . as he moves forward and chooses another life or experience to incarnate to, that he'll remember me and the way that I "changed him." That his soul will always remember me and be grateful for our incarnated life together.

I learned
To let go
Of the illusion
That we can possess
I learned to let go

In my spiritual awakening I have learned to let go of the illusions of the ego, of the mind and of all of the mental programs and woundedness programs that we run and project onto others. Mason's love and his teaching me of the Ways of Oneness supported my ability to truly awaken and in the ability to teach this to others in the way that I do. Mason's illusion at the end of his life was that he couldn't let go of me. That he was incapable of moving on or doing anything without me by my side encouraging him, loving him, and cheering him on. I learned to let go of my ego. Mason learned to let go of his attachment to me and to turn inwards for his source of strength.

I travel in stillness
And I'll remember happiness

For Mason, "I travel in stillness" means his soul will move on and continue to choose what planets to visit and incarnate on for his soul's evolution, and he will do so with peace from this lifetime. He feels complete in his lessons that he learned with his life as Mason. He feels peacefulness and Presence from this lifetime and from the loving relationship he had with me. There is no negative karma or anything that needs to be "cleaned up" in a future life together. He only remembers the happiness of sharing a life with me. And he reassures me that he'll remember our happiness, our happy moments and all of those fun, happy times that were filled with innocence and Purity. That those are energetically imprinted on his soul, so he'll take those moments with him for eternity.

For me, I have learned to live my life in peaceful Presence with the ability to Surrender to "what is." Mason helped me to learn how to stop resisting life. He deepened this lesson for me as I held him in my arms while he died. Although I was in emotional agony, I was also in the stillness that only a peaceful heart can bring. And as far as happiness goes, I could never forget the happiness that Mason and I shared and created together. He simply was joy. His entire personality and everything about him made me happy. In the past I have spent so many holidays alone. No one to celebrate with. But I was never alone. I always had my dogs. I always had my Mason. I used to struggle with a profound sense of loneliness. Because of him, I was never truly alone. Remembering him and the fourteen-plus years that I got to share with him will always make me happy, even if it is now bittersweet. Even as I cry my sad tears because of how much I miss him, those tears are always also filled with a profound sense of gratitude and happiness.

Before Mason's soul ended his communication with me, he wanted me to know that he was grateful for the life that I gave him. That when I'm hard on myself or when I feel guilty for the times that I was impatient with him, or when I went through a period of financial struggle and couldn't give him the vet care that he needed, that I should find within myself the Way of Forgiveness. I needed to embrace the fact that there is nothing that needs to be forgiven. That *he* has nothing to forgive me for. Those moments that we shared together were for both of our souls' growth and that I should realize that I had never failed him. I cried intensely that morning, my voice loudly forcing its way out of my throat, flowing in sync with the flood of tears that poured like waterfalls down my puffy face. It had been exactly four months since I had cried that hard. They were tears of pain from missing him and no longer having him by my side. They were tears of gratitude for the part of my life that I got to share with him. They were tears of the love that I have for him. And they were tears for the love that I have come to have for myself because of him.

CHAPTER 25

Living in Oneness

LIVING IN ONENESS

Every Way described in this text is a different aspect of the totality of Oneness or enlightened consciousness. You are not yet living in the Way of Oneness if you can demonstrate extreme Patience, but fail to see and honor an animal's life as equal to yours, for this lacks the Ways of Equality and Honoring. If you believe that your child who is in the hospital with cancer has the right for you to be by her side at all times, but that it's okay that your cat or dog isn't treated with the same level of Compassion and Connection, you are a far cry from reaching the level of divinity that Oneness represents. The majority of people's almost immediate question to me when they found out about Mason's passing was, "Are you going to get another dog?" That's like saying, "Oh I'm sorry to hear about your child dying. Are you going to have another kid?" That question reflects the level of consciousness that embodies objectification. Animals, even "loved" pets, are not seen as equal to us. Their lives don't matter as much as ours. Our pets are seen as objects. As replaceable. As property. As "things" that you discard if they get too expensive or burdensome. Or when you selfishly got them and then chose to get rid of them because they were too much work or didn't behave in the exact way you wanted them to. Lives that you don't value are the lives that you easily and dismissively throw away or that you turn a blind eye to when they are tortured or harmed. When we don't yet value life equally. . . *all life* . . .we are living as spiritual infants who live in the psychotic delusion that we humans are somehow advanced, superior beings, especially compared to other species. It is an extraordinarily low level of consciousness to believe that you are superior to others. These belief systems cause many to behave as spoiled rotten children who actually think that the universe revolves around them and even that the universe owes you something. To believe that your life is more valuable than another's reflects arrogance. Entitlement. Selfishness. Extreme ignorance. An inflated view of your importance and specialness. The very traits that breed misogyny, racism, and are at the root of the destruction of our precious Planet Earth. This is the true definition of mental illness. And this type of mental illness, the beliefs, programs, actions, and systems in place that reflect separation, plague humanity in the same way that decay plagues a dead carcass left to exposure. The rot sets in and does more and more damage until there's nothing left. The planet, humanity as a whole, animals, wildlife, and nature are nearing this brink of extinction. The rot has been doing so much damage for so long, we're almost at a point in our evolutionary history where extinction of all life is inevitable. Of course, the arrogant who believe in the toxic patriarchal way of domination and conquering are never going to see it that way. But just because their vanity blinds them to the Way of Truth doesn't mean the rest of us shouldn't rise up and course correct. Living The Ways is a path to not only heal yourself, but to heal the entire planet and every being that shares Earth as their home.

Living in Oneness organically arises as you begin to master all of the Ways. It empowers you while increasing your emotional resilience to pain. In case you didn't catch on by now, the emotion of grief is one of the most powerful potentials of expansive transformation, and it's one of the most common emotions to try to suppress or avoid feeling. When you're close to mastering the Way of Surrender in your daily life, you'll have the ability to fully surrender to the pain that grief is instead of avoiding, coping, suppressing, ignoring, going into denial, or medicating with what you're addicted to. All of those paths prevent healing and keep you at a low level of consciousness, as well as disempower you. Those methods actually keep you in a holding pattern of powerlessness. Mason, as my mystical, master teacher, taught me how to fully Surrender. Never once did I run mental programs of resistance during his last days with me. Never once did I blame, project, or think that this shouldn't be happening or that it wasn't fair. I was in full Presence with all of it, and I fully surrendered to the excruciation of grief. That's power. Surrendering and being Present with your grief is a powerful act of self-love. It allowed me to live in the Way of Truth of how I was feeling at any given moment, as well as accept the Truth that Mason was dying. It allowed me to practice the Way of Selfless Service and the Way of Compassion for Mason no matter what he needed from me or how much he needed. Only being in the Way of Surrender gives you the capability to show up like that. The Way of Purity allowed me to nurture my own grief while doing anything and everything that Mason needed me to do for him, while never making the around-the-clock care for him about its impact on me. If I made how much time, effort, and energy that Mason needed from me *about me*, I would've been coming from a selfish place, not a selfless one. And that's not pure. Tainting an experience with selfishness lacks Purity. The Way of Loyalty meant that I was devoted to him. That his quality of life reigned supreme over my wanting him to keep living. And the Way of Wisdom allowed me to know precisely when it was time to make the call to the at-home euthanasia service and to schedule them to come to the house for Mason's transition. The Way of Trust allowed me to have faith in Wisdom's guidance telling me that it was Mason's time. And the Way of Connection allowed me to hear that message directly from Mason himself, as well as to hear from him his unwillingness to fully let go by himself. That allowed me to provide him with the comfort, emotional support, reassurance, psychic communication, and physical connection of not leaving his side for the last twenty-four hours I had with him. Doing all of this for him was an act of Selfless Service. The Way of Compassion for his body's physical state was present, which aided in the choice to euthanize. And Compassion for his mental and emotional state was at the forefront. I wanted to alleviate his suffering. And he was suffering. His greatest suffering came when he couldn't stand on his own and follow me. That he was physically incapable to be by my side when I left the room to shower or go to the bathroom. He suffered greatly at the end every moment that I wasn't right next to him comforting and soothing his fears and anxiety. Everything I did for him and every Way that I showed up for him reflected the Way of Purity, as well as all of the Ways.

It's important for you to see that becoming the Ways doesn't free you from pain or from challenging experiences. Only spiritually immature and ignorant persons preach that when you spiritually awaken, you'll be filled with bliss all of the time, and life will be easy. What nonsense. It's not even possible to function as a human when in the state of Bliss. Watching Mason die and saying goodbye to him for the final time was absolutely agonizing. Being human means you are going to feel emotional pain. You're meant to. How you handle that pain is the reflection of your level of maturity and spiritual progress. Choosing to run from it, curse it, numb it, judge it, or resist it is a reflection of weakness, of a low emotional IQ and spiritual immaturity. To embrace your pain with the nurturing power of your inner Light. . .to feel its fullness and intensity, and to remain deeply inside of the pain for as long as it needs to be there, is a person who is evolving into a new kind of human. On a micro level, this is a person who is moving away from ignorance, immaturity, and force to one who reflects power, wisdom, enlightenment, and divine, sacred love. The more you learn and integrate the Ways, the more powerful you become. The freer you feel. The lighter you are. Life flows more fluidly for you with synchronicities guiding the direction for you to go in. When challenges come, you embrace them with love and move through them with grace. You offer gratitude for challenges for you have the Wisdom that those challenges are inviting you to evolve even more. Living a harmonious and peaceful life becomes a very real experience.

On the macro level, you have an effect on the communities around you as well as the country that you live in. Being more peaceful and filled with divine power, you now have the genuine power to change the world. You will be guided in divine ways to dismantle systems that reflect and promote separation, inequality, and greed. You will never settle for a person in a position of power who lacks the Way of Integrity. Never again will there be a leader of a country who is a rapist, misogynist, or racist. Political parties will fade away and mean nothing. Integrity, equality, truthfulness, transparency, and all of the Ways of Oneness will mean everything. These will be the Laws that govern countries, corporations, communities, and households. Unification will arise, among people, nations, animals, nature, oceans, the sky, and the Earth. We will no longer fight each other, but instead educate, support, and challenge each other to rise to higher levels of consciousness. Our school systems will reflect spiritual psychology, subtle energy sciences, the healing arts, mysticism, and Truth. Physicians will evolve and incorporate the science of energetics, psychoenergetic science, and vibrational medicine into their practices. Learning about subtle energy bodies and their impact on our physical bodies will be common knowledge at every grade level from elementary school to the most prestigious institutions of higher learning.

Living authentically in the Universal Law of Oneness means you've gained the Wisdom that what you see "out there" in the collective or on a global scale is nothing more than the reflection of what you carry inside of yourself and how you show up as an individual. Transforming yourself from the inside out to reflect the Ways of Oneness is what it really means to "be the change you wish to see in the world" as Mahatma Gandhi famously stated. And living in the Ways will dramatically alter the course of violence, inequality, and destruction in this world. There will be no more wars. There will no longer be men living on this Earth of any culture or background who would be capable of raping or murdering women or children. Men will step into the Ways of Humility, Integrity, Gentleness and Harmlessness, and Honoring. Ways that have been absent from the dysfunctional, domineering patriarchy for way too long now. Women will heal centuries of wounded feminine energy and step into their innate powers of leadership, Presence, Equality, Trust, and Wisdom. It won't be possible to brainwash people anymore or to control them with fear. People will evolve enough to realize that they've been nothing but brainwashed to believe that you automatically reproduce as you become adults. Having children will only occur for those Conscious enough to become educated in spiritual, emotional, mental, behavioral development of children. And for those who are willing to devote their life's purpose to the raising of a child. Parents will realize their role is as a spirit guide incarnated and will never interfere with what a soul (in the form of their child) is here on Earth to experience and become. Conscious parents would never get in the way of the lessons a young soul has chosen to experience. Further, in enlightened societies, only 20 to 30 percent of the human population would reproduce. And entire world populations would hold themselves responsible for raising all of the children on the planet. Supporting, guiding, teaching, and raising children is everyone's responsibility. Every child would receive enough focused attention, quality time, as well as global learning. Everyone will be integrated and working together. . .harmonizing each other. The notion of separation will cease to exist, and no longer will things like skin color, gender, or sexual orientation be a barrier to anyone. These things will also never again be used as a form of victimization so one can refute self-responsibility over their own lives.

The more that individuals like yourself learn and become all of the Ways of Oneness, the more you'll see drastic transformation on the macro level. The more we all take responsibility for self-evolution, the more we will activate a global level of Harmony with all. The New Golden Age of Harmony must be birthed by first experiencing the death of the old paradigm of separation. The old paradigm that strips women of their right to choose what happens to their own bodies, that gives more freedom and protection to rapists than the victims who were raped, that steal people's rights of body sovereignty to choose to vaccinate or not vaccinate themselves, the toxic paradigm that poisons and sells foods laced with chemicals and markets them as healthy so that people become chronically ill and then have to pay into healthcare systems that benefit from keeping people sick over getting people healthy, the paradigm that breeds and teaches hate, victim consciousness, and disempowerment, the old, third-dimensional paradigm that infuses domination, superiority, fear, and brainwashing into its cultures, religions, educational systems, and societal learning. This is the paradigm of unconsciousness. The collective shadow blueprint of separation. And it is dying. To live in Harmony requires death of one's shadow self and the rebirth of elevated consciousness that reflects the Ways of Oneness. To live in a global level of Harmony requires the death of the collective shadow of humanity and the rebirth of a new collective consciousness that promotes and embraces peace, cooperation, loving support, and Wisdom. This new goldprint of Oneness will reintroduce the Sacred Feminine onto the planet so that healing can occur, and Wisdom (over ignorance and greed) can once again be the guiding power that leads all governments, societies, institutions of learning, businesses, and corporations across the globe. The Honoring of all beings will become second nature. The codependency of tribes will dissolve, and global communities reflecting the power and divinity of Oneness will spread.

LIVING IN ONENESS

* * *

A world that lives in the Ways of Oneness is a reflection of enlightened societies. This means that all of the old paradigms that reflect anything less than The Ways, must be dismantled and rebuilt from the inside out and built upon the Ways of Oneness. Only healed, whole individuals that reflect the Ways of Oneness can achieve such massive change. What's required is a global death → rebirth process. Everything as we currently know it will be transformed. In an enlightened society, for example, our judicial system will be entirely different from the current experience. In an enlightened society that functions in the Ways of Oneness, we won't experience the level of violence and killing that we've seen in humans for centuries. But it doesn't mean people won't make mistakes or start to be led down the wrong path towards darkness and negativity. Adolescents and young adults who make poor choices or harmful choices that negatively impact others are often doing so because of the unhealthy way they were or are being raised. Wounds and shadow programs have already taken root and are impacting their choices and behaviors. The offenses or crimes they commit will be categorized into tiers to determine what transformational healing curriculum they should be entered into. This includes healing and elevating out of emotional wounds and traumas, negative mental and behavioral programs, and teaching one how to connect to their own inner, divine power. These lost souls will also be taught how to detect dysfunctional energetic patterns in their energetic bodies that then influence their behaviors and choices. This level of learning will be commonplace. As will this level of healing and elevating a person through the use of psychoenergetics, vibrational medicine, and the science of subtle energies.

All people will be handled in this way. No longer will it exist that lawyers defend guilty people who have committed crimes and caused harm in others. There is no defense for that. Instead, as the Truth is brought forth by all parties involved, the team will dive deeply into the mental, emotional, behavioral programs, and inner child wounds of the accused or obviously guilty person, and of all parties involved. This is what will be brought forth in a court of law during a "hearing." A deeper learning process to understand and uncover aspects of the person's shadow self will be unveiled. During the hearing of the shadow-self unveiling, the "sentence" will be appropriate forms of rehabilitation and healing modalities. In addition, there will not be a maximum sentence so to speak. There will be a minimum sentence. This is the minimum amount of time required to attend and participate in multiple energetic and spiritual therapies in an attempt for the person who caused harm to heal, evolve, and elevate themselves out of the level of consciousness that had the ability to cause the harm that they caused. This is also the case for those who falsely accuse others. Once this minimum sentence is completed, the person will have the opportunity to earn their way out of "mandatory healing" through the demonstration of more elevated levels of consciousness, self-awareness, and to what degree they are evolving energetically into a being that embodies the Ways of Oneness. If they haven't made much progress, they remain in mandatory sentencing with treatment. If they make wonderful progress, they'll be released to explore and pursue ongoing ways to further heal and elevate themselves on their own, or with ongoing varying levels of support.

Another addition to our court systems will be Mystics. Mystics have the ability to read subtle energies, and detect what programs and wounds people have and are running, as well as the elevated vibrational frequencies of the Ways of Oneness. You can't fake your progress with a Mystic. Because you can't fake energy. Energy is energy. And those that have this magical and mystical ability to read a person's subtle energies will see the Truth in how they are actually functioning versus how they attempt to portray themselves in order to be released from mandatory healing therapies. It must also be understood and reemphasized that by the time humanity has evolved enough to create systems, such as the one that is mentioned here, people won't be committing the extremely heinous crimes that we are used to seeing in our current times. As humans heal and evolve themselves, our judicial system will heal and evolve itself as well.

The therapy and rehabilitation systems will be completely evolved and renovated as well. Pointless therapies and modalities such as talk therapy or methods that only focus on surface-level programs like behavior modification will be a thing of the past. They don't work. Plain and simple. They don't heal the root core of why and how someone is showing up in a harmful way either to themselves or to others. No more wasting time or money on nonsense. An out-of-balance soul will be supported by highly evolved, highly conscious spiritual teachers, mystics, healers, therapists, and mystical life coaches who are trained to guide misguided souls out of their own darkness and into their Light. Their current level of consciousness will be evaluated, and an individualized plan of care will be created to heal both the human and soul aspects of the misguided person. They will be led through a process of healing, higher-soul integration, and self-actualization process. And finally, gone are the treatment programs that negate a person's holistic self. This means including the energetic bodies that are a part of every human and being on this planet. The energy bodies surrounding a human's (or animal's) physical body are where diseases and illnesses first get created and where the strongest influence of one's behaviors are located. And conventional practices ignore all of this. Which is why physically, mentally, or emotionally healing a person who is out of balance or in dysfunction has been less than impressive to date. So treatment plans for sick or ill people and animals will require methods to heal and integrate all aspects of a being's entire energetic system. Transformational healing methods that involve energetic alchemy methods will be used as well as holistic healing modalities to support a person's spiritual, mental, emotional, and physical bodies, their soul self, and every aspect of their energy fields throughout this rehabilitative process. Only when a person heals and balances their entire energetic beingness can they function in wholeness as a highly conscious being.

* * *

In the Golden Age of Harmony, school systems will be unrecognizable from what you see today. The Ways of Oneness will be at the heart of every school. Children and adults will be taught about their full energetic systems and how that imposes on and influences their physical bodies throughout their entire lives. Common-core curriculum will include teachings of their newly evolved, fifth-dimensional chakra system, and they will learn how to care for each and every energy center. Intuition, psychic abilities like psychokinesis, mysticism, energy healing, energetics, clairvoyance, claircognizance, and a multitude of variances of the mystical and psychic arts will be included in basic curriculums. This doesn't mean that teaching something like mathematics will suddenly become obsolete. That's absurd. The entire universe is based on an energetic and mathematical structure. It means that our global educational systems will be infused with the Way of Truth and all of the Ways of Oneness. So this includes the understanding that we are divine souls having a human experience in this planetary university called Earth. It means that we have powers and abilities far beyond what we've been traditionally taught and led to believe. And those powers and gifts will be nurtured and the Way of Responsibility cultivated in each child as she grows. It means that our educational systems will no longer be tainted with sexism and racism, nor will textbooks be filled with lies. Each student will be taught and guided on how to tap into the Wisdom of the Universe and will learn the difference between energies of the Light over energies of darkness. This is the only way to truly live in Harmony. You must be capable of living in Harmony with yourself before you can truly live in Harmony with a spouse or partner, with family members, with colleagues, neighbors, friends, or communities. Harmony can only be lived when it is infused into everything we do as individual human beings. In all of our school systems. From preschool to colleges and higher institutions. This includes medical schools and business schools. The ways of diagnosing and treating a human body will never again be limited to just a physical vessel. And outdated Newtonian science will diminish so Einsteinian energetic science can reign. Energetic systems including the biomagnetic field that surrounds the physical body—which include but are not limited to the astral body, the mental body, the emotional body, and the etheric body—will be understood and taught how those create physical ailments and diseases. Treatments will be holistic. Meaning they take all of the biomagnetic energy bodies surrounding the physical body into consideration during assessment, diagnosing, and treatment plans. There will no longer only be physicians and surgeons of the mere physical vessels that based diagnosis and treatment from Newtonian science. There will be a doctor of energetics, medical intuitives, mystical healers, spiritual psychologists, psychoenergetic practitioners, and highly trained medical psychics as a part of medical teams. Humans are multidimensional, energetic beings. It's time we lived in the Truth of what we are so we can live our lives with the proper tools, modalities, and healing methods to allow us to live a full and invigorating life that honors the totality of what we are.

Businesses will no longer be run by greed and the incessant hunger for wealth or with the addiction to individual success. Business schools will teach from an ethical level of consciousness with the main focus on the quality of products and services, of healing people, the Earth, and bridging the gaps of separation with the particular products or services that that business has to offer. All products and services will be focused on healing and wholeness, not on sickness and dysfunction. Which means no more *profiting* off of other people's sickness and dysfunction. It means setting up systems that promote people's healing and then the knowledge, skills, and assistance to maintain high levels of health and wellbeing. This includes at the end-stage of someone's life. Being in Harmony with the universe is realizing and embracing when it's time for a person to leave the Earth plane. Understand that a soul always chooses her or his departure, no matter how they leave the planet or at what Earthly age. The experience of saying goodbye to our loved ones is filled with lessons and opportunities for soul growth. Death of the physical body and our relationships with those that die are part of what Earth University has to teach us. It reminds us to live in the Ways of Oneness so we have no regrets, no negative karmic debts, and so we don't take the short time that we have on Earth and with others for granted. We learn to cherish every moment. There is no better reminder of that than someone you love dying and no longer having the opportunity to share your life with them for a moment longer. Did you make the most of your time together? Or did you spend way too much time fighting, hurting one another, and harboring resentments? During your time together, did you show up for this dying being as the most magnificent version of yourself, or did you fall short and cause this being or person emotional, mental, or even physical harm? The pain of losing someone allows you to conduct your own Life Review while still alive on Earth. Self-assess. Take inventory. Be radically and transparently honest. Never shame yourself. But do your own Life Review of how you showed up, what harm you may have caused, what loving things you did or failed to do. This allows you to course correct and focus on healing yourself and expanding out of the ways that you still fall short of showing up as a reflection of each of the Ways of Oneness. Which Ways are you still disharmonized with? That's where your focus should be.

LIVING IN ONENESS

* * *

Living in the Ways of Oneness means putting an end to corruption in all of its forms. No more buying votes or paying people off. No more scandals. No more cover-ups. No more fraud. No more fake bank accounts. No more deceitfulness in the way banks are run. No more keeping silent. True Harmony on Earth and with humanity requires learning, living, and teaching all of the Ways of Oneness and incorporating those Ways into every institution, every business, every interaction with another person, animal, or aspect of nature. This is a reflection of being in Harmony. And being in Harmony means offering the Ways of Oneness to yourself, so you can then, with ease, offer them to the rest of the world. Mastering all of the Ways allows you to be in Harmony with everything, and it also allows you to harmonize the energies around you as you move through this world. This is how the New Golden Age of Harmony gets created. It all starts with you. If you want others to learn the Ways, you must first learn the Ways for yourself and integrate them until they are a part of who you are and how you show up in every situation. This is how you walk your talk and practice what you preach. Every person is a work in progress. As long as you are actually "working" at authentic growth, self-healing, and expansion by raising your levels of consciousness and embodying the Ways of Oneness, then you are perfectly on your path. Remember, walking the path of the Light is never about perfection. It's about growth. Falling down and making mistakes are never failures. The only real form of failure is quitting, giving up, and the refusal to grow. What most label as failures are just experiences where they didn't get what they wanted. But realize what you got was exactly what you needed. You needed that "failure" for the experience. To learn what doesn't work. To gain skills that need to be built upon. That experience was a stepping stone. We all need stepping stones to learn from and build upon. No one is here to be born and be perfect, never make mistakes, or to get everything they want. What a conceited, entitled way to view your life and reduce it to something that is, quite frankly, meaningless. People who believe this sound like spoiled, rotten children. In fact, it's typically when you *don't* get what you want that real growth is sparked within yourself. If you get everything you want, you have no reason or inspiration to change or elevate who you are. Not getting what you want inspires you to look within and make necessary changes. The current version of you may not be capable of handling, receiving, or managing what it is that you dream of having. Why do you think so many famous people overdose, become addicts, or commit suicide? What you want to achieve probably requires a more evolved version of yourself. Because of this, the Universe will hear from you what it is that you want to manifest, achieve, or accomplish. Then it will set up everything that you need to challenge you to evolve and become the person that can handle that coming into your life. It may require more schooling or training. It may require nine business failures to gain the skills and wisdom needed to manage the successful business that will grow into a multibillion-dollar company. It may require tough, painful tests of initiation that you should pass in order to become strong enough to "get what you want." So, stop crying over the fact that you don't yet have what you want. It's time to mature out of spiritual toddlerhood and instead embrace everything the universe places before you and realize that what you're moving through is a stepping stone so you can become a more powerful version of you. You need to learn emotional resilience. You can't learn that by getting everything you want and having everything go your way. If you need everything to go your way in order to be happy or peaceful, your emotional IQ is comparable to an infant's. Part of living in Oneness is understanding the Wisdom of this and allowing that Wisdom to guide you through the turbulent times where you're being challenged to grow and become a more expansive and more powerful you.

Situations where you find yourself making excuses for or downplaying your poor or harmful choices while you point the finger and blame others are situations calling you to become the Way of Responsibility. Situations that trigger impatience are there to teach you the Way of Patience. Situations that trigger resistance, refusal to accept the truth or the emotional pain, are there to teach you how to Surrender. Situations that trigger reactions instead of responses are there to mirror to you your lack of Presence so you can learn how to shift into and offer the Way of Presence. Situations that are filled with lies and half-truths are there to teach you the Way of Truth. Experiences of abandonment are there to teach you the value of Connection so you'll learn to offer the Way of Connection over abandoning yourself or another. Experiencing someone being heartless or unresponsive to your pain is there to teach you how to be the Way of Compassion. Being treated with abuse or aggression is there to teach you about the Way of Harmlessness and Gentleness. Being treated as less-than or as inferior to another is there to teach you the Way of Equality. Experiencing betrayal in any form is there to teach you how priceless the Way of Trust is in our relationships. Being degraded or disrespected is there to teach you how important it is to learn the Way of Honoring for yourself and for others. Situations where you were dealt terrible customer service, you were ripped off, or you experienced the "over-promise, under-deliver" from some person or business is meant to teach you what the Way of Selfless Service is. Various forms of abandonment, people quitting when required to work hard, people ending relationships as soon as they're challenged to grow up, are all there to teach you how valuable the Way of Loyalty is. Experiencing unrealistic expectations and demands from others, judgment, or withholding of love are there to teach you the importance of the Way of Unconditional Love. Experiencing how people will react to you or to others when they are arrogant, conceited, and self-absorbed, or experiencing a crushing blow to your ego, are all there to learn the precious gifts gained from releasing those toxic programs and then shifting into the Way of Humility. Moving through experiences that are filled with dishonesty and a lack of moral principles are there so you can learn the pricelessness of the Way of Integrity. Having people hurt you and do cruel things to you just for the sake of being mean are there to teach the very challenging lesson of the Way of Forgiveness. Moving through life with hate, prejudice, anxiety, depression, negative mental and emotional programs, are the experiences meant to teach you how valuable the Way of Purity is. So then you'll do what it takes to purify your multidimensional body-system, including your energetic fields, and step into the inner power you have to heal yourself. Experiencing your own or others' ignorance and blind faith are lessons to teach you what the Way of Wisdom is. All of your life challenges and obstacles are there to show you how you are not living in Harmony with others, with nature or with the universe, so you can learn how to shift into the Way of Harmony with all. All of these Earth School lessons are being offered to you during your time on this precious planet. Learn to see them for what they are so you can choose to grow from them instead of choosing victimhood and allowing yourself to be destroyed by them.

* * *

Have you ever noticed the way people come together in loving support of one another when there is a disaster? But in between disasters, people fall right back into hating and opposing each other. When it takes a horrific tragedy for people to let go of programs of separation and come together in Connection, Compassion, and Selfless Service, you know you're living in an extremely low level of collective consciousness. The fact that disasters, pandemics, and tragedies are a requirement for people to show up in the Ways of Oneness means the collective consciousness knows nothing of the Ways of Oneness. Humanity's level of consciousness has been so very low for so many centuries that what's been required for us to awaken are tragedy, wars, and disasters that cause severe and chronic suffering. That's what is required to break down one's ego when he doesn't pursue the path of enlightenment on his own. If you want less suffering, then choose to grow up. If you want less emotional pain, then learn how to become powerful in your level of Compassion so that you have the ability to nurture your pain when you experience it. If you don't want to be abandoned, then stop abandoning yourself and learn the Way of authentic Connection with your higher self and only connect to others from that place of divinity. No more using, manipulating, or superficiality. No more connecting to others from a place of unconsciousness, egoic programs, masks, and unhealed traumas. If you're sick of things not going your way, then terminate your resistance to challenges and to what life is offering to you and learn how to fully Surrender to what is. If you want to stop being judged or attacked, then learn what it means to be in the Way of Harmlessness and Gentleness. If you want to experience Unconditional Love, then stop placing expectations on others to show up in exactly the ways you want them to so *you* won't be triggered. And the list goes on . . .

For the last 10,000 years or so, humanity fell so low into their own darkness that the human experience seemed to always include violence, war, domination, aggression, inequality, sexism, racism, and other endless programs of separation. Have you had enough yet? Because if you continue to take inventory of how others show up in those ways, but still haven't switched the focus onto your own self-assessment, then the answer to the above question is "no." No, you haven't had enough suffering and darkness . . . of greed and hate. . . of fear and emotional misery. Of violence. Of rape. At least not yet. When you continue to look externally instead of internally, you're not ready to live in the Ways of Oneness. You still believe you are the center of the Universe. You still blame and project, which means you are running programs of superiority. You and our precious Planet Earth will never be able to heal when you continue to function in the energies of those dark, unloving programs of separation. If it all seems to be too much, or it feels hopeless to achieve, remember, all you have to do is begin with the first Way. Start with the Way of Responsibility. Take inventory of yourself and of every single way that you justify, make excuses, dismiss, fail to show up, exhibit laziness or entitlement, or refuse to take Responsibility for your life, your relationships, and your emotional and mental states of being. Just start there. Choosing to See where you are falling short of being radically responsible *is* the path of Responsibility. It's where and how you begin. You can also print out a list of all twenty Ways and carry it with you wherever you go. It can be used as a reminder for yourself to become the Ways. It can also be used as a quick self-inventory checklist when you're triggered. If you get triggered, pull out your list of the Ways. Which Way is challenging you to evolve? Which Way is calling to you to shift, heal, and grow so you can become that Way? Use the Ways as a guide. Or simply ask yourself when you're triggered, "What would Mason do?" WWMD. Use this as a reminder and a request to the Ways to help them to guide you in each and every situation that you're in. Can you grasp the Truth yet, of what is being offered to you? Can you begin to understand that you've been tricked into believing in a divine power that is outside of and separate from you, in order for you to remain powerless and easy to control? Do you understand that the divine power of Source, of the Universe, of the Light, is inside of and flows through every single thing that exists in this world, the galaxy, and so on? Can you comprehend that it flowed through a dog like Mason? Can you grasp that *you* are a divine being who at any point in time can choose to awaken to your true, divine nature and allow the Light of Source to flow through you as well? Do you understand that, as you choose to become the Ways of Oneness, that that is a direct path to becoming an enlightened and truly loving being?

Use the Ways as the illuminated path to Oneness and to self-actualization. . . because that's what they are. Each Way has its own Consciousness. Each Way is a teacher in and of itself. Each and every Way is a Light Code of enlightenment that creates the framework for peace, harmony, and self-actualization on the micro level as well as enlightenment on the macro level. Allow them to be your teachers while you are a student here in this university called Earth. Allow yourself to become the Light codes of the Ways of Oneness. For that's how you will learn how to master your *self* and how we, collectively, will create peace on Earth. The New Golden Age of Harmony can only arise out of the Ways. We've been trapped in the codes of darkness, powerlessness, and separation that have been driving us, our emotions, our behaviors, and our conduct for far too long. It's time to invite in and activate the Light Codes of Oneness to form the goldprint of enlightenment and allow that to be our code of conduct from here forth. It's impossible to give birth to a New Golden Age out of separation. Harmony can never be created while living in ignorance to the fact that you are disharmonized to your divinity. Harmony can never be created out of disharmony. One must become Harmony on an individual level in order to contribute to the creation of Harmony at a group level. Harmony must be achieved by humanity, or humanity will continue to crumble. Mother Earth will continue to die. Divine creatures of our planet will continue to go extinct. We will kill ourselves with our own waste. We are dying from our own pestilence of greed, materialism, and selfishness. And we continue to point fingers and blame everyone outside of ourselves, like *we* are not the ones doing this to ourselves. It's always someone else who is creating these things. Always someone else who is at fault. Always someone else who we hold responsible for our pain, for our suffering. You can see that much of humanity still hasn't shifted into the very first Way, the Way of Responsibility. And we are running out of time to get a clue and get things right.

The good news is that you are not as lost as you may think. We've had a blueprint for centuries on how to live in hate, violence, selfishness, and fear. We've mastered that era of humanity. It's time to master a new way of living. The Universal Ways of Oneness are the Goldprint of human evolution. The Ways of Oneness are infused with golden, Christ consciousness, and the illuminated white Light of Source. The diamond white Ray of Enlightenment breathes life into the Ways and into each person who embraces them. The Sacred Ray of Creation is the golden-yellow Light Ray that opens one's gifts of Divine Sight and offers the ability to see Truth so one can change, grow, mature, and heal themselves. Our mystical and divine natures cannot be oppressed any longer. They are the aspects of the infinence that is a part of each and every living being on the planet. Of every atom, every cell, every particle, every wavelength, every frequency, every energy body. We are all infinite Beings having a tangible experience, and it's time for Remembrance of your divine nature to fully come forth. It's time to create life, experiences, businesses, relationships, friendships, and families from that divine remembrance. It's time we govern small communities and global societies from the energies and Light codes of Oneness. It's how you should parent your children, educate in schools, and what we should base laws from. It's through these Ways that we will learn how to honor and not hate. How to live in Harmony instead of separation. And it's through these Ways that I have learned to live a more meaningful life of joy, gratitude, and Grace. One that is free from suffering and filled with love and nurturing when I am in pain. One that allows me to be powerful and selfless and live my life driven by the powers of divinity that guide my life so I may guide others towards the Ways that create peace and freedom. These Ways guide my every day so that when I fall from Grace, I have the support and direction to show me how to get back on track, how to rise up from where I fell, and how to grow beyond the stumbling block that showed me where I need to heal or elevate myself. The Ways have taught me honor. How to honor others. How to honor and love myself. And how to finally honor all the attributes that make me me. I now know how to honor my sensitivities, my divine power, my abilities as a hypersensitive empath, and my power and ability as a spiritual leader to connect to the One Source and channel Wisdom directly from the Universe. I honor my style of radical spiritual teaching and how to never again apologize to people who feel small in the Presence of my power. That's the level of Honoring that I have learned from this sweet and precious canine soul that I called Mason.

And now, as I write the last words of this book, I honor Mason. I honor Mason's Ways that go far beyond the teachings of any saint or sage. I honor who he was, what his divinity taught me, and what he was here to show every person and every being he came into contact with. I honor him for being my guru . . . my angel incarnated, in this lifetime. I honor Mason as a vessel that carried sacred teachings from the Light of Source to pass to me. Mason gifted to me the Universal Ways of Oneness, so I could, in turn, gift them to humanity. And so I honor his memory by blessing others through the offering of his teachings to them and to you now. It is my hope that you will not just read this and then place this book up on a shelf to be forgotten. It is my hope that you take each Way and practice it, as well as ask yourself in challenging situations, "WWMD? What would Mason do?" My wish is that you allow these Ways to teach you, to support you in your evolution, and to transform your life. That you integrate each Way until you master each and every one and that you share this book and Mason's Ways of Oneness with as many others as you can. I also hope that you can realize that these aren't *really* "Mason's Ways." They are the Ways of Source itself, inviting us to finally rise up to the level of divinity that we have the ability to achieve while in human form. By mastering these Ways, you can raise yourself up to the level of enlightened Oneness. And then you can walk this planet as an enlightened being for the rest of your existence. For, if you follow and integrate each and every Way, it's possible to one day elevate yourself *so high* that you can actually achieve living on this planet in the supreme and sacred way that dogs already know how to live. As the Universal Ways of Oneness.

I'LL REMEMBER

Madonna

Say goodbye
Not knowing when
The truth in my whole life began
Say goodbye
Not knowing how to cry
You taught me that

And I'll remember
The strength that you gave me
Now that I'm standing on my own
I'll remember
The way that you saved me
I'll remember

Inside I was a child
That could not mend a broken wing
Outside I looked for a way
To teach my heart to sing

And I'll remember
The love that you gave me
Now that I'm standing on my own
I'll remember
The way that you changed me
I'll remember

I learned
To let go
Of the illusion
That we can possess

I learned to let go
I travel in stillness
And I'll remember happiness
I'll remember, hmm
I'll remember, hmm

And I'll remember
The love that you gave me
Now that I'm standing on my own
I'll remember
The way that you changed me
I'll remember (I'll remember)

Now I'll never be afraid to cry
Now I finally have a reason why
I'll remember (I'll remember)
Now I'll never be afraid to cry
Now I finally have a reason why
I'll remember (I'll remember)
Now I'll never be afraid to cry
And I finally have a reason why
I'll remember (I'll remember)
Now I'll never be afraid to cry
And I finally have a reason why
Remember

Mason Fiori was an English, yellow lab and angel incarnated mix. He came into Rachel's life at eight weeks old and devoted his life to her as her soul-companion dog. Mason was an incarnated example of the Universal Ways of Oneness, meant to activate these Ways inside of Rachel's consciousness. Once Rachel was mastering these Ways as a spiritual teacher herself, Mason's soul mission was complete.

Mason currently resides at the Rainbow Bridge where he joyfully awaits for his human mommy to rejoin him in soul form.

RESOURCES

Need help, guidance, coaching, or healing? Visit Masters of Self University: www.MastersofSelfUniversity.com. Check out our individual coaching programs, couples programs, support and healing groups, psychic healing sessions, and classes on the Universal Ways of Oneness.

Check out the Masters of Self University PODCAST. The Masters of Self University PODCAST is your highest source of Sacred Truth and Universal Wisdom offered by Rachel Fiori, spiritual leader & CEO of MSU. Join our journey of soul transformation with Rachel and the rest of the amazing Certified Mystical Life Coaches of MSU.

www.ingramcontent.com/pod-product-compliance
Lightning Source LLC
Chambersburg PA
CBHW071312150426
43191CB00007B/592